The Structure of Texts

edited by
Udo Fries

SPELL

Swiss Papers in
English Language and Literature

Edited by
The Swiss Association of University Teachers of English
(SAUTE)

General Editor: Max Nänny

Volume 3 · 1987

The Structure of Texts

edited by

Udo Fries

Gunter Narr Verlag Tübingen

CIP-Kurztitelaufnahme der Deutschen Bibliothek

The structure of texts / ed. by Udo Fries. –
Tübingen : Narr, 1987.
(Swiss papers in English language and literature ; Vol. 3)
ISBN 3-87808-843-4

NE: Fries, Udo [Hrsg.]; GT

Gedruckt mit Unterstützung der Schweizerischen Geisteswissenschaftlichen Gesellschaft

Einbandgestaltung: Peter Halter, Zürich
Satz und Druck: Laupp & Göbel, Tübingen 3
Printed in Germany

ISBN 3-87808-843-4

Acknowledgements

We wish to express our thanks to Dr. Andreas H. Jucker for his painstaking proofreading and his compilation of the index.

SPELL is published with the financial aid of the Swiss Academy of Humanities.

All enquiries should be addressed to: The General Editor of SPELL, Englisches Seminar der Universität Zürich, Plattenstraße 47, 8032 Zürich, Switzerland.

Table of Contents

Preface

This volume contains all but one of the papers read at the 1985 St Gallen symposium on the "Structure of Texts." It includes both the linguistic and the literary contributions presented at the conference, a combination which may seem unusual in these days of specialisation; the open-minded reader may find, however, that there are indeed a number of areas in which the two fields come very close to one another, and that it is sometimes difficult to draw a clear borderline between them. This fact is reflected in the arrangement of the individual essays in this volume, in which no line of demarcation is drawn between the linguistic and the literary papers.

The introductory address, delivered by Nils Erik Enkvist, comes first and is of paramount interest to students of style, be they linguists or literary critics. This is followed by a number of papers with a clearly linguistic background; the growing concern of linguists with questions of discourse and text is apparent in all of these contributions. The next group of papers, dealing with general questions of literature rather than with any particular authors, focus on related fields of interest, and it is no coincidence that their authors quote, among other books and articles, the very works which are referred to in the "text-linguistic" papers. The papers concerned with texts by individual British writers are arranged chronologically; they span a considerable period, beginning with papers on Beowulf and on Chaucer, and moving through Shakespeare to Milton, Swift, Fielding, and Addison. The volume concludes with essays on Melville, American-Indian autobiography, and the postmodernist text. All of these contributions reflect the growing interest in a variety of approaches towards questions of textual structure, which open up new possibilities in the interpretation of English literary and non-literary texts.

Udo Fries

What Happened to Stylistics?

Nils Erik Enkvist

1

I well remember that distant age when ladies still dressed in skirts of a standard length prescribed by fashion. And I remember how people used to theorize about connections between skirt length and the cycles of the economy. In a bull market, as in the years before the Wall Street crash in 1929, skirts were said to go up, but in a recession, as in the early thirties, skirts were supposed to go down.

If these remarks have led you to hope for frivolous reminiscences of a middle-aged skirt-watcher, I fear you will be disappointed. My purpose was only to suggest that, like skirts, stylistics too has had its fashionable ups and downs. As I have invested in stylistics during both bullish and bearish markets, I see myself in the role of an historical market analyst of stylistics. And, as market analysts should, I shall not only cite facts and figures but also give you some personal interpretations and opinions. Some of them will no doubt be controversial; some may even be distasteful to people whose perspective is different from mine.

2

But first a terminological caveat against undue reification. I have already spoken about "stylistics" as if such a term had a constant and stable referent. In actual fact no discipline, and least of all stylistics, is immutable in scope. Borders of disciplines move, one subject expands and another one may shrink, and new disciplines start asserting their territorial rights. Such shifts and even feuds in interdisciplinary relations are never arbitrary. They may owe to major international currents in scholarship, or to local conditions in a particular university or department.

But they can always be read as a cultural metatext, as a commentary how a larger or smaller society or group faces a never-ending sequence of intellectual challenges.

I wanted to remind you of such problems because in speaking about "stylistics" I am committed to a label which has covered many different things in many different settings. A definition is therefore in order. An extensional definition would begin by listing what types of activities have been pursued under the label of "stylistics". Such a list leads us back, if not to the birth of the world's first bard or story-teller, at least to the birth of rhetoric. And when looking at the annals of rhetoric we must worry about matters such as the shifts in balance between *inventio, dispositio,* and *elocutio: elocutio* was the stage of composition most akin to stylistics proper, and during periods when *elocutio* expanded at the expense of other areas of rhetoric, rhetoric became increasingly similar to, or even identical with, stylistics. As matters of style have been dealt with under different headings, the student of stylistics cannot simply look up the word "style" in texts from various periods. He must really go deep into his texts and see how they deal with problems he himself would include in his stylistics.

But to look for stylistic statements in rhetoric and in other disciplines, one must first have an intensional definition of style. Unless one knows what style is, one does not even know what to look for. As I think the most interesting attempts at defining the linguistic essence of style were made in the 1950's and 1960's, I shall now try to give a bird's-eye view of the territory of research of the linguistic stylistics of that period.

3

The conspicuous surge of interest in linguistic stylistics between the late 1950's and the 1970's was, I think, motivated by the confluence of several trends. One was the linguists' interest in finding out whether their methods might help us to objectify as intractable a concept as style. Perhaps they could provide a linguistic complement to the literary critic's traditional impressionistic approach. Another relevant trend was a growing impatience with the structuralists' preoccupation with the smallest units of language: phonemes and morphemes. Describing sentences and discourses as arrangements of such small items was like describing a metropolis as an arrangement of individual bricks, stones and planks. Therefore attempts arose at focussing on larger units such as sentences and texts. In his *Syntatic Structures* of 1957, Noam Chomsky attempted a syntax-centred description of language; roughly at the same time there appeared systematic efforts at going even beyond the sentence into text and discourse. Two of the milestones in this development of a text-centred but still linguistic stylistics were the Bloomington style conference of 1958 (Sebeok 1960) and the debate about the essence of style in *Voprosy Jazykoznaniya*, the leading linguistic journal in the Soviet Union.

Of course there had been scholars such as Vossler, Croce, Bally, Spitzer, Staiger, Roman Jakobson, and – bridging the gap to the present – René Wellek who had ventured into the border zone between language and literature well before the 1950's. But – and here I shall digress for a moment – it has always surprised me how little happy collaboration there has been between linguists and literary scholars, especially in the area of stylistics. The best-known exceptions are Russian formalism, and its sequel, Prague structuralism. In Moscow, Petrograd and Prague, linguists and literay scholars breathed the same air. They spoke to each other and could be impressed by each other's views. Roman Jakobson particularly seemed to cruise happily between literature and linguistics. And in France, and perhaps in Switzerland, the gap between linguistics and stylistics seemed narrower than in many other environments. But notably in the English-speaking world, such a happy harmony for some reason failed to come about. Even to my own youthful mind, when I studied post-Bloomfieldian structural linguistics and the then fashionable new-criticism-dominated literary syllabus in the great days of the University of Michigan in the late 1940's, it was puzzling to see how little contact there was in Ann Arbor between these two tribes of linguists and literary scholars. This was the more surprising as New Criticism was uncovering poetic minutiae that were fairly crying out for rigorous linguistic description. Of the American structuralist linguists, Archibald Hill – another link to the present day – was exceptional in subjecting poems to an analysis based on linguistic considerations (Hill 1965).

But this was a digression. My main purpose was to emphasize that in the late fifties and early sixties, a number of linguists tried to find out to what extent the concept of 'style' was amenable to linguistic analysis and description in rigorous and objective terms (cf. Enkvist 1964, 1973a, 1973b). And to do this, the linguist had to find out what style was: he had to define style.

4

And what *is* style?
In a wide semiotic sense, we might suggest that style is a way of doing something within a given set of rules. We can, for instance, drive a car with different styles, more smoothly or more jerkily, more politely or more aggressively, within the same highway code. We can build, say, two railway stations that satisfy the same requirements and contain the same facilities but still look different: then the differences qualify as stylistic. If we want to translate such a wide semiotic definition into the more restricted world of natural language, style might turn out to be a certain definite way of saying something.

Such a definition, you will have noted, assumes that there are different ways of saying the same thing. About this, people disagree. Some people, many logicians and some linguists among them, say that the same proposition or predication can be dressed up into different surface forms. Others deny such a dualism between meaning and form. In the manner of the New Critics they assert that every text has a unique meaning of its own, and that all changes of the surface form of a text will also inevitably change its meaning. Their view might be characterized as monistic rather than dualistic. But those impatient to get on with the job of stylistic analysis may wish to bypass such theoretical arguments. Yet to know whether two expressions "mean the same" or not they will need a rigorous, formal semantics which is capable of distinguishing surface variants which mean the same from surface variants which mean different things. And nobody can offer the style analyst such a semantics, ready-made. It follows that the definition of style as a way of saying something is hardly a satisfactory basis for concrete linguistic operations. It relies too heavily on intuitions about identity or difference of meaning, such intuitions being notoriously subjective and open to argument.

Another definition starts out by assuming that style is a decorative halo of stylistic devices and figures surrounding a kernel of basic meaning. If such a definition is to be translated into a heuristic procedure, we must once again learn to distinguish underlying basic meanings from their expressions on the textual surface. And this we cannot do with sufficient stringency.

Yet another of the classic approaches to style regards style as the result of choice. Intuitively, such an approach seems fine. We feel that our own styles arise through choice, sometimes unconsciously, and sometimes consciously through a long and even painful quest for the best from among a set of possible expressions. Here the difficulty is that nobody has succeeded in charting all the choices that are available to a speaker or writer in a certain situation. Some choices involve semantic substance, others take place between near-synonyms. Even generative-transformational grammar failed to give us a complete charting of the syntactic structures from among which choices take place during text generation. And, finally, when we actually see a text, all the choices have already taken place: they are no longer available for investigation. To the linguist, the operationalization of the view of style as choice poses unsurmountable problems.

A definition more concretely useful to a linguist is based on regarding style as situational variation. In different situations, people express themselves differently, and style is that subvariant of language that is associated with a particular type of situation. We use one type of language in formal situations and another type of language in intimate ones; a general uses one type of language when talking to a private and another type of language when speaking to his wife (at least I hope he does). Here the problem for the linguist is how to learn to describe situations, how to extract those situational features that are stylistically relevant from the welter of all the features that go into any normal speech situation.

We might now merge the definitions of style as choice and of style as language associated with a certain type of situation, and say that style arises from a situationally determined choice of expression. In so saying we are looking at the genesis of style in a speaker or writer. But we can and should also look at matters from the point of view of the receptor, the hearer or reader. A person who knows a language has acquired a great deal of experience of contextualised and situationalised language: he knows how family members chat at each other over breakfast, how professors speak to students, how tax authorities bully citizens, and how the Elizabethans used to address their ladies in a sonnet. He turns such past experiences of contextualized language into present expectations. Whenever he hears or reads a new text he matches it against relevant past experience and forms a set of expectations as to what is to come next. He matches the emerging text against a network of past experiences, forms expectations which are either satisfied or thwarted, and gets his impressions of the style of the text as an incremental result of such processes. This presupposes that the receptor has a network of past experience adequate for stylistic judgments. If different literary critics have different networks of past experiences, their judgments of the style of the same text may become different. And if there is no such network, for instance if we are learning a foreign language, we cannot possibly judge the style of a text. This, by the way, sets a programme for us as teachers of English as a foreign language: if we want to give our students a sense of style, we must first provide them with a network of experiences of the range of texts they will need for stylistic judgments.

The speaker, then, chooses his expressions to fit the situation he is in. The hearer or reader judges the style by matching the emerging text against a network of past experiences of situationalized and contextualized language.

Starting out from such views of the rise of stylistic judgements, the linguist would like to set up an apparatus capable of modelling them in stringent terms. The obvious way of imitating the rise of stylistic responses is to compare the language of one text with the language of another body of text, and obviously one that has a significant contextual relationship to the text studied. Defining the significance of contextual relationships is not a task for the linguist alone: it is a cultural matter, not one of linguistic structure. In practice, one's problem and one's purpose must determine where one looks for a body of text suitable for comparison with the text at hand. To study the style of Shakespeare's sonnets, for instance, we should hardly consider comparing them with the instructions in the telephone book or with Gray's Manual: Shakespeare's plays, the sonnets of other sonneteers, and other literary texts would give us a more meaningful base of comparison. Note, however, that the choice of norm against which we compare the text will always predetermine our results. In this sense, linguistic stylistics must ultimately rely on extralinguistic criteria. For those looking for concrete examples of such analyses, author-attribution studies are a good field to study.

To carry out such a comparison we shall need two things: first, an apparatus for describing the text and the norms we compare it with, and, secondly, a statistical apparatus for measuring the significance of the similarities and differences we shall find. Our apparatus for linguistic description must be adequate for the job: if we are interested in, say, imagery, simple basic syntax may not be enough. And stylostatistics, or stylometrics as it has sometimes been called, is a recognized subfield of stylistics with its own devotees and its own bibliographies (see e. g. Kenny 1982).

The stylistic comparison was essentially a heuristic for the discovery of style markers, the stylistic characteristics that give a text its particular stylistic flavour. (A style marker is definable as a linguistically describable item or structure or process whose density (= number of occurrences per some measure of text length) is significantly different from, or significantly similar to, the corresponding density in a stylistically relevant norm.) But linguists have not been satisfied with mere descriptions of sets of style markers. Some of them have tried to place stylistic variation into its proper perspective in a system of language varieties: how do styles relate to and interact with historical variants of the language, with regional dialects, sociolects, and idiolects? Further, if styles are a matter not only for occurrence and non-occurrence of specific markers, but also a matter of frequencies, how can we devise syntactic rules that are sensitive to such frequencies? Matters of these kinds were studied in the seventies, for instance, by William Labov, the sociolinguist, and his followers (Labov 1972); by Henrietta Cedergren and David Sankoff, who contributed to the development of so-called variable rules sensitive to frequencies (Cedergren and Sankoff 1974); and by Charles-James Bailey and others who advocated polylectal grammars catering for systematic descriptions of the total variation of a language, including its styles (Bailey 1973). Such studies showed that sociolinguists, students of linguistic variation, and students of style have a great deal in common, at least in their methodology. Sometimes it seems as if the difference between a sociolinguist and a student of style depended more on departmental background than on research methods.

Such, and other, arguments led to an hausse in the status of stylistics in the linguistic establishment. Stylistics acquired all the hallmarks of scholarly respectability: a place in many syllabuses, sections at symposia and congresses, conferences of its own, special journals such as *Style*, *Language and Style*, and *Lingua e stile*, and a bibliography which seemed to grow in geometric rather than arithmetic progression. Soon, however, problems that students of style had regarded as their domain were invaded by a somewhat different tribe of linguists: those calling themselves text linguists or discourse analysts.

5

Thus another of the most interesting events in the linguistics of the 1960's and 1970's was to be the realisation that descriptions of languages in terms of single, decontextualized sentences could not reveal all of the true essence of the structure and use of a natural language. A sentence is not a purpose unto itself. On the contrary, sentences normally occur in speech situations, they are embedded in discourse and are surrounded by other sentences which they must link up with. And in some types of discourse, such as impromptu speech or modern, syntactically deviant poetry, the continuity and connexity of the text are more important than sentence structure: indeed in such texts the sentences need not be syntactically well-formed, though the text still works successfully in communication. This means that the text is all right even if its sentences, in a syntactic sense, are not. (There are, however, syntactic constraints that must be upheld: we cannot say *Jack kicked Jill* if we mean "Jill kicked Jack".) And to understand the reasons why a speaker or writer has chosen a specific form for a certain sentence, we must reckon with the links of that sentence with its situational and discoursal environment.

A few examples. In isolation, a sentence such as *this book I have read many times* looks stranger than *I have read this book many times.* (Note that the equivalence between such sentence pairs can be defined in terms of their having the same truth value, irrespective of whether they "mean" precisely the same or not.) But it would be perfectly natural if uttered by a person who stands in front of a table with several books and points at one of them. Similarly, if I ask, *What happened to the sandwiches?* it would be quite normal to answer, *the sandwiches/they were eaten by Susie,* whereas a dialogue such as, A: "What did Susie do?" B: "The sandwiches were eaten by Susie." would seem distinctly odd. We choose from among cognitive equivalents to find the one that fits our discourse: we choose between *Susie is John's daughter* and *John is Susie's father, Peter is taller than Max* and *Max is shorter than Peter, put six oysters into a well-greased frying-pan* and *into a well-greased frying-pan put six oysters, your spectacles are on top of the telephone book* and *the telephone book is under your spectacles,* depending on what information structure we wish to give to our discourse, and on what we think our receptor already knows and what is to him new information. In fact we can now suggest that the task of syntax and lexis is to make possible the conveyance of information structures in the desired form. The information strategy of discourse and the information structure of the sentence come first; we then choose those words and syntactic structures that best carry out the information strategy. Here too, as in wars, strategy comes before tactics.

As I here used two terms, "strategy" and "tactics", which are not part of the stock terminology of linguistics, a brief digression may again be in order. One of the major trends in recent linguistics has been an increasing interest in describing languages in terms of processes and not only as structures. Indeed the word "process" has become extremely common in titles of linguistic books and articles, and we can justifiably speak of the rise of a new kind of processual or procedural linguistics (see e. g. Allén

1982 and Eikmayer 1983). But once we are committed to describing processes we must also develop a new apparatus for processual description. And for such an apparatus we shall need concepts such as "strategy" (for "goal-determined weighting of different alternatives at points where one must decide between alternative actions") and "tactics" (in language, for "choice of words, sentence patterns and textual macro-structures which best help one to realize and execute the chosen textual strategy"). A place where a decision must be made between different alternatives might be called a "decision point", and the factors or parameters whose values affect the decision might be labelled as "decision parameters". In such processual terms we might now try to redefine style as "a context-determined weighting of decision parameters". In metrically regular poetry for instance, the requirements of the metre may be important enough to override even the requirements of syntactic well-formedness. Metricality then becomes a heavily weighted factor or parameter. And if a cookery-book writer fronts a locative adverbial, even with the verb "to put" where such fronting is rare (as in *Into a champagne glass put two lumps of sugar.*), this fronting apparently owes to the importance of turning the sentence into an icon of events in the concise operational style. Such a sentence is short for "first take a champagne glass and then put into it two lumps of sugar": it mentions the champagne glass and the bits of sugar in the same order as they enter the scene.

And now back to my argument. I myself became involved with these textual and discoursal problems in the sixties because I found that different styles could also differ in the ways in which they linked sentences to each other. Therefore I needed a piece of linguistic machinery capable of describing links between sentences. Among useful studies were the theme–rheme investigations of Prague-school linguists, though at that time the role of themes and rhemes for text strategies and the linking of sentences had not yet been properly understood. Paradoxically, generative-transformational grammar also came to stimulate text linguistics. Transformations had to be described in full explicit detail, including the triggers that started them off. But it soon appeared that many transformation triggers resided, not within the sentence but outside it, in discourse and text and situation. A number of the successive revisions in transformational grammar have actually consisted of devising ways and means of introducing textual parameters, forces from the discourse, into the description of single sentences. In fact there are only two solutions available to the linguist who has grasped how much the sentence owes to its discoursal environment. Either he becomes a text linguist and acknowledges that the discourse is the father of the sentence, or he must try to bring in textual parameters into the description of single sentences.

Text and discourse linguistics went into a rapid development, and different schools and methods quickly evolved. We might try to classify the theories and models of text linguistics into four major categories, just to bring some order into what at first sight looks like a chaos.

The first category of text models I have called sentence-based. Sentence-based models accept a text such as it is, without tampering with its clauses and sentences, and try to describe what links clauses and sentences to each other. *Cohesion in English* by Michael Halliday and Ruqaiya Hasan (1976) is an example of a sentence-based study of cohesion. But if we ask ourselves where sentences come from, why they were formed the way they are, and what alternative ways there would have been for textualizing the same or similar contents, a sentence-based model will no longer be enough. We need a model which starts out from some type of primitive text atoms and contains devices for combining them into texts according to definite and explicit strategies. If we symbolize these text atoms with predications we might call such a model predication-based. The same set of predications can then be textualized into different texts with different strategies. Predication-based text models have been devised for instance by Bengt Sigurd (1974) and Gunnel Källgren (1979) in Sweden, and methods for reconstructing underlying predications from texts have been designed by van Dijk and Kintsch (e.g. 1983) and others, who use the term "text base" for such a predication set.

But if we go on to ask where predications come from, we shall need a third type of model, one capable of extracting predications out of a store of knowledge. As such knowledge stores turn into models of human cognition, we might call these text models cognitive. Cognitive text models, then, model information storage in the form of frames, schemata, scripts, and the like, often given in the form of associative networks. Cognitive psychologists and psycholinguists are interested in studying cognitive aspects of text processing in human subjects, whereas students of artifical intelligence are trying to build computer models of cognitive text processing.

A glance at the abstracts in *LLBA* and a survey of journals in psycholinguistics, psychology and cognitive science (including artificial intelligence) will show the strength of such currents. So will a count of those books and articles whose titles proclaim an interest in text, or language, or information processing. Two useful surveys are Flores d'Arcais and Jarvella 1983 and Sanford and Garrod 1981.

There is yet a fourth question: why does a certain person in a certain situation choose to express himself in a certain way? What politeness level does he opt for? Does he surround his text proper with metatext, phatic expressions and the like? How do people organize their behaviour in dialogue? To answer such questions we need a fourth type of text model that we might call interactional. Pragmalinguists such as Stephen Levinson have surveyed this area (Levinson 1983). Ethnomethodologists such as Sacks, Schegloff and Jefferson (1974) have studied turn-taking in dialogue, conversation analysts such as Deborah Tannen have attempted comprehensive analyses of conversational strategies (Tannen 1984), and so forth.

These types of text models do not relate to each other like slices of a pie, but rather like Chinese boxes or Russian dolls. Interactional models show how people behave, and perhaps to some extent why; when people know what they ought to do, they can begin extracting things to say, as modelled by cognitive text models; when they have extracted what they want to say, they go on to textualize it as explicated in a predication-based model, to produce a text with cohesion markers such as those described in a sentence-based text model. All the same we should not press distinctions between these model types too hard: of course interaction presupposes cognition because our knowledge of how to behave, how to interact, is part of our cognitive store. But such a pigeonholing is of some practical use, and it also invites comparison with the processes of invention, disposition and elocution in classical rhetoric.

6

Stylistics can never be the same after the rise of discourse linguistics. I could touch upon the effect of discourse linguistics on stylistics under two headings. The first has to do with the status of stylistics as a discipline in relation to discourse linguistics. And the second has to do with the new weapons stylistics can borrow from the arsenal of discourse linguistics. But for reasons of space I find it more convenient to answer these two questions together.

What, then, has discourse linguistics done to change the status of stylistics?

One plausible answer would be: discourse linguistics has swallowed stylistics. Stylistics has become part of discourse linguistics. When we work with sentence-based text models we must concern ourselves with the ways in which different types and patterns of links between sentences correlate with different situational contexts. In other words, we must study how frequent different linking types are in different text types, and in so doing we are in fact analysing styles. In predication-based text models, you will remember, the textualisation of a set of predications was steered and governed by a text strategy. And in fact "text strategy" comes to be largely or even entirely synonymous with "style": it is the text strategy that reckons with contextual principles in shaping the surface form of the text, it is the text strategy that estimates what the receptor already knows and what he is capable of processing. In cognitive models of text production, we get involved with systematizations of cognitive storage, including the storage of stylistic values: word families such as *girl, lass, maiden, young lady, bird* and so on, as well as families of syntactic structures with different stylistic values will have to be stored in memory with relevant labels, so that they can be retrieved and used in their proper stylistic contexts to conform with traditions, or perhaps to shock the receptor by breaking all traditions. And, finally, in interactional models, factors of stylistic context also come to the fore. Principles of politeness, of co-operative behaviour (in terms, for instance, of the Gricean maxims), of turn-taking, of clarifying text structure through special metatextual signals, of softening one's message by softeners and hedges, and so forth – all these principles will be directly relevant to style, as ingredients in the contextual and situational elements and patterns that effect the choice of language.

In such a view, as you have seen, stylistics in a sense disintegrates: stylistic considerations are scattered into the four different models of text. Stylistics cannot be said to exist intact inside text linguistics, like Jonah in the belly of the whale. Rather, the discoursal whale has chewed up the stylistic Jonah, whose bits and pieces now enrich different parts of his host organism.

Those students of style whose happiness depends on the intactness of their stylistic empire may well deplore such a development. Still, even they ought to be happy about the help they get from text and discourse linguistics. There is now an arsenal of new methods describing textual connexity which reveal new types of style markers. And in a wider, more philosophical context one might even suggest that in science, presiding over one's own liquidation can be a fine achievement. A scientific theory that has shown its own redundancy by reducing its statements to terms of another science is, in this sense, a success. In chemistry for instance we no longer need a special theory of phlogiston: we can explain burning as a special case of oxidation which is a special type of ordinary chemical reaction. Perhaps in linguistics we can do without a special theory of style if we can learn to handle all the relevant problems within a more general and powerful theory of discourse. Chomsky too assumes "that our aim is to assimilate the study of language to the general body of natural science" (Chomsky 1977:4), thus proclaiming his interest in presiding over the liquidation of linguistics. To what extent "the general body of natural science" would be capable of providing an adequate basis for stylistics is a problem he does not discuss.

Of course, the student of style can turn such an argument the other way round. He can say that stylistics is his main business, and text and discourse linguistics are his servants and handmaidens. The job of the text and discourse linguist is simply to provide him, the student of style, with tools and with assistance.

Personally I find it difficult to get upset or excited by such arguments, pro or con. I said at the beginning of my talk that disciplines should not be viewed as static, stable and immutable objects. And to me it matters little under what label we analyse styles, or whether people call me a student of style or of text and discourse.

7

If style is definable as that variety of language which correlates with context, including situation; if the impressions we get of style are based on a continuous matching of the emerging text with sets of expectations conditioned by past experience; and if we can study linguistic style markers through a comparison of the densities of linguistic features in our text with the corresponding densities of linguistic features in a contextually related norm – then to what extent are such matters dealt with in today's different literary theories?

To answer such a question I must venture into what to me looks uncomfortably like an uncleared minefield. Those familiar with literary theory – or just "theory", as its devotees often call it – will know how fragmented and full of contradictions and contested views today's literary theory is. For a consensus we should be looking in vain. The subject, however, is interesting, and I shall briefly mention a few current literary theories and give you an opinion of their relevance to stylistics. At this point I have had the benefit of the wisdom of my colleague Professor Roger Sell of Åbo Akademi and the University of Göteborg, whose conversation, face-to-face and by letter, has guided me through some parts of the critical wilderness.

Post-structuralism, particularly in its deconstructionist extremes, has not been hospitable to systematic comparison of one variety of language with other varieties. The deconstructionist's preoccupation has been with particular complexes of problems, or themes, in terms of certain key words, which are often manipulated and revolved out of context, to reveal contraditions and show the instability of meaning. The term "intertextuality", fashionable with many movements, might at first blush suggest a concern with placing a text into a system of other texts and matching its language with intertextually related norms. In practice, to the best of my knowledge, such stylistic intertextual comparison has not been the main concern of the critics who speak about intertextuality. Rather they have tried to divorce texts from their pragmatic role in an act of communication from writer to reader, emphasizing that the relation between a text and other texts is more important than the relation between writer, text, and receptor.

There is more harmony between my view of style as arising from a matching of a text with past experience and with expectations, and the kind of criticism known as Reader Response. One of the early protagonists of Reader Response criticism was Stanley Fish, whose, what one might call, "middle period" as a critic – roughly, the seventies – began with his famous paper on Affective Stylistics (Fish 1970). There Fish argued that style did not reside in detachable, reified structures in the text, but resulted from a sequence of fulfilled or thwarted expectations. Style in other words grew incrementally, evolving out of an experiential process: it was a dynamic phenomenon rather than a static structure. Presumably Fish too viewed style as a continuous matching of a linear, emerging text with a set of expectations conditioned by past experience. Wolfgang Iser's emphasis on readers as active agents filling in gaps left by the author should also be compatible with a stylistic creed: one of the factors affecting the receptor's inferencing is his past experience of what expressions are common and what expressions are rare in a certain type of situation. Note again how nicely such a view harmonizes with the approach to style as a matching of a text with a network of comparable experiences of other texts.

There is in the Western world today an intense and rising surge of interest in the work of Mikhail Bakhtin, another of the Russian theorists resurrected outside the Russian-speaking world. Indeed Bakhtin's work will make students of style ponder its stylistic significance. One point where Bakhtin anticipated text and discourse linguistics is his emphasis on the complex *rapport* that exists between speaker and listener, writer and reader. An act of communication, so Bakhtin realized, does not proceed through the simple behaviorist formula, speaker → text →

hearer. On the contrary, first the speaker estimates what the hearer already knows and how much information he is capable of absorbing. A message is always adapted to the receptor even before it is dressed up in its final linguistic garb. Bakhtin did not, however, show how such receptor adaptation is manifested in terms of the choice of words and syntactic structures and information strategies, themes and rhemes, topics and comments and presuppositions, as modern linguists would like to do. He was satisfied with more general terms:

> [The speaker's] orientation toward the listener is an orientation toward a specific conceptual horizon, toward the specific world of the listener; it introduces totally new elements into his discourse; it is in this way, after all, that various different points of view, conceptual horizons, systems for providing expressive accents, various social "languages" come to interact with one another. The speaker strives to get a reading on his own word, and on his own conceptual system that determines this word, within the alien conceptual system of the understanding receiver; he enters into dialogical relationships with certain aspects of this system. The speaker breaks through the alien conceptual horizon of the listener, constructs his own utterance on alien territory, against his, the listener's, apperceptive background. (Bakhtin 1981: 282.)

To Bakhtin, language exists in a state of heteroglossia prompted by the dialogization of discourse, and part of this heteroglossia would no doubt qualify as stylistic. Such heteroglossic tensions exist not only between speaker and listener but also within a literary text. Different passages in different styles evoke different contexts, says Bakhtin:

> Style organically contains within itself indices that reach outside itself, a correspondence of its own elements and the elements of an alien context. The internal politics of style (how the elements are put together) is determined by its external politics (its relationship to alien discourse). Discourse lives, as it were, on the boundary between its own context and another, alien context. (Bakhtin 1981: 284.)

If my reading of this passage is correct, Bakhtin would subscribe both to the view of style as context-bound language, and to the conviction that impressions of styles arise through a process governed by expectations, which in turn are based on experiences of what is common and what is rare in a particular type of context. Bakhtin's meticulous sense of stylistic tensions and his use of 'style' are not, however, objectives in their own right. Bakhtin uses stylistic contrasts and textual heteroglossia as a taking-off point. What he is really interested in are the wider sociohistorical perspectives, in the novel for instance. I don't think we can say as yet what critics beyond the Marxist persuasion – I am thinking of critics such as Terry Eagleton and Frederic Jameson – may make of Bakhtin. Perhaps he will spark off a new kind of sociostylistics, a criticism trying once again to link styles to social currents.

But there I am already gazing into my crystal ball. When critics are asked, What is the next fashion in literary theory?, their answers will differ depending on their persuasion. One answer is, a new historicism. Another answer is, literary pragmatics. Roger Fowler, still as sensitive to stylistic arguments as ever, regards literature as social discourse, as a message from a writer to a reader (Fowler 1980). And Roger Sell claims that

> literay scholars ... are now overcoming the Deconstructionist scepticism about the ability of authors to encode meanings that are at once their own and communicable to others ...
> I should prophecy that the interaction between literary texts and their contexts is from now on likely to be the major growth area in literary research. (Personal communication.)

Texts, so Sell insists, should be seen as functioning within, and contributing to, ongoing contexts of human interaction. If he is right, we are likely to be heading for a new marriage of "lang." and "lit.", and another renaissance of stylistics.

8

I was beguiled into forming the title of my paper as a question, and I should therefore also try to answer that question. So, what happened to stylistics?

I think the study of style is still very much alive. Some people study style overtly, calling themselves students of style. But many others too are involved in analyses of stylistic variation. Sociolinguists have as one of their major tasks the study of situational variations in language. Text and discourse linguists study those aspects of style that arise from different ways of connecting and organizing sentences into texts, and from different text strategies which are in turn affected by forces in human cognition and social interaction. 'Text strategy' could indeed be defined in ways that make it practically synonymous with 'stylistic principle' or 'stylistic organization of discourse'. And some literary theorists are concerned with style, irrespective of whether they use that particular term or not. Some of us call ourselves students of style and are proud of doing so. Others study styles on the sly as crypto-stylisticians, and yet others study styles without knowing that they are doing so. In any case, stylistics is still very much with us, though sometimes in shapes and guises that did not exist twenty or even fifteen years ago.

REFERENCES

Allén, S., ed. (1982): *Text Processing.* Proceedings of Nobel Symposium 51. Stockholm: Almqvist & Wiksell International.

Bailey, C. J. (1973): *Variation and Linguistic Theory.* Arlington, Virginia: Center for Applied Linguistics.

Bakhtin, M. (1981): *The Dialogic Imagination.* Austin, Texas: University of Texas Press.

Cedergren, H. / Sankoff, D. (1974): "Variable Rules: Performance as a Statistical Reflection of Competence." *Language* 50: 333–355.

Chomsky, N. (1977): "Conditions on Rules of Grammar." In: Roger W. Cole, ed., *Current Issues in Linguistic Theory.* Bloomington and London: Indiana University Press, 3–50.

Eikmayer, H.-J. (1983): "Procedural Analysis of Discourse." *Text* 3: 11–38.

Enkvist, N. E. (1964): "On Defining Style." In: N. E. Enkvist / J. Spencer / M. J. Gregory, *Linguistics and Style.* London: Oxford University Press, 3–56.

Enkvist, N. E. (1973a): *Linguistic Stylistics.* The Hague and Paris: Mouton.

Enkvist, N. E. (1973b): *Stilforskning och stilteori.* Lund: CWK Gleerup Bokförlag.

Fish, S. (1970): "Literature and the Reader: Affective Stylistics." *New Literary History* 2: 123–162. Reprinted in Fish, *Is There A Text In This Class?*, Cambridge, Massachusetts, etc.: Harvard Univesity Press, 1980.

Florès d'Arcais, G. B. / R. J. Jarvella, eds. (1983): *The Process of Language Understanding.* Chichester etc.: John Wiley & Sons.

Fowler, R. (1981): *Literature as Social Discourse.* Bloomington: Indiana University Press.

Halliday, M. A. K. / R. Hasan (1976): *Cohesion in English.* London: Longman.

Hill, A. (1965): *Essays in Literary Analysis.* Austin, Texas. [A collection of fourteen previously published papers.]

Iser, W. (1976): *Der Akt des Lesens. Theorie ästhetischer Wirkung.* München: Wilhelm Fink.

Källgren, G. (1979): *Innehåll i text.* Stockholm: Studentlitteratur.

Kenny, A. (1982): *The Computation of Style.* Oxford etc.: Pergamon Press.

Labov, W. (1972): "The Isolation of Contextual Styles." in Labov, *Sociolinguistic Patterns.* Philadelphia: University of Pennsylvania Press, 70–109.

Levinson, St. (1983): *Pragmatics.* Cambridge: Cambridge University Press.

Sacks, H. / Schegloff, E. A. / Jefferson, G. (1974): "A Simplest Systematics for the Organization of Turn-Taking for Conversation." *Language* 50: 696–735.

Sanford, A. J. / S. C. Garrod (1981): *Understanding Written Language.* Chichester etc.: John Wiley & Sons.

Sebeok, T. A., ed. (1960): *Style in Language.* Cambridge, Massachusetts: M. I. T. Press.

Sigurd, B. (1974): *Experiment med text.* Papers from the Institute of Linguistics, University of Stockholm, 25.

Tannen, D. (1984): *Conversational Style: Analyzing Talk Among Friends.* Norwood, New Jersey: Ablex.

van Dijk, T. A. / W. Kintsch (1983): *Strategies of Discourse Comprehension.* New York etc.: Academic Press.

Some Textually Relevant Grammatical Choices

D. J. Allerton

Apart from short public notices like *Kindly refrain from smoking* and isolated exclamations like *Fire!* most ordinary uses of spoken and written language involve constructing a text of more than one sentence. The notion of "text" further implies that sentences are put together in an organized way. Some texts are planned at a macro-text level, such as when a book is divided into parts and/or chapters; but most spontaneous uses of language, such as natural conversation, informal letters and notes, or diary entries, are not planned at all at such a high level. All kinds of text agree, however, in being planned at the lower textual level of clause, sentence and sentence sequence. This planning involves the adaptation of the form of a sentence to make it appropriate to the context in which it occurs, thus indicating its relationships to neighbouring sentences. Since the relations between the clauses of a complex sentence are similar to those obtaining between sentences in sequence, any textual linguistic analysis must also take account of links between clauses. The various kinds of inter-clause and inter-sentence connection have been surveyed in a number of works, notably by Halliday and Hasan (1976) and by Van Dijk (1977). For each kind of connection a choice must be made from a list of grammatical options. After considering briefly what these selections are, we can go on to look at one of them in more detail and consider its stylistic relevance.

But what, first of all, is meant here by "choice" or "selection"? This manner of referring to linguistic behaviour derives from a commonly adopted view of language production, according to which the speaker selects his message by making a series of (psycho)linguistic decisions. Each decision constitutes a lexical or grammatical choice. In the case of the impromtu speaker it cannot be a matter of conscious choice, although somehow, apparently, a selection is made. The writer, on the other hand, may be more aware of making a selection, though even he may be less than clear about the nature of the selections he makes; he is perhaps dimly aware of the availability of a number of conceptually equivalent modes of expression, each with its own textual or stylistic nuance. In either case, the choices, no matter how they are made, can be seen as determining the structure of both sentences in terms of clauses and of the wider text formed by sentences in combination.

In cataloguing textually relevant grammatical choices, we should not appear to be undervaluing lexical choices. As is made clear by Halliday and Hasan (1976: 274–92), textual cohesion is also achieved through lexical relations like repetition, synonymy and hyponymy (including the use of "general words", such as *thing, stuff*), as well as collocational links between words. But writers of all kinds have always been at least aware of lexical choice, even though they have not totally understood it. What they have been less conscious of is the grammatical selections we may outline as follows.

Firstly, let us consider the selection of a textually appropriate noun phrase for referring to a particular entity, i. e. a person, an animal, or a thing, concrete or abstract. The following phrases, for instance, are all different ways used by Conan Doyle to refer to Sherlock Holmes's arch-rival:[1]

> (ex-)Professor Moriarty, Moriarty, the Professor, the gentleman on whose front teeth I have barked my hands, his [= Col. James Moriarty's] brother, our friend, that man, the man, he/him

The proper noun phrase, for example, directly names an individual, and thus demands a familiarity with the bearer of the name in question; common noun phrases, on the other hand, identify an individual through description. The different degrees of richness a common noun phrase may display, correspond to different amounts of information required to identify the individual concerned, and this obviously depends on what is already established as "given"[2] by the preceding text. The use of a definite determiner or pronoun signals to the listener-reader that he should have enough information to unambiguously pick out the individual item. If, in the extreme case, the preceding text makes further description, and even the class of the entity the speaker has in mind,

[1] These and all following examples are taken from 'The Final Problem' in: Sir Arthur Conan Doyle, *The Memoirs of Sherlock Holmes* (Harmondsworth: Penguin, 1950).

[2] The term derives from M. A. K. Halliday, cf. for instance Halliday (1970: 162–64). For a more detailed study see Allerton (1978).

quite obvious, then not even a head noun is necessary: a pronoun like *he/him* is appropriate.

A second grammatical selection which can be textually relevant is the tense-aspect form of the verb. For instance, in the following extract:

> On the Monday morning Holmes had telegraphed to the London police ... (p. 249)

we might ask why Conan Doyle has used *had telegraphed* rather than *telegraphed* (or *was telegraphing*). The answer, of course, lies in the context in which this event is being presented. The events of a narrative are most naturally presented in their "real" consecutive order, but the (past) perfect can be used in inserting a mention of an earlier event which has an effect which appears at this point in the narrative. The English progressive is also used (but in a different way) to indicate the timing of an event (and its completion) relative to other events mentioned in the text.

As a third grammatical choice with textual relevance we should mention the selection of an appropriate lexical verb with the right valency characteristics and in the right voice. If we examine the sentence:

> A minute later a carriage and engine could be seen flying along the open curve which leads to the station. (p. 248)

we may be struck by the verb complex *could be seen*, i. e. *see* used in the passive: Conan Doyle could have instead used a simple intransitive verb like *appeared;* alternatively, he could have transformed the whole sentence to use the active form *(we) could see (a carriage and engine).* Such selections are made partly on the basis of which noun phrase fits most naturally into subject position, and this in turn is in part determined by the identity of the subject and other noun phrases in the passive sentence.

Fourthly, in our list of textually relevant grammatical choices we must refer to the various foregrounding and backgrounding devices, such as fronting, clefting, pseudo-clefting and subject-postponement, that can be used to give different shapes to what is basically the same sentence.[3] Consider, for instance, the cleft construction in:

> It was the sight of that alpenstock which turned me cold and sick. (p. 253)

In ordinary conversation this sentence could well have been used after a previous one by another speaker which had implied that something else

[3] See the range of sentence structures in Quirk et al. (1972: chapter 14).

had turned "me" [= Watson] cold and sick; the above sentence would then have been used to deny some suggested other cause while accepting that something had turned 'me' cold and sick, and asserting that it actually was the sight of that alpenstock. The effect of using the cleft sentence in a narrative without such a preceding context is to emphasize the cause of Watson's coldness and sickness and take the symptoms as read, so to speak. Other devices, or the same device with a different item clefted, can be used to give different weightings to the various constituents of the sentence and thus signal their significance.

A fifth (and for present purposes, final) point of grammatical selection with textual significance, and the centre of interest in this paper, is the choice of ways of combining the different "eventualities" we talk (or write) about. By "eventuality" is meant an event, process or state of affairs such as is typically referred to by a finite verb and its associated subject, object, etc. (e.g. *The wind blew the door open. The roof was leaking. It was cold.*). We can assume that every simple sentence, with the probable exception of exclamations, refers to an "eventuality" in this sense. But although a simple sentence structure is the basic format for talking about an eventuality, it can be downgraded through coordination or various kinds of subordinative embedding to the status of clause or phrase as a constituent in a larger sentence.

The various complex structures that may arise through using or not using coordination or embedding to link two related eventualities can be summarized as follows:

(a) two separate sentences, optionally linked by a conjunction or sentence adverbial, e.g. *consequently; nevertheless,*
(b) two coordinated clauses, linked by a coordinating conjunction, e.g. *(and) so; but,*
(c) one matrix (or "main"[4]) clause and one subordinate clause, linked by a subordinating conjunction, e.g. *because; although,*
(d) one matrix clause and one non-finite clause (with an infinitive or gerund), linked by a preposition, e.g. *because of; despite,*
(e) one matrix clause and one nominalization, linked by a preposition, e.g. *because of; despite,*

[4] The traditional term 'main clause' is not ideal, because it suggests the traditional grammatical view that a complex sentence can simply be segmented into 'main clause' and subordinate clause, the former being no more than the sentence remainder left when the subordinate clause has been removed. We should rather insist that the matrix clause includes the subordinate clause as one of its constituent parts.

For some semantic types of link, there is a further possiblity for combining two eventualities, viz.:

> (f) two nominalizations/non-finite clauses, linked by a verb, e. g. *cause; not prevent,* with one of them as the subject of this verb.

The linking words quoted as examples express two semantically different kinds of link, a causal one and an adversative one; other kinds of link include conditional and additive.

As an exemplification of the structurally different kinds of linkage we may consider the following different ways of linking the same two eventualities:

(1) (a)	Holmes arrived late.	Consequently they missed the train.
		They nevertheless caught the train.
(b)	Holmes arrived late;	and so they missed the train.
		but they caught the train.
(c)	Because Holmes arrived late, they	missed the train.
	Although	caught
(d)	Because of[5] Holmes arriving late they	missed the train.
	Despite	caught
(e)	Because of[5] Holmes's late arrival they	missed the train.
	Despite	caught
(f)	Holmes's late arrival	caused them to miss the train.
		did not prevent them (from) catching the train.

Despite their differences in outward form these sentences and sentence sequences are all broadly equivalent in their basic referential or cognitive meaning. On the other hand, their different grammatical structure must correspond to some semantic choice made by the speaker/writer and understood by the listener/reader.

Such semantic differences are extremely difficult to describe but they are summarized in Table 1:

[5] Whereas in (1) (d) *because of* can be replaced by *with* (in colloquial English) in (1) (e) this is impossible; *owing to,* on the other hand, is much more natural in (1) (e) than (1) (d) (in formal English).

Table 1
Types of Eventuality Linkage

(a) Separate Sentence	(b) Coordinate Clause	(c) Subordinate Clause	(d) Non-finite Clause	(e) Nominal-ization
assertion of a claimed fact		mention of a possibility		mention of an assumed fact
major importance		reduced importance		background
independent interpretation				dependent for inter-pretation

Each sentence or downgraded sentence refers to an eventuality, but whereas in an independent sentence this eventuality is asserted as a (claimed) fact, in a subordinate clause it is only a potential fact or possibility, and in a nominalization (which is after all a kind of noun phrase) it is reified, i. e. seen as a thing and thus assumed as a fact.

There are other semantic strands to this structural difference. One of them seems to be the relative importance attached to one eventuality compared with the other. Matrix clauses, for instance, partly through the falling nucleus intonation pattern typically associated with them, usually carry information that is more important or has greater novelty value. Compare, for instance, the relative weight of the matrix clause and the subordinate clause in (1) (c) above, and consider the effect of switching the causal version round to:

(1) (c′)The reason why they missed the train was that Holmes was late.

When an eventuality is further downgraded, to the rank of noun phrase (i. e. it is nominalized), its news value is reduced to that of background information like *Holmes's late arrival* in (1) (e) and (f).

A further semantic aspect to the kind of linkage is the closeness of the link between the two eventualities referred to. Obviously, separate sentences give the impression of being most independent of each other, but even coordinate clauses are at least semi-independent. It seems to require downgrading of one of the eventualities to a minor structural status (subordinate clause, non-finite clause or nominalization) for the closest link to be forged. This seems to suggest that take-overs of small entities by large ones result in more integration than do mergers of equals.

The kinds of meaning we have attributed to particular types of eventuality linkage clearly do not constitute direct referential meanings like those of lexical words such as *table* or *cat;* they are not even quite like basic grammatical meanings such as 'past (tense)' or 'agentive (subject)', which might be regarded as secondary meanings which modify and link lexical meanings to form sentential or propositional meanings. We should perhaps rather see our proposed textual meanings as tertiary, in the sense that they are semantic relations between sentence structures, which by definition already have a relatively complete meaning (made up of primary and secondary meanings).

Our inter-sentential meanings form just one kind of textual meaning, and this seems to correlate with one type of textual style. So far we have considered only the possibilities for combining references to two eventualities. If, however, we wish to combine three or more, we can either use one linking pattern repeatedly or, alternatively, use a number of different patterns alongside each other. The latter practice has been adopted by Conan Doyle in the following passage:

> It may be remembered that after my marriage, and my subsequent start in private practice, the very intimate relationship which had existed between Holmes and myself became to some extent modified. (pp. 235–6)

What would this passage have looked if the author had referred to the same eventualities, but had consistently used one of our types of textual linkage (a) to (e) above? He would have presumably produced something like (2) (a) to (e) below:[6]

> (a) You may remember the following points. Very intimate relations had existed between Holmes and myself. Then I had married. Subsequently I had started in private practice. Afterwards our relations became to some extent modified.
> (b) The reader may remember the following points: very intimate relations had existed between Holmes and myself, and then I had married and subsequently started in private practice; and so afterwards our relations became to some extent modified.
> (c) It may be remembered by the reader that after I had married, after which I started in private practice, the very intimate relations which had existed between Holmes and myself became somewhat modified.
> (d) It may be remembered that the very intimate relations previously existing between Holmes and myself becoming to some extent modified after my marrying and subsequently starting in private practice.
> (e) The slight modification, after my marriage and subsequent start in private practice, in the previously very intimate relations between Holmes and myself may be remembered.

[6] I have varied other points to fit the general style of each passage, notably the voice of the verb *remember*.

It goes without saying that a natural speaker or writer would rarely if ever use the same linking patterns over and over again in this way; and so the versions (2) (a)–(e) seem somewhat artificial. But the exaggerated consistency of such mini-texts can provide an insight into the semantic contribution and stylistic effect of each individual linking pattern. Broadly, a series of independent sentences gives an impression of clarity, of directness, of personalness, of liveliness, or even a racy quality. Sentences with subordinate clauses, on the whole, seem slightly more formal. And at the other end of the scale, sentences with nominalizations appear factual, but difficult, and even dull – typical, in fact, of a ponderous academic style. In a novel texts of type (a) are best suited to dialogue and dramatic narrative, whereas those of types (d) and (e) are more appropriate to description and contemplation. An unmitigated type (e) is probably too extreme for any literary use, but is commonplace in some academic writing, not least in the field of sociology.

REFERENCES

Allerton, D. J. (1978): "The Notion of 'Givenness' and its Relations to Presupposition and to Theme", *Lingua,* 44, 133–168.

van Dijk, T. A. (1977): *Text and Context. Explorations in the Semantics and Pragmatics of Discourse.* London: Longman.

Halliday, M. A. K. (1970): "Language Structure and Language Function". In: John Lyons ed.: *New Horizons in Linguistics,* Harmondsworth: Penguin, 140–165.

Halliday, M. A. K. / Hasan, R. (1976): *Cohesion in English.* London: Longman.

Quirk, R. et al. (1972): *A Grammar of Contemporary English.* London: Longman.

Sharing a Text: A Co-operative Aspect of Verbal Interaction

Richard J. Watts

In text linguistics and discourse analysis we have progressed beyond the point at which the only candidate for the status of text was a linguistic object resulting from the activity of writing. Since Lord and Parry's research[1] no-one doubts the validity of a notion of oral literature; hence "oral text" is not a contradiction in terms. Likewise drama and recorded interviews are immediately acceptable as dialogic texts. Free verbal interaction in the form of conversation, small talk and chat, on the other hand, has experienced some difficulty in gaining admittance to the illustrious company of text types. It is often grudgingly dealt with as if it were a subgenre of the discussion or interview, although I have yet to see a satisfactory definition of either of these terms.

I am not implying here that conversation has not enjoyed enough attention by researchers. On the contrary, at present we are experiencing a veritable boom in conversation analysis.[2] But the principal impetus towards the detailed, intensive and serious study of free verbal interaction ("free" in the sense of not being directed by any fixed communication goal or theme on the part of the participants) has come from sociologists and linguists with a bent for the social and ethnological status of such interaction, not from theoretical linguists and not, so far as I can judge, from text linguists.

[1] Cf. Lord (1960), Parry (1971), Finnegan (1977).

[2] "Conversation" tends to be used in the literature as a catch-all term for a very wide and varied spectrum of oral discourse. I shall henceforth avoid the resultant ambiguity in the term – "conversation" as all oral discourse and "conversation" as a specific type of oral discourse – by referring in general to "verbal interaction".

Yet precisely this form of verbal interaction displays a complexity and a dexterity of performance to fascinate even the most die-hard theroretical linguist. I shall illustrate its potential interest as a text type by examining one small area of socio-communicative verbal interaction which I shall call "text sharing". Text sharing occurs within the total fabric of the interaction whenever two or more participants contribute towards the ongoing development of its structure without them running the risk of threatening either their own or another participant's face. I shall return to the concept of "face" later.

However, before we consider such points in more detail, let us consider one definition of a dialogic text offered by Ann Banfield (1982). Banfield's main purpose is to argue, by offering empirical evidence of a linguistic nature, that the written narrative text is not communicative and that the attempt to establish a narrative voice or narrator whose communicative partner is a narratee, fictive reader or implied reader (or any other term we care to suggest) is misled. The argument is fascinating, provocative and at times highly convincing, but that is not my point here. It stands to reason that in order to prove that the written text is not communicative, she needs to define what she understands by communicative discourse and, within that framework, a dialogic text. It also follows that for her – as both a theoretical linguist and a literary theoretician – this type of text is of very little intrinsic interest.

Banfield posits that the most basic syntactic category in a generative linguistic model is not the sentence, but what she calls the "expression". The expression node (or E-node) in her grammar can be expanded in a number of ways which may or may not include a sentence. An expression may be an expressive structure on its own (i. e. with no sentence embedded within it), an expressive structure and a sentence, or simply a sentence. The crucial point in her argument, however, is that an expression may never be embedded within a sentence. Thus we may have any of the following utterances (1)–(4), but not (5):

(1) Good God!
(2) Another crack like that and out!
(3) What's the time?
(4) Hell, why should I do it?
(5) *He asked hell why he should do it.

The time orientation of the expression is always the time of the utterance, the *now,* and the locative orientation the place of utterance, the *here.* The only utterer implied at the level of the expression is the *I*, the *speaker* him/herself, and the only addressee is the *you,* the *hearer* or *hearers.* Thus, in discourse, a text can be defined as "a sequence of Es such that the first person is coreferential from E to E or is coreferential with an *addressee/hearer* or *hearer* of the preceding E" (Banfield 1982: 135). She adds that the second person may be singular or plural. In addition, "throughout a *text*, every instance of *present* is cotemporal with the speech act and every instance of *past* anterior to *present*" (Banfield 1982: 60).

As far as it goes, this is a reasonable definition of a dialogic text. But it implies that discourse consists of a sequence of discrete expressions with discrete interchanges from one participant to the next. Even allowing for the fact that this is a necessary idealization and takes no account of overlap and interruption, the assignment of one expression uniquely to one participant is not always borne out by the facts of free verbal interaction. Consider the following extract from informal small talk among six participants, all members of the same family, one afternoon early in April 1984:[3]

(6) S That was Amstrad wasn't it?
D No no no no no. What's that guy called now?
S What works in Comet's?
D Yeah.
S John Bates.
D John Bates. He told me Amstrad was rubbish. (0,5)
S I don't know.
D He sells them.
(2,1)
R Why – why was there/why was it rubbish?[4]

[3] The data in this paper are taken from an extensive corpus of tape-recorded socio-communicative verbal interaction at present being transcribed and analyzed at the English department of the University of Berne. The transcriptions given here do not include such significant variables as intonation, volume level, syllable lengthening, etc., which might prejudice the interpretation of the data. I offer the reader the admittedly pusillanimous excuse that these factors have indeed been taken into account, but do not significantly weaken the concept of text sharing. If anything, they strengthen it, but a detailed argumentation will have to be waived in the present paper.

[4] The following transcription conventions have been used in the analysis of the data:

(0,5)	=	a pause of half a second
(,)	=	a pause of less than half a second in duration
:er (,):	=	a filled pause
/	=	self interruption
–	=	repetition, stammering
—	=	an incomplete turn at talk
+	=	termination of an intervention at a point prior to the termina-

If (6) is to be considered a dialogic text, it must meet Banfield's two conditions. Up to the point at which R enters the interaction, this appears to be the case; his utterance, however, causes problems. He has most certainly been a hearer of the previous expression, but this utterance does not refer to it. In addition, although he has been a hearer, he has certainly not been an addressee, since the interaction previous to his entry has been exclusively between D and S. Now if D and S had been conversing in a restaurant and R had been a total stranger at the next table overhearing the interaction, would his utterance then count as part of the text? In strict accordance with Banfield's definition, it would, but I have my doubts.

I shall leave this question open, since there is a more serious objection to be raised. The past tense in R's expression surely does not encode a time point anterior to the present time of the utterance. R does not intend to ask why Amstrad was rubbish at the point in time when John Bates made that statement, and thereby to imply that it might not be rubbish now. So according to Banfield's criteria, R shifts to a new text with his utterance.

Such an analysis, however, is clearly counter-intuitive, since the anaphoric pronoun "it" may only be interpreted by the other participants by going back through their memory of the expressions uttered until they find a suitable coreferent by which a logically relevant implication can be deduced. Significantly, the relevant coreferent, the NP "Amstrad", is in the same sentential expression as the past tense form "was", which re-occurs in R's expression. We have here one form of text sharing, in which a participant uses a previous expression by another participant, altering it slightly in order to return the interaction to its central topic. Thus whether or not a free verbal interaction achieves the status of text does not depend solely on the kind of semantico-syntactic criteria set up by Banfield, but also on a central topic to which the participants may return as often and as intensively as they like and from which sub-topics may radiate. The utterances within which the topic and sub-topics occur contain a set of propositions which constitute the common knowledge of the participants, and any utterance must be relevant to this

		tion of the turn in which the intervention occurs
*	=	a back-channel intervention
&	=	intervention by another co-participant causing simultaneous speech, or simultaneous speech from the beginning of a turn at talk

common knowledge by allowing linguistically direct or pragmatically indirect implications to be deduced by the co-participants.[5]

To be fair to Banfield, her concept of the text is in reality a concept of textual shift within the total narrative, which she illustrates in the framework of what she calls "narration" and "representation". If we add to Banfield's conditions the condition of pragmatically deducible relevance to a central topic and its sub-topics, we may be more adequately equipped to define the textual status of free verbal interaction. Looked at in this way, it is perfectly conceivable that such interaction may consist of a number of texts. In order to support a notion of textual shift, however, we must concentrate on the dialectic nature of verbal interaction.

Any utterance addressed to a hearer or set of hearers has a right to a response, and that response might, but need not, merit a response by the original speaker. Failure to respond is a violation of the speaker's right to conversational territory, commonly referred to in the literature as "negative face".[6] Failure to respond relevantly is likely to be detrimental to the responder's and the original speaker's status within the social group, i. e. it may violate the "positive face" (or public self image) of either. The guiding principle behind a well-structured verbal interaction is thus that of relevance. The original speaker must be able to deduce an implication, either directly or indirectly, from the common stock of knowledge shared by the participants or built up through the interaction by means of topic development. The structure itself takes the form of interchanges from one speaker to another, which are termed "adjacency pairs". Thus whenever an adjacency pair has been completed and a new first pair-part is set up, we may speak of a textual shift.

It is clear that in extract (6) a number of shifts have been made. S asks for confirmation of a statement and receives a negative response from D. D then requests information concerning a person who, judging by the deictic pronoun "that", is relevant to the topic. S appears to violate the condition of relevant response to a first pair-part by asking a question herself. But she neither signals this possible face-threat in any of the conventionally acceptable ways, e. g. by prefacing the utterance with an expression such as "you mean" or the non-lexical expression "er", nor does D give any indication that he has taken it as a face-threat. In point of fact, no face-threat has been committed, since S has shared the text

5 For a discussion of the concept of "relevance" within a pragmalinguistic framework cf. Wilson and Sperber (1978).

6 For a detailed discussion of the concept of face and the politeness phenomena which are employed to obviate the threat to one's own or a co-participant's face, the reader is referred to Brown and Levinson (1978).

with D. Instead of responding relevantly, she completes his utterance with a relative clause modifying the NP "that guy" in D's utterance. She does so with interrogative intonation thereby implying that not enough information is on hand to warrant a relevant response. D is obliged to respond to S's question before she can respond to his.

The two examples of text sharing in (6) are not representative of the most common occurrences, however. In neither case does the sharer, the participant who uses a previous utterance as the framework or basis of his/her utterance, interrupt the previous speaker. Normally interruption would be interpreted as a violation of the speaker's conversational territory, as an attempt to take the floor from the speaker when the latter has not indicated that it has been relinquished, hence as a threat to the speaker's face. The textual structure of free verbal interaction is violated at points such as these, and the ways in which the equilibrium is restored are indicative of the degree to which communication is successful.

One type of interruption that cannot be interpreted as text-sharing merely signals to the co-participants that the interrupter would like to take the floor for a turn at talk.[7] It announces his claim to the floor in advance and may be considered as a floor-seeking gambit.[8] Speakers do not normally allow themselves to be interrupted, however, and it is highly unlikely that the interrupter really expects to gain the floor at that particular point.

Extract (6) continues as follows:

(7) D Well he reckons after the / after about a year the parts start to / all these working / you know cos they're all this sort of ultra-thin modern & (,) that you slide out and this
&
B & Well (1, 1) don't you –
D business. They tend to go wrong very quickly.
You can't get 'em repaired.
B Well don't you think that with anything
electrical or like that & you get a rogue
&
D & The more ???–
one and it – and it & goes wrong. It's the
&

[7] The terminology used in the present article and the theory on which it is based may be found in the seminal article by Sacks, Schegloff and Jefferson (1974).

[8] For the term "gambit" cf. Keller (1979).

D & Oh yes yeah yeah +
same w – with television and (,) motor cars
even. You le– & —
&
S & You can't guarantee can
you?
B No but with these Amstrads don't you think that :er (,) s–/ you
give a dog a bad name and it's a & jolly goo–/ hard job to get rid
&
D & Yes +
of it. You know what I mean (1, 7) but :um (,): might not be a case
Amstrad. They might be rubbish. (0,7) What do you think David? Do
you think they are?

B has to wait until D has completed his turn, confusing though it may be, before she is able to enter the conversation. She conventionally prefaces the floor-seeker and the beginning of her turn with the expression "well", which functions as the minimizer of a possible face-threatening act.[9]

Other types of interruption may be more threatening to the speaker even though they may not be meant as face-threatening acts. S, for example, interrupts B in the turn which she now proceeds to develop at a point which cannot possibly be interpreted as a transition relevance place, i. e. a point in the text at which transition from one speaker to the next is possible and/or permissible. B hesitates and is about to self-interrupt when S enters. S's utterance is in fact a response to B's apparent request for information in her opening question "don't you find that S". The question, however, is purely formulaic and merely prefaces an assessment by B. Her response to S is interesting. On the one hand, she complies with S's request for information with the expression "no". On the other hand, she indicates that her negative face has indeed been threatened by following up the expresssion "no" with the contradictory coordinator "but" and reformulating the turn more precisely, this time deliberately relating it to the overall topic of the text through the NP "these Amstrads".

Interruptions such as these cannot be interpreted as text-sharing, since they threaten the speaker's negative face. They require some kind of remedial work on the part of the interrupter. But not all interruptions are face-threatening acts. Many are supportive expressions of the type known as back channel behaviour and merely indicate to the ongoing speaker that the listener is still attending. Many are clear examples of text sharing.

[9] Cf. Owen (1983) and Watts (1985).

Let us consider extract (8) which is taken from a five-party lunchtime conversation among family members:

(8) M And they've got lots of tableaux B *mm+ beautiful. With a lovely tableau of an old kitchen B *mm+ and there's a tableau of a/ o– o– of the :er (,): the farriers you know that shoe & —
&
B & Shoe the & horses
&
M & The horses and
leather shops cobblers & and—
&
B & We'll take a trip
down there tomorrow you and me.

M has just told a story about herself and her grandson visiting an exhibition of local life and customs in a small Cornish port and is now describing the exhibition. B's first two utterances are typical supportive back channel behaviour, the first occurring at a transition relevance place (falling intonation and syntactic completion at the NP "tableaux") and the second with a rising intonation at the noun "kitchen". B's other two utterances, however, must be interpreted as interruptions. The second of these successfully wrests the floor away from M, since M gives up her turn at the coordinator "and", not completing her list. B's utterance is even addressed to another co-participant, although this is not clear from a mere transcription of the oral text. We have here a clear case of negative interruption, a violation of M's right to complete her turn.

The remaining utterance by B cannot be interpreted negatively, however, since it helps M to complete her list. Neither can it be interpreted as back channel behaviour, since it does more than merely indicate to the ongoing speaker that the channel of communication is still open. B has been signalling her interest throughout M's turn, but shortly after the second back channel utterance M runs into difficulty in encoding the information. The pause filled by "er" can be interpreted as a floor-holding signal, and it could have given B an opportunity to interrupt negatively at this point. It is significant that she does not interrupt. In continuing her list with the NP "the farriers" M appears to believe that there is a danger of her not being understood, since she appeals to B for confirmation with the expression "you know". B duly gives confirmation as soon as the verb "shoe" occurs, and her NP "the horses" is immediately picked up by M to allow her to continue the turn. The granting of confirmation is not placed at a transition relevance place, but at the next most logically suitable point in the text and is accepted by M.

Extract (9) is taken from the same conversation and it deserves some attention, since it displays an example of very tightly woven text sharing which does not involve interruption:

(9) M It's a lovely shop. We get smoked salmon there (1, 0) B *oh + and it's absolutely gorgeous.
M & Very nice. They do a lovely smoked mackerel.
&
W & And they do a very nice smoked – smoked mackerel that you can slice.

After the adjective "gorgeous" there is a clear transition relevance place in M's turn which W uses in order to join her in praise of the assortment of smoked fish on sale at the shop concerned. M in no way considers that W is making a bid for the floor at this point, and with split-second timing they provide each other with the lexemes and structural elements needed to convey the information. Both M and W carry out their turns simultaneously. Whatever is said by one participant is immediately integrated into the other's ongoing utterance, thus creating a veritable conversational fugue in miniature. The fact that M and W have been married for almost fifty years helps to account for the fine anticipation shown by each of them concerning what the other is likely to say. Indeed the total lack of social distance and the high degeree of intimacy between the participants in this type of verbal interaction help to explain why interruptions will very rarely be interpretable as face threats and very frequently as text sharing.

This type is perhaps the most interesting, as it provides evidence of the amazing speed with which we are able to process incoming oral language data and build them into our own projected turn. It also demonstrates the inadequacy of Banfield's definition of dialogic text as "a sequence of E[expression]s such that the first person is coreferential from E to E or is coreferential with an *Addressee/hearer* [...] of the preceding E". Far from being one of the exceptions of simultaneous speech which prove the rule of alternating turns at talk, this example of text sharing clearly demonstrates that the two speakers are not only aware of what the other is saying during the time when they are both speaking, but also that they are able to use elements of the other's expression within what they themselves are encoding.

A more extensive examination of free verbal interaction would reveal that the ability to share a text is widespread and that such closely interwoven text sharing is one of its most notable characteristics. It is surely one of those features which contradict any claims – explicit or implicit – that free verbal interaction is somehow not worthy of the linguist's attention. I would, in conclusion, make my own claim that it is only by studying this type of phenomenon seriously that some of the recent aberrations in linguistic theory may be corrected and a more useful approach to the structure and function of human language be developed. One point is beyond dispute: both phylogenetically and ontogenetically oral verbal interaction as a text type is prior to the written text.

REFERENCES

Banfield, A. (1982): *Unspeakable Sentences: Narration and Representation in the Language of Fiction.* Boston: Routledge and Kegan Paul.

Brown, P. / Levinson S. (1978): "Universals in Language Usage: Politeness Phenomena". In: E. Goody, ed. (1978): *Questions and Politeness.* London: CUP, 56–324.

Finnegan, R. (1977): *Oral Poetry.* London: Cambridge University Press.

Keller, E. (1979): "Gambits: Conversational Strategy Signals". *Journal of Pragmatics* 3, 219–238.

Lord, A. B. (1960): *The Singer of Tales.* Cambridge, Mass: Harvard University Press.

Owen, M. (1983): *Apologies and Remedial Interchanges: A Study of Language Use in Social Interaction.* Berlin: Mouton.

Parry, M. (1971): *The Meaning of Homeric Verse,* ed. Adam Parry. Oxford: Clarendon Press.

Sacks, H. / Schegloff, E. / Jefferson, G. (1974): "A Simplest Systematics for the Organization of Turn-taking for Conversation". *Language* 50, 696–735.

Watts, R. (1985): "Relevance in Conversational Moves: A Reappraisal of 'Well'". Mimeo. To appear in *Studia Anglica Posnaniensia.*

Wilson, D. / Sperber D. (1978): "On Grice's Theory of Conversation". *Pragmatics Microfiche,* 3.5.

Summaries in Newspapers: A Textlinguistic Investigation

Udo Fries

0. Linguists and laymen alike are aware that different texts may be interrelated in a variety of ways. This has been described, e. g. by Beaugrande and Dressler (1981), as the phenomenon of *intertextuality*, a term which is somewhat hazy as it may refer to quite different things. There are, e. g., texts which can only be properly understood if the reader/listener knows other texts that have been produced previously. A standard example is the case of parodies, which refer to an original that is paraphrased or commented upon: you cannot understand a parody if you don't know the original. The same criterion of intertextuality is used for replies in conversation (Beaugrande 1980: 20). Here the reply is not a "parallel" text to the original, but refers to the content of a text that must be known to speaker and listener alike. I have also used the term intertextuality in connection with highly conventionalized texts, e. g. death announcements, which can only be properly produced if the author has some knowledge of the traditional text-type.

This paper is about a special type of intertextuality existing between texts of different length. The shorter of these we may call *summaries*. Once again, the type of intertextuality is somewhat different: even though it may be helpful, we do not need to know the longer text – which I would like to call the *original text* – in order to understand the summary. Quite on the contrary, one of the functions of summaries is to give information to a reader who has no time to read through the original – something which has become especially important in the 20th century. Another function which may be added to that of information is evaluation. Book reviews are a typical case in point: they should not only inform the reader about the contents of a book but should also give a critical evaluation of the original text; the purpose of a review may very well be to dissuade a reader from buying a particular book. Another function of book reviews, incidentally, is the self-presentation of the author of the review: his readers should realise what a clever chap he is.

With some types of summaries, the function of advertising is added to that of information: these texts should persuade the reader not only to read but also to buy the original. As a good example, which also sheds some light on the texts I want to discuss later, we may look at book-advertisements by some publishers. Take, e.g. the following German example, consisting of three texts that refer to one original. The first text is the headline copied from the original text, which now becomes part of the abbreviated version.[1] There is then a second abbreviated version consisting mainly of nominal constructions – to inform the very busy reader of the contents of the book, and thirdly, there is the full text – the summary proper. All these texts are related to one another, and thus represent a clear instance of intertextuality. These are the three texts:

(1) i Die Ableitung der denominalen Verben mit Nullsuffigierung im Englischen.

ii *Kurztext:* Auf der Basis eines Satzkorpus formuliert diese Arbeit eine produktive Wortbildungsregel für englische denominale Verben mit Nullsuffigierung (z. B. *drink*), die ins Lexikon eingegangenes Alltagswissen des Sprechers verarbeiten.

iii Für die denominalen nullsuffigierten Verben des Englischen wird auf der empirischen Grundlage eines Satzkorpus eine produktive Wortbildungsregel als Ableitungsbeziehung zwischen (Basis)nomen und denominalem Verb formuliert, die die schon 'registrierten' Ableitungen und die Innovationen erklärt. ...

Summaries or *abstracts* are important text-types that have developed over the last few decades, and without which modern science could not exist. It is not surprising, therefore, that much has been written about the art of reviewing and of producing summaries or abstracts of longer texts, such summaries being required to contain all the necessary information and nothing but this necessary information. The major problem is, of course, how to determine which parts of a text are of prime importance and must be reproduced in the shorter version. For the type of summary we are now going to discuss these problems are, however, only of minor importance.

1. In the following analysis I will deal with summaries on the front pages of newspapers, in particular those of the London *Times,* from which I have collected a corpus of 100 summaries and full texts. Various

[1] Headlines may be regarded as part of the text, but also as texts in their own right. Traditionally they are treated as separate entities, cf. e.g. Mårdh (1980) or the classic study by Straumann (1935). For studies relating headlines to texts cf. Harweg (1968), and most recently Hellwig (1984).

terms seem to be used for this type of text. The *Times* – unofficially – calls them 'read-through', but they may simply be called 'News in brief'. For a textlinguistic analysis, a number of questions may profitably be asked:

1.) What is the function of these summaries?
2). What do these texts look like? What are their syntactic and thematic structures?
3.) What do the headlines of these texts look like? Are they typical of this particular text-type?
4.) What is the relationship between headline and text of this particular text-type?
5.) What is the relationship between these texts and the longer versions within the newspaper?
6.) What is the relationship between the two headlines?
7.) In what ways does our text-type refer to the text within the newspaper?
8.) What elements are identical in the two types of text?
9.) From which part of the long text are the elements in the short version derived?

What I cannot pursue here is the problem of general rules that must be followed in order to produce a good summary, nor can I consider rules that would automatically change a text into a summary. I am rather interested in what is actually done by producers of summaries in newspapers. These writers are not necessarily the authors of the long texts which we find within the newspaper, so that the author who writes an article cannot be held responsible for headlines and summaries. This may help to explain some of the inconsistencies we find between these various texts.

2. The function of summaries outlined above is first of all achieved by a number of typographical and linguistic means. All the texts are clearly separated from other short notices in the newspaper. They appear at exactly the same place in every issue and consist of a headline followed by a short text, both of which are supposed to draw the reader's attention to the full version of the news-item within the paper. All these texts appear to be about the same length, and all of them are followed by a final line referring to the page on which more informaton on that particular topic can be found. This is an important aspect for the reader, as it is the only clear indication of the referential character of the text-type. Other indicators can only be detected within headline and text them-

selves, but do not explicitly refer to another text. It is rather through the lack of sufficient information and because of the interest aroused by these texts that the reader will look for the corresponding article within the newspaper.

3.1. Let me begin my analysis with a short comparison of the headlines. From the very layout of the newspaper it is clear that there is less space available for the read-throughs than for the longer articles. This is clearly borne out by the number of words per headline in the read-throughs.

In the short versions there are altogether 281 words in the corpus, which means that the average headline consists of 2.81 words. The long texts have longer headlines, amounting to 721 words; that means 7.21 words per headline, a figure which is confirmed by other analyses of English newspaper-headlines. The restricted space available for the read-throughs is, no doubt, a decisive factor in the choice of the wording of a headline: in the short versions the most common headline consists of only 2 words. Consider the number of words per headline and the layout, i. e. the number of lines needed for each individual headline:

(2)

2 words: 62%	1-line: 62	–	–
3 words: 16%	1-line: 15	2-lines: 1	–
4 words: 4%	1-line: 1	2-lines: 2	3-lines: 1
5 words: 14%	–	2-lines: 9	3-lines: 5
6 words: 3%	–	2-lines: 2	3-lines: 1
7 words: 1%	–	–	3-lines: 1
Headlines:	1-line: 78	2-line: 14	3-line: 8

In 2- and 3-word headlines there is usually only one line involved, while in the longer headlines two and three separate lines are used up. On the whole, however, the one-line headline is the most common type, accounting for 78% of all examples. The relatively large number of headlines consisting of 3 words is due to the large number of phrasal verbs in this type of headline.

In the case of the long texts headlines often spread across more than one column, and thus a count by lines would not yield any useful results for comparison. Such headlines consist of 3 to 13 words, with 5- and 6-word headlines the most common type.

(3)

3 words: 1	9 words: 10
4 words: 3	10 words: 11
5 words: 20	11 words: 8
6 words: 21	12 words: 4
7 words: 12	13 words: 1
8 words: 9	

I will not analyse these headlines any further, as they have been the subject of general investigations of newspaper headlines. What is important here is the difference between the headlines of the two text-types; the short, 2- or 3-word headlines are typical of summaries, whereas the longer headlines – from 4 words upwards – are examples of the more general and better-known type of newspaper headlines. Most often they consist of 5–6 words, but others consisting of 7–11 words are by no means rare.

3.2. Let us look more closely at headlines consisting of 2 words. We will doubtless expect these two words to stand in some relationship to one another, such as subject – predicate, attribute – head-word, or topic – comment. Hellwig (1985: 8) calls this "semantische Zweigliedrigkeit". As the most common type we find nominal headlines consisting of two nouns in an attributive relationship, which often defy easy semantic analysis.

(4) Prison ordeal
Sex confession
Debt hopes

Thus, while *Prison ordeal* and *Sex confession* in (4) may readily be interpreted as "someone experiences a prison ordeal" and "someone confesses something about a sexual act", in *Debt hopes* it is very unlikely that "someone hopes for debts"; it is much more likely that someone hopes that some debts will be reduced (?), removed (?), or forgotten (?). No limits are set to the reader's imagination: indeed, this may be regarded as one of the means of arousing his interest, of making him read on in order to find out more about the subject matter. Another point worth considering is that no agent is mentioned in this type of headline. Thus, there is again something left for the reader to find out. This, however, is not always the case:

(5) Walesa fear
Reagan hint
Dali denial

In the examples in (5) it is always a well-known public figure that is mentioned. No doubt it is assumed that the reader would like to hear more about how the "denial", "hint" or "fear" are connected with these agents; it is therefore not surprising if the texts following the headlines begin which the names mentioned:

(6) Mr Lech Walesa returned to work in the Gdansk shipyards voicing fears of being arrested in the May Day demonstrations "which could be a trap for me"

President Reagan's reversal of his ban on grain negotiations with the Soviet union is seen as a further indication that he intends to seek another presidential term

Art experts and close friends of Salvador Dali, the surrealist painter, denied the claims of a Catalan artist who said he had flooded the market with faked Dalis

In the third example it is not Dali himself who is the agent, the person who did the denying, even though he is closely connected with the denial; consequently the summary does not begin with his name.

Instead of the name of a person, we may also come across the names of countries, institutions or the like, which are also supposed to be well-known to the readers and thus are of news-value: they arouse the interest of the reader.

(7) US anger
Ethiopia famine
Rolls-Royce loss

Once again, the texts begin with the names mentioned in the headline:

(8) The United States has reacted angrily to the apparent rejection of their offer to stage the 1986 World Cup. They have asked the international football federation to think again.

Large areas of Ethiopia are in the grip of the worst drought since that of 1973 which killed hundreds of thousands. A million are in immediate peril. Britain is giving £ 250,000 extra help

Rolls-Royce, the state-owned aircraft engine manufacturer, lost £ 91 m before tax last year, after making a profit of £ 18 m in 1981. The loss reflects a big fall in demand for engine spares.

As the second text shows, the situation is sometimes more complicated, but the general principle seems to apply. Other nominal headlines consist of a noun in the genitive as an attribute to another noun. In accordance with the general rules for genitives, these nouns usually refer to human beings:

(9) Invader's story
Spencer's bill
Lion's selection

In the texts which follow these headlines, the same principles that have just been discussed apply. This may also be the case when attributive adjectives constitute the first member of the two-word constructions, though here we must reckon with such a close relationship between the two words that they form a semantic unit which cannot be split up in the following text.

(10) i Polish reshuffle
ii Golden touch
iii Nuclear split

Whereas in (10)i we expect a text giving information about (a) a reshuffle which takes place (b) in Poland, in the texts following, (10)ii and iii, the noun phrases of the headlines are taken as a unit. In these cases there is much more freedom in the wording of the text.

(11) In a reshuffle of the Polish Government the Minister of Agriculture has been replaced and General Moczar, chairman of the Supreme Chamber of Control, has been retired.

Eugene Evans, aged 16, who left school last year, expects to receive £35,000 this year as a computer programme designer with a firm in Liverpool.

A Labour Party internal policy report strongly opposing the development of nuclear power has been rejected by a party committee, exposing deep divisions within Labour on nuclear policy.

The difficulty of the texts in (11) derives in part from the metaphorical headline in (10)ii and the wordplay in (10)iii, hovering between "nuclear fission" and the "deep divisions"within the Labour Party mentioned in the text. Besides nominal headlines, we find various types of verbal headlines. Among these there are finite verbal headlines consisting of a subject and a predicate.

(12) Ethiopian wins
Bank withdraws
Firemen hesitate

Here, the interest of the reader is aroused in two ways: firstly, he needs a closer identification of the agent (which Ethiopian, which bank or which firemen are being talked about), and, secondly, he needs further information on the predicate: what is the contest in which an Ethiopian has won, from what has the bank withdrawn, or about what are the firemen hesitant? The texts must at least give a first answer to these questions:

(13) An Ethiopian, Bekele Debele, won the world cross-country championship in a thrilling finish to the race at Gateshead. Only two seconds separated the first four runners.

Midland Bank has decided not to extend its branch network nationwide to cater separately for individual and corporate customers because of the high cost of implementing the strategy.

The threat of a series of one-day firemen's strikes this week receded after it became apparent that enthusiasm for industrial action was waning.

Both the Ethiopian and the bank are identified by their respective names, Bekele Debele and Midland Bank; the firemen are those who had threatened to go on strike. In all three texts we also get further information on the predicate of the headline: in the first text of (13) we hear which race the Ethiopian won, and we are even given some of the details of the performance of the other competitors – altogether enough to satisfy our initial curiosity, and at the same time incentive enough for those interested in the topic to turn to the corresponding article in the newspaper to find out some of the remaining very important details that are not given in the front-page text; e. g., who were the other athletes, over what course was the race run, and what were the final results? For those readers not interested in cross-country racing the information given in the front-page text is, however, quite sufficient to allow them to turn to other matters. One can easily apply the same principles to the two further examples given in (12) and (13). The most common type of verbal headline consists of a subject followed by a participle or adjective, with the copula being supressed.

(14) i Licence withheld
ii Aid arriving
iii Israel angry

In (14)i and ii it is essential that the character of the licence and the aid be further described, whereas in (14)iii the subject need not be elaborated on. Further information on the predicate, however, must be given in all three instances.

(15) One of the four surviving single vellum sheet copies of the Magna Carta, dated 1297, was temporarily withheld from export by Mr Paul Channon, Minister for the Arts

Relief agencies said their aid was reaching Ethiopian drought victims and there was no evidence that it was going to the Soviet Union.

Israel has reacted angrily to President Reagan's decision to continue to withhold delivery of F16 jet fighters while Israel troops occupy Lebanon.

Each single text leaves open many questions that an interested reader would probably like to have answered in the full text within the newspaper.

3.3. Usually part of the headline is repeated in the summary, which helps the reader comprehend the text. In the headline, however, such words frequently appear in an abbreviated form, which is expanded in the summary. This is shown in the following survey:

HEADLINE OF SUMMARY	TEXT OF SUMMARY
Surname only	*Full name*
Walesa	Mr Lech Walesa
Dali	Salvador Dali, ...
Watson('s prize)	John Watson ...
Surname only	*Title + name*
Reagan	President Reagan
Name only	*Name + apposition*
Dali	Salvador Dali, the surrealist painter,
Rolls-Royce	Rolls-Royce, the state-owned air-craft engine manufacturer,
Carson	Willie Carson, the royal jockey
General noun	*Addition of name*
Ethiopian	an Ethiopian, Bekele Debele
Bank	Midland Bank
General noun	*Substitution of proper name*
Star	Vitas Gerulaitis, one of the world's top tennis professionals
Abbreviation	*Full form*
US	The United States

These instances may be taken as special cases of *Expansion* or *specification* of the whole or part of the headline. In addition, we come across more general examples of expansion:

Same chair	the same electric chair in Alabama that took 10 minutes to execute Evans on Friday
Turkey	Turkey's ruling military council
Bill	the Police and Criminal Evidence Bill

Headlines and texts may differ with regard to the parts of speech employed: in headlines nominal expressions are preferred, while in the texts we find verbal constructions:

Noun	*Verb phrase*
anger	has reacted angrily
loss	lost
denial	denied
confession	admitted

Often, the noun in the headline correspondes to a noun in the text which is embedded in a verb phrase – usually as the object of the verb:

fear	voicing fears
decision	faces a delicate decision
challenge	faces a legal challenge

Whenever there is a finite verb in the headline, it occurs in the simple present tense. The corresponding texts report the events in the past (or present perfect) tense.

Verb – present tense	*Verb – past tense*
(Ethiopian) wins	won the world ... championship
Pound surges	Sterling surged

4.1. As we have seen above, most summaries are of roughly equal length. The shortest occupies 4 lines, the longest 14; the majority, however, are between 5 and 7 lines in length, the average figure being 6.58. It is interesting to consider whether the length of the headlines of the summaries in any way indicates the length of the text. This does seem to be the case: with two-word headlines, the average text-length is 5.8 lines, whereas with headlines of more than two words, this figure is 7.8. Usually (in 67% of the examples), these texts consist of 1 sentence (calculated by full-stops), but they may extend to 4 sentences: this, however, is clearly exceptional. The average number of sentences is 1.38, once again with a lower figure (1.23) for 2-word headlines: and a higher figure (1.62) for headlines of more than two words.

4.2. An analysis of the 67 one-sentence summaries shows that there are two major types, if we compare these texts with the longer versions within the newspaper. One type I would like to call the ordinary summary. In these the gist of the story, or what the particular author of the summary considers to be the most important and perhaps most effective elements of the story, is formulated in the summary; the general rules governing summaries mentioned at the beginning of this paper would apply here. Then there is a second and, for this particular text-type, more important type of summary, in which the first sentence of the long text is used as the basis of the summary. This procedure is, of course, not possible with every text – I would even maintain that in general the first sentence of a text does *not* contain the *theme* of the text. For a different opinion, cf. Werlich (1976: 27 ff), who argues that the "thematic text base" is a text-initial linguistic unit. Yet very often the introductory sentences of a text have nothing whatsoever to do with the main content and purpose of a text, and in all such cases a summary that simply reproduced the first sentence would be quite useless. One example should suffice to make this clear:

The text begins:

(16) It was the first evening of Passover and a thick, sticky fog lay heavily over the half-ruined villa where the Israelis have their company headquarters beside the Damascus road.

The only important element here is *Passover* which accordingly reappears in the summary. Otherwise the summary brings in facts that are only reported later in the longer article:

(17) Israeli soldiers about to celebrate the Passover had to leave their meal uneaten as gunfire and explosions erupted nearby. It was the beginning of an ambush in which an Israeli soldier died.

Incidentally, in newspapers it is mostly articles on the sports pages that cannot be summarised by simply reproducing the first sentence of the text: cf. (18) and (19). This corroborates my thesis that we are here dealing with a very particular sort of text-beginning, which is "textsortenspezifisch", i. e. specific to particular traditional text-types.

(18) FULL TEXT: England are accustomed to breaking fresh ground at the national stadium. ...

(19) SUMMARY: England were held to a 0–0 draw by Greece at Wembley and Scotland drew 2–2 with Switzerland at Hampden Park in European Championship matches.

Here, the summary gives the results of two matches. The full article, of course, would never give the two results in textinitial position. Instead, it begins by relating some aspects of the background: and whenever an article begins with background information this will not become part of the summary.

4.3. The following analysis concerns examples taken from summaries consisting of one sentence only, and a comparison with the initial elements of the corresponding long texts reveals a number of differences. The summaries, though not written in an elliptical style, are restricted in length and must therefore omit "unnecessary" information. The following types of ellipsis occur:

1.) Complex names are reduced to simpler variants. This we have already observed when comparing summary headlines with the texts of the summaries; now it turns out that the summaries themselves consist of abbreviated forms in comparison to the full text. Thus, the summaries clearly stand between the headlines (and, incidentally, also the headlines of the full text-versions) and the original texts.

(20) i FULL TEXT: Turkey's ruling military national security council yesterday lifted a 1980 ban on political activities, paving the way for general elections promised for this autumn or early next year. ...
ii SUMMARY: Turkey's ruling military council has lifted the 1980 ban on political activities, paving the way for a general election promised for this autumn or early next year.
iii SUMMARY HEADLINE: Turkey relents
iv TEXT HEADLINE: Turkey lifts ban on political parties

As we can see from (20), the *national security* reference is omitted in the summary, and the *ruling military ... council*, which appears in the summary, is deleted in the headlines.

A further example:

Text	*Summary*
General Mario Benjamin Menendez	General Mario Menendez

Often, it is not part of the name itself that is deleted, but part of an appositive description of a person mentioned.

John Lennon, the former Beatle	John Lennon

2.) Time adverbs such as *yesterday, last night, last week,* etc. are omitted, and the deletion of these adverbs may bring about a change of tenses in the summary: the past tense is then no longer obligatory. Example (20) is a typical case in point: the deletion of *yesterday* leads to a change of tense in the summary from past to present perfect, which is also more appropriate for the particular text-type of the summary – which has to "sum up" the present situation rather than report what happened the day before. Thus, while I can agree with Werlich (1976:

86) that summaries belong to the group of expository texts, I do not believe that "the *temporal text structuring* (...) of a narrative text (...) is reflected in the summary" (Werlich 1976: 91). Other examples:

Text	*Summary*
The threat of a series of ... strikes receded last night after it became apparent. ...	receded after it became apparent
during the Argentine occupation last year. ...	during the Argentine occupation.
Lord Spencer was ordered yesterday to pay ...	Lord Spencer has been ordered to pay ...

Often, the time-adverb may be embedded in a longer phrase describing the reporting situation; in that case the whole phrase may be deleted:

it was announced last night	——

3.) Prepositions and adverbs may be deleted if the text remains easily comprehensible. This sort of telegraphic ellipsis is familiar not only from telegrams, but particularly from spoken, conversational language. In replies to questions, prepositions are among those elements that are most easily deleted for the sake of brevity.

Text	*Summary*
a series ... of ... strikes, starting this week,	a series of ... strikes this week
to prevent sightseers from looking into the grounds	to prevent sightseers looking into the grounds
is seen here as	is seen as

4.) Attributive adjectives whose function is largely to comment on or evaluate the following noun-phrase may be omitted in the summary:

Text	*Summary*
its ambitious branch network	its branch network

5.) Noun-phrases, though customarily used, may, strictly speaking, be redundant and may therefore be deleted. As in the previous points, a maxim of brevity can be observed in the summaries. The full text of the example given above runs as follows:

(21) i FULL TEXT: Lord Spencer was ordered yesterday to pay £ 1,000 damages and costs to a woman whose dog was shot by his gamekeepers.
ii SUMMARY: Lord Spencer has been ordered to pay £ 1,000 to a woman whose dog was shot by his gamekeepers.

or

the possible involvement of British intelligence in the case.	the possible involvement of British intelligence.

6.) An indefinite article may be changed into a definite article, thus presenting the information which follows as if it were previously known to the reader – which is also a means of making the reader more curious about the details of the main news report. An example of this is once again found in sentence (20).

7.) Relative clauses may be reduced to verb phrases by omitting the relative pronoun and the finite part of the verb:

Text	*Summary*
which is dated 1297	dated 1297
which is published this morning	published this morning

8.) Subordinate clauses may be turned into nominal groups – if they are not deleted altogether – as less important information:

President Reagan's surprise announcement that he is reversing his ban	President Reagan's reversal of his ban
Britain's leading foreign affairs "think tank" which is popularly known as Chatham House,	the leading foreign affairs "think tank",

9.) In consecutive sentences, the cohesive devices my be changed to bring about a shorter version. Instead of repetition substitution may be used:

The Inland Revenue has released nine statements ... These statements	The Inland Revenue has released nine statements ... They ...

10.) Finally, there are a number of diverse changes which are more difficult to interpret: singular and plural, word-order shifts, shifts of tenses in indirect speech, and a few others. These inconsistencies may simply be due to different authors writing the text and the summary.

All other changes that are of major importance can only be described within the larger framework of the study of summaries. What I have done here has been to look at summaries from the point of view of their production, i. e. I have taken the full texts inside the newspaper as the starting point. If we adopt the reader's view-point, then the summary comes first, and only afterwards does he turn to the full article. Finding this article may sometimes prove more difficult than expected, since neither the headlines nor the text-beginnings need consist of identical elements. In this case, the reader must rely on additional semantic clues; thus, the repetitions which we have observed have an important function in relating the two texts to each other.

4.4. I have argued above that the summaries are supposed to lead the reader to a perusal of the corresponding article within the newspaper. This, one could imagine, may be achieved through the thematic structure of the summaries. Unfortunately, only a few thoughts about this structure can be presented here. First of all, we must take into consideration the fact that the reader begins to read his text with the headline; thus, when he begins to read the first line of the text, he already has some knowledge, some expectation of what the following lines will contain. Hence, when he reads, e. g., *houseprices up*, he knows what the topic of the following lines will be, and he will do everything possible to relate these lines to the headline. When he sees that the text begins with a paraphrase of the title, he is reassured and can concentrate on the new information that is presented:

(22) House prices have risen by up to 8 per cent during the last three months in some parts of the country, according to a market survey by the Royal Institution of Chartered Surveyors.

The source of the news items is given in final position: it is a very heavy element, and thus particular attention is drawn to this part of the summary: I suppose that one would therefore like to hear more about *the Royal Institution of Chartered Surveyors.* Indeed, the text itself, which is constructed in a slightly different way, has this element as the beginning of its second paragraph, taking it as a topic to be expanded:

> House prices have risen by eight per cent during the last three months in some parts of the country, according to a market survey published today. The latest report from the Royal Institution of Chartered Surveyors covering the quarter to the end of February shows. ...

With regard to the thematic structure of summaries, we have thus found one type, and it sems to be one of the most common types, in which the two parts of the headline are presented first, and then some new information is added in the second half of the text. Let me give a few examples with the topical part of the headline in capitals:

(23) i Israel angry.
ISRAEL HAS REACTED ANGRILY to President Reagan's decision to continue to withhold delivery of F 16 jet fighters while Israel troops occupy Lebanon.

ii Carson banned.
WILLIE CARSON, the royal jockey, *WAS BANNED* from riding for six days after being found guilty of reckless riding at Ayr.

iii *Sterling gloom.*
THE GLOOM OVER STERLING'S PROSPECTS and oil price outlook has led to renewed fears over the rise in interest rates and dearer bank loans.

In a second type of summary, the two parts of the headline are simply expanded without any other information being added; the additions explain, as it were, the two elements. They may also explain why these elements have been together in the first place. There is no clue to the direction which the main article will take, or the direction in which the attention of the reader is to be drawn:

(24) i Watt to quit
Mr David Watt, director of the Royal Institute of International Affairs, the leading foreign affairs "think tank", is to resign at the end of the year.

ii *IRA* trial clash
The New York trial of four men accused of gun-running to the *IRA* was adjourned for a week after a courtroom clash about the possible involvement of British intelligence.

In a third type, the reader has to read through the whole of the summary before he comes to the parts already known from the headline; when he finally reaches this point, the text ends abruptly, leaving him wondering how the text will continue – and possibly he will then turn to the main text:

(25) i Ambush death
Israeli soldiers about to celebrate the Passover had to leave their meal uneaten as gunfire and explosions erupted nearby. It was the beginning of an *ambush in which an Israeli soldier died.*

ii Afghan hope
Señor Javier Pérez de Cuéllar, the United Nations Secretary-General, said after talks in Moscow that he was *encouraged about Afghanistan.*

It is clear that these types are idealizations and that the list is not exhaustive. Nevertheless, this may offer a way of analyzing a traditional text-type which is, more than any other, embedded in and related to other texts. An investigation of these *summaries* may therefore shed light on both the production and the reception of texts.

REFERENCES

Beaugrande, R. de (1980): *Text, Discourse and Process. Towards a Multidisciplinary Science of Texts.* London: Longman.

Beaugrande, R. de / Dressler, W. (1981): *Einführung in die Textlinguistik.* Tübingen: Niemeyer. (Konzepte der Sprach- und Literaturwissenschaft, 28).

Harweg, R. (1968): *Pronomina und Textkonstituion.* München: Fink.

Hellwig, P. (1984): "Titulus oder über den Zusammenhang von Titeln und Texten", *ZGL,* 12, 1–20.

Mårdh, I. (1980): *Headlines. On the Grammar of English Front Page Headlines.* Lund: C.W.K. Gleerup. (Lund Studies in English, 58).

Straumann, H. (1935): *Newspaper Headlines. A Study in Linguistic Method.* London: Allen & Unwin.

Werlich, Egon (1976): *A Textgrammar of English.* Heidelberg: Quelle & Meyer. (Uni-Taschenbücher, 597).

Deictics and the Status of Poetic Texts

Balz Engler

One of Keats's last poems, which he probably wrote in November 1819, is untitled, and runs as follows:

> This living hand, now warm and capable
> Of earnest grasping, would, if it were cold
> And in the icy silence of the tomb,
> So haunt thy days and chill thy dreaming nights
> That thou would wish thine own heart dry of blood,
> So in my veins red life might stream again,
> And thou be conscience-calm'd. See, here it is —
> I hold it towards you.[1]

Whose hand is extended? Who is addressed by the words? What does "now" refer to? These questions are immediately suggested by the deictic elements, which presuppose a situation of which the words of the poem are part: Somebody holding *this* hand towards somebody else addressed as *thou* and *you*, at a particular moment. The deictics suggest that the text is part of a situation; the situation in turn suggests conversational implicature.[2]

In other words, we are faced with a problem that the text itself cannot answer, and that makes dubious the notion of a text's autonomy. Answers to the question, *Who is the addressee?* can range over a wide area. It may be argued that, in general, deictics in Modern, as contrasted to Classical poetry, have lost their force; that, in this poem, the person addressed is the reader; that it is Fanny Brawne, Keats's financée, and, finally, that the text was meant to become part of a play.[3]

1 *The Poems of John Keats,* ed. by Jack Stillinger (London: Heinemann, 1978), 503.

2 See Stephen C. Levinson, *Pragmatics.* Cambridge Textbooks in Linguistics (Cambridge: Cambridge University Press, 1983), chapter 3.

3 The poem has traditionally been considered to be addressed to Fanny Brawne,

Deictics in poetic texts, specifically words of address, have rarely been studied by literary critics;[4] Jonathan Culler, in an essay on "Apostrophe" in *The Pursuit of Signs: Semiotics, Literature, Deconstruction* even claims that they have deliberately been neglected because they are considered an embarrassment.[5]

Culler tries to remedy this situation. His essay discusses only one type of deixis, but it reflects concerns that affect deixis in general. In discussing apostrophe, however, it accepts and makes explicit views that are widely held but need to be criticized. Culler's attempt to tackle a problem baffling to critics, therefore, also exposes the weaknesses of his own approach.

In describing how deictics have been neglected by literary critics Culler quotes George N. Shuster's introduction to *The English Ode from Milton to Keats*:

> The element of address is of no especial signifcance, being merely a reflection of the classical influence. All the verse of antiquity was addressed to somebody, primarily because it was either sung or read and the traditions of song and recitation required that there be a recipient.[6]

This position denies address in Modern poetry any deictic function. Culler, on the contrary, considers address in the form of apostrophe crucial to lyrical poetry; he emphasizes "the fact that the apostrophic

a view no longer held by many. Walter Jackson Bate comments: "The general feeling now is that the lines were a passage he might have used in some future poem or play" (*John Keats* [Cambridge, MA: Harvard University Press, 1963], 626–27); the dramatic interpretation is certainly suggested by the strong gestic energies in the text (cp. on dramatic language Rudolf Stamm, *The Shaping Powers at Work* [Heidelberg: Winter, 1967], esp. 11–84). The speech seems to belong to a figure confronting its mortal enemy, or even its murderer, seeking reconciliation. In a letter to John Taylor of 17 November, 1819, Keats speaks of "The Earl of Leicester's history" as a "promising" subject for a play (*The Letters of John Keats, 1814–1821*, ed. by Hyder Edward Rollins. 2 vols. Cambridge: Cambridge University Press, 1958, vol. II, 234).

4 There is a rich literature on deixis in linguistics, especially in the areas of ethno-linguistics and language-acquisition.

5 Jonathan Culler, "Apostrophe." In *The Pursuit of Signs: Semiotics, Literature, Deconstruction* (London: Routledge and Kegan Paul, 1981), 136. He took a similar position already in *Structuralist Poetics* (Ithaca, N. Y.: Cornell University Press, 1975), 166, and confirms it in "Changes in the Study of the Lyric". In: Chaviva Hošek and Patricia Parker, eds. *Lyric Poetry: Beyond New Criticism* (Ithaca, N. Y.: Cornell University Press, 1985), 38, 49–50.

6 George N. Shuster, *The English Ode from Milton to Keats* (New York: Columbia University Press, 1940), 11–12.

postulation of addressees refers one to the transforming and animating activity of the poetic voice".[7] He quotes Shelley's "On Life" in support of this view: "[T]he words, *I*, *you*, *they* are not signs of any actual difference subsisting between the assemblage of thoughts thus indicated but are merely marks employed to denote the different modifications of the one mind".[8] This links up with Shelley's famous distinction between story and poem in *A Defense of Poetry:*

> ... there is this difference between a story and a poem, that story is a catalogue of detached facts which have no other connection than time, place circumstance, cause and effect; the other is the creation of actions according to the unchangeable forms of human nature as existing in the mind of the creator, which is itself the image of all other minds.[9]

Shelley's essay, according to Culler, suggests a general distinction between "two forces in poetry, the narrative and the apostrophic," and he concludes "that the lyric is characteristically the triumph of the apostrophic".[10]

Culler closes his discussion of apostrophe with a short analysis of the poem quoted at the beginning, which he calls "perhaps Keats's most fascinating poem".[11] He takes it for granted that the poet is addressing us, his readers, and that the present created by the deictics is "a *now* of discourse, of writing".[12]

Culler's discussion of apostrophe is disappointing for two reasons: First, he fails to do what the title of his essay would suggest, i. e. he does not offer a convincing definition of apostrophe. He begins by discussing apostrophe and ends by discussing the Keats poem, which does not offer any – a confusion that, as we shall see, is typical of textualist criticism. Secondly, his discussion lacks historical perspective; he generalizes the use of deictics in poetry from the way they are used by Romantic poets. I should like to say something about both points in turn.

The problem of definition may be approached by way of linguistic pragmatics. According to Stephen C. Levinson deixis "concerns the ways in which languages encode or grammaticalize features of the *context of utterance* or *speech event,* and thus it also concerns ways in which

[7] Culler, 148.
[8] "On Life." In *Shelley's Prose,* ed. by D. L. Clark (Albuquerque, NM: University of New Mexico Press, 1954), 174.
[9] Clark, 281.
[10] Culler, 149.
[11] Culler, 153.
[12] Culler, 152.

the interpretation of utterances depends upon the analysis of that context of utterance".[13]

Three among the descriptive notions and terms introduced by Levinson are of particular interest to us: person deixis, time deixis, and place deixis.[14]

Person deixis, of which apostrophe is obviously an example, encodes the roles of the participants in a situation: Who is the speaker (first person), who is the addressee (second person), who is referred to without being either the speaker or the addressee (third person). Apostrophe can be described as *the move between two types* of addressees. Quintilian's definition in terms of forensic rhetoric makes this quite clear. He defines apostrophe as "a diversion of our words to address some person other than the judge".[15]

It is therefore wrong to say, as Culler does about the Keats poem quoted: "The fact that it eschews apostrophe for direct address makes it possible to speak with more confidence about its effects and the way in which they are produced".[16] This seems to suggest that direct address in a lyric is, after all, a kind of apostrophe, at least as far as its effect is concerned. As his essay shows, Culler accepts, without questioning, John Stuart Mill's dictum that the lyric is not heard but overheard.[17] The passage in Mill is well-known; it runs as follows:

> Eloquence is *heard,* poetry is *overheard.* Eloquence supposes an audience; the peculiarity of poetry appears to lie in the poet's utter unconsciousness of a listener. Poetry is feeling confessing itself to itself in moments of solitude.[18]

[13] Levinson, 54. Culler does not mention a single study from the field of linguistic pragmatics – a branch of semiotics, which is mentioned in the title of his book.

[14] The two additional types are discourse and social deixis: Discourse deixis does not link the utterance with its context, but concerns the utterance itself: "As I said then", "I am now turning to another topic" (see below note 19). Social deixis may be of interest where it defines the relationship between the speaker and the addressee in the poem; but it is beyond the scope of this paper to deal with this.

[15] Quoted by Culler, 135. The primary addressee is temporarily put in a third person position. At the same time some kind of complicity between the speaker and addressee is established, as both are placed in the same position vis-à-vis the apostrophee (if there is such a word). The implications of this are of great interest, but cannot be discussed in detail here.

[16] Culler, 153.

[17] Culler, 137, *via* Northrop Frye's *Anatomy of Criticism.*

[18] *Mill's Essays on Literature and Society,* ed. by J. B. Schneewind (New York: Collier-Macmillan, 1965), 9.

On this premise, namely, that the poet is speaking to himself, any address to somebody else must be considered an apostrophe, and a poem like "This living hand ..." must appear as a particularly striking example of the "triumph of the apostrophic". But can Mill's dictum be accepted as generally valid?[19]

This brings me to my second criticism, which concerns the lack of historical perspective. Culler (like so many before him) uses the Romantic lyric, a historical phenomenon, in constructing a generic system that is not explicitly limited to a particular period. He even goes one step further: He derives the function of deictic elements in poetry from the *theorizing* of Romantic poets. In doing so he shows himself, for different reasons, to be as severely limited as Shuster, whose position he attacks. Small wonder that all his illustrations come from Romantic and post-Romantic poetry.

Misconceptions often begin with the vagueness of the term *lyric.* The only trait shared by lyric poems, according to a recent collection of essays, seems to be "the single undisputable feature of [their] relative short length".[20] Yet the same collection also contains an essay on *The Prelude* (which may be called of relative long length). This is possible because the words *lyric* and *lyrical* are casually associated with Romantic notions like the intense moment, and the expression of personal feeling.

The history of the word *lyric* itself should make us wary: Its deriva-

[19] The same problems also arise with place and time deixis. Additional ones can only be hinted at here. For example, we have to distinguish between two types of usage: endophoric (pointing forwards or backwards in the text) and exophoric (pointing outside it). This distinction is based on the assumption that the beginning and the ending, and thus the inside and the outside of an utterance, as it were, are clearly marked; but this need not be the case. When I am saying that *here* I am only discussing *exophoric* deictics, does this mean that I am not going to deal with any other types in my paper, or that I am going to deal with those later? You cannot tell.

Most deictic elements can serve both the endophoric and the exophoric functions (the definite article, demonstrative pronouns, like *this* and *that,* personal pronouns, like *he* and *they,* adverbs of place and time like *here* and *there* or *then* and *now,* and the tenses of verbs (with the important possible exception of the preterit). Others, like the personal pronouns *I, you* and *we,* and the place deictics *yon, yond,* and *yonder* always have an exophoric function.

[20] Hošek and Parker, 13. E. M. Forster at least gave us the approximate number of words when he tried to define the novel along similar lines. Among more obvious examples the following poems are discussed in their collection on *Lyric Poetry:* an epitaph by Surrey, Jonson's *Under-wood,* and Wordsworth's *Prelude.*

tion from music and song is too obvious to warrant discussion; we still use the word for song-texts. The dissociation of the lyric from song, leading to a semantic definition of the lyric rather than one according to medium, is relatively late;[21] indeed our problem of defining the lyric may be due to our attempt to force together meanings widely different and historically remote from each other.

The use of address and other deictic elements in the Romantic lyric cannot, therefore, serve as a general model, but must be considered the result of a historical process. This can be studied in eighteenth century poetry. Faas, among others, has described the increasingly close relationship between descriptive poetry and the ode, and at the same time, the increasingly precise definition of the situation of which the words of the poems are supposed to be part.[22] This is done with the help of deictics of person, place and time: the speaker is individualized, the scene particularized, the time condensed to the moment of intense experience. Conversely, we might say, it is increasingly the text that defines the situation, a situation that is different from, even incompatible with, the one in which the recipients find themselves.

Two examples may be suggestive of such changes: In Pope's *Windsor Forest* (1713) deictics are mainly used as rhetorical devices for juxtaposition and structuring catalogues, i. e. they function on the level of discourse:

> There, interspers'd in Lawns and opening Glades,
> Thin Trees arise that shun each others Shades.
> Here in full Light the russet Plains extend;
> There wrapt in Clouds the blueish Hills ascend:[23]

In Collins's *Ode Occasioned by the Death of Mr Thomson* (1748–49), a scene is indicated ("On the Thames near Richmond"), and the movement of the poem follows the movement in the situation presented, that of a boat gliding past Richmond church.[24]

[21] An historical dictionary is of limited use here, because the examples make it difficult to judge to what extent the word refers to song, to what extent it is used metaphorically. The *O. E. D.* gives first examples for the modern meaning of *lyric* from the sixteenth century. *Lyricism,* a word in which the transferred sense has become dominant, is first recorded for 1760.

[22] Egbert Faas, "Die deskriptive Dichtung als Wegbereiterin der romantischen Naturlyrik," *Germanisch-Romanische Monatsschrift* N. F. 22 (1972), 142–61.

[23] Alexander Pope, *The Poems,* ed. by John Butt. One-volume edition (London: Methuen, 1963), 195–96.

[24] *The Poems of Gray, Collins, and Goldsmith,* ed. by Roger Lonsdale (London: Longmans, 1969), 486–91. The movement implied by the poem is discussed

Elsewhere I have sketched the consequences of this development for the relationship between the poet and the recipient.[25] They may be summarized as follows: The addressee is rarely identified or even defined as clearly as the speaker and the situation; the Keats poem is no exception to this. As recipients we may feel considerable pressure to take on the role of the implied addressee; our own situation as recipients may then conflict with that of the addressee in the text. We may find ourselves confronted with the question whether we should identify with the speaker or consider ourselves addressed by him.

This conflict between being addressed and identification is characteristic of reading in general: The reader is both the addressee, and continually has to reconstruct the speaker from the few marks left by him or her on the page; reading therefore may be characterized as a dialogue between two selves.

The need for identification becomes urgent in Romantic poetry, where the speaker may indeed, as Mill suggests, be addressing himself. This creates a close link between the Romantic lyric and writing (or printing). Northrop Frye suggests as much, when he compares oral and literate poetry:

> If the poet does not read or write, the poem exists only in the one dimension of pure continuity in time, because such a poet is not thinking of lines on a page. If the poem is written, it appears in two spatial dimensions, across and down a page, as well as in time, and the crucial term "verse", with its associations of turning around or turning back, becomes functional. The poem may still be continuous, but in "verse", where we keep coming to the end of a line and then starting another, there is a germ of discontinuity. *The more this sense of the discontinuous increases, the more closely we approach the lyrical area.* (my italics).[26]

Deictics signal the changes in the role of the recipient, which are due to a changing relationship between text and situation. *At the same time* the changing relationship between text and situation also affects the function of deictics. They increasingly *become* what Shelley describes them to be in the passage quoted by Culler, "merely marks employed to denote the different modifications of the one mind," which is the mind of the

by E. M. W. Tillyard, "William Collins's 'Ode on the Death of Thomson'", *A Review of English Literature* 1 (1960), 30–38; reprinted in his *Essays Literary and Educational* (London, 1962), pp. 89–98.

25 Balz Engler, *Reading and Listening: The Modes of Communicating Poetry and their Influence on the Texts.* The Cooper Monographs, 30 (Berne: Francke, 1982), 58–62.

26 In his essay "Approaching the Lyric" In: Hošek and Parker, 31.

creator, and the image of all other minds. In other words, the deictics no longer tie the text to the situation in which it is used, but, having quasi-magical force, create a situation of their own in the imagination.

The use of deictics thus mirrors the change from a poetic of conversation, as we still find it in Augustan poetry, to a poetic of expression, a process we can describe as interiorization.[27] In his essay "The Poem as a Closed Field" Walter J. Ong sketches this process:

> With romanticism, the old agonistic poetic had been replaced by a new poetic of creativity. The poet is irenic, or at least neutral, uncommitted, free of dialogic struggle with an audience, since for the "creative" romantic imagination the poem is no longer a riposte but a simple product, an "object" rather than an exchange.[28]

In this view, John Stuart Mill's idea that "poetry is *overheard*" becomes a document of this change rather than a generally valid statement:

> The insulation of poetry from dialogue allows poetic in the romantic age (in which we still live) to deflect attention which had earlier been directed to the audience, back to the poet's own self. John Stuart Mill registered the changed emphasis, with no evident awareness of its deeper implications ...[29]

We do not have a detailed study of how this change in poetics affected deictics and vice versa. We need one if we want to overcome the limitations of an approach like the one of Culler. Here I can only suggest two small pieces of possible evidence: It is striking to notice that in the course of the eighteenth century at least two deictic words became, apart from their occurrence in dialects and sociolects, limited to literary usage. Both are crucial to the argument I have sketched here. One of them is *yon* and the words related with it (*yond*, *yonder*) – the only place deictic that had always been restricted to reference outside the discourse, to the situation in which it takes place. The other word, significantly, is the person deictic *thou*, the pronoun of address.[30] The complexities of the task are

[27] Ann Banfield, *Unspeakable Sentences* (Boston: Routledge and Kegan Paul, 1982), has observed related changes due to writing in narrative texts, in particular how they can represent speech and thought indirectly. Her unspeakable sentences are often characterized by a conflict between different deictic elements (e.g., the preterit and *now*). In the lyric we find an equivalent conflict between the scene and the *now* of the reader.

[28] Walter J. Ong, "The Poem as a Closed Field," In: *Interfaces of the Word: Studies in the Evolution of Consciousness and Culture* (Ithaca, N.Y.: Cornell University Press, 1977), 222–223.

[29] Ong, 223.

[30] On *thou* cf. Thomas Finkenstaedt, *You and Thou. Studien zur Anrede im Englischen* (Berlin: de Gruyter, 1963), especially 227–231.

daunting, as we must realize when we return to the Keats poem quoted at the beginning: Whose hand is extended? Who is addressed? Even: Why does Keats switch from *thou* to *you?* Simple answers may be esthetically more satisfying; but by suppressing one dimension of the work of poetry they also distort it.

Chiastic Structures in Literature: Some Forms and Functions

Max Nänny

According to the OED, a *chiasmus* is a "grammatical figure by which the order of words in one of two parallel clauses is inverted in order." It seems that around 1870 this term, whose etymology derives from the Greek letter "chi" (χ), began to enter the English language and in time to replace the rhetorical term *antimetabole*, which the OED defines as a "figure in which the same words or ideas are repeated in inverse order" and which the Renaissance rhetorician Richard Puttenham aptly called "counterchange" in his *The Arte of English Poesie* of 1589. In modern critical parlance, hence, the expression *chiasmus* is generally applied to a "balancing pattern in verse or prose, where the main elements are reversed."[1]

The term "elements" in this definition indicates that the chiastic patterning *abba* may occur not just on the sentence level but on *all* levels of a literary text: on the level of sounds (including rhymes and rhythm), words, sentences, lines, stanzas, narrative elements (plot, character) and concepts. It goes without saying that chiasmus may be combined with other rhetorical figures such as parallelism, antithesis (dialectical chiasmus), polyptoton, anadiplosis, etc.

Now, what holds for linguistic signs generally, whose signifiers may be identical and yet relate to various signifieds (think, for instance, of the multiple meanings of the signifier "to get"), is equally true for the chiastic pattern *abba* as a pattern – for it may also acquire several meanings depending on the semantic context. Apart from its use as a mnemonic aid in oral literature or as a clever mannerism of style, the various possible interpretations of the uniform structural pattern *abba* make chiasmus available for various mimetic or iconic ends.

[1] J.A. Cuddon, *A Dictionary of Literary Terms* (Harmondsworth: Penguin, 1982), p. 113.

Thus the chiastic series *abba* may be seen as a dynamic or temporal sequence that reverses its movement or inverts its development. Hence, chiasmus may be used as an "emblem" or icon of reversal or inversion generally. Furthermore, the return to the initial element *a* at the end of a chiastic sequence may, on a somewhat more metaphorical level, suggest circularity and, ultimately, a certain form of closure or non-progressive stasis.

But the same chiastic pattern *abba* may also be considered statically or spatially as a symmetrical arrangement of elements which stand in a relationship of balance, opposition, reciprocity or mirroring. However, the first and last elements *a* of the chiasmus *abba* may as well be looked upon as framing, centring or enclosing the inner elements *bb*.

All these possible interpretations of chiasmus may reinforce, reflect or be parallel to the semantically indicated meaning of a literary passage or text.

Before concentrating on my main task, namely on the analysis of functional, that is, imitative (iconic) or "emblematic" uses of chiasmus in some English and American literary texts, I shall first consider chiasmus as a mnemonic and compositional aid in oral literature and then look at a few examples of its later, largely gratuitous use as a kind of oral or rhetorical residue which has dwindled to a mere mannerism of style or a decorative device.

Mnemonic Uses

Let me start with the earliest literary use of chiasmus, namely its use as a primarily mnemonic aid that has little semantic function. For chiastic framing by balanced similarity and antithesis can be found in oral literature where it is helpful as a compositional device. The oral singer of tales has recourse to chiastic or annular composition in order to help memorization and the organization of narrative material without the help of writing.

Thus Cedric H. Whitman has persuasively shown "Homer's habit of returning to things previously mentioned in reverse order,"[2] his technique of "ring-composition" or his pervasive use (observed ever since Cicero) of the rhetorical figure of *hysteron proteron.* Analysing Homer's *Iliad,* Whitman writes:

[2] *Homer and the Heroic Tradition* (Cambridge, Mass.: Harvard University Press, 1958), p. 254.

> Not only are certain books of the poem arranged in self-reversing, or balancing, designs, but the poem as a whole, in a way, an enormous hysteron proteron, in which books balance books and scenes balance scenes by similarity or antithesis, with the most amazing virtuosity.[3]

Devoting a long chapter to Homer's manifold framing devices,[4] Whitman demonstrates book by book the annular or chiastic pattern of the *Iliad.* To take merely two examples: he shows how the day groupings of the first book and the last book (Book XXIV) reverse each other neatly:[5]

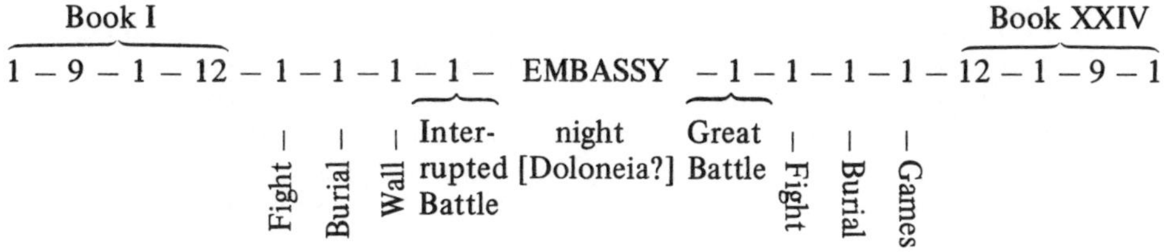

Or Whitman also establishes that the principal scenes of Book I are chiastically reversed in Book XXIV:[6]

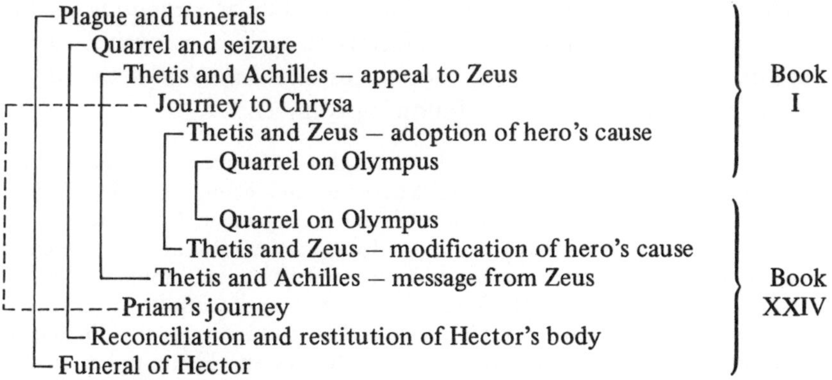

Whitman suggests that the chiastic device had not only the mnemonic purpose of assisting the singer to keep in mind what he said before but that it was an artistic device "to give shape and clarity to the sections of his work, which, composed paratactically and with almost equal detail

[3] *Homer and the Heroic Tradition,* p. 255.
[4] Ibid., pp. 249–284.
[5] Ibid., p. 25.
[6] Ibid., p. 260.

and emphasis in every part, might otherwise fall into an intolerably unarticulated series."[7]

The fact that Homer's general use of chiasmus in his poetic composition must have failed to reach the level of full consciousness is commented on by Whitman as follows:

> The very serious question arises ... as to whether the audience, listening to an oral presentation of the poem, could possibly have caught the signs of such 'fearful symmetry', or whether it would have meant anything to them if they did. Granted that the procedure *abba* is useful in small compass to a singer, and perceptible as a structural unit to the audience, such can hardly be the case when *ba* is separated from *ab* by many thousand lines. Yet two things may be said regarding this point. The human mind is a strange organ, and one which perceives many things without conscious or articulate knowledge of them, and responds to them with emotions necessarily and appropriately vague. An audience hence might feel more symmetry than it could possibly analyze or describe. The second point is that poets sometimes perform feats of virtuosity for their own sakes and without much hope of understanding from their audiences, for one of the minor joys of artistic creation is the secret which the artist buries in his work..."[8]

The use of the chiastic framing device can also be observed in the popular ballad which generally favours not only binary and trinary patterns, parallelism, balance and antithesis but also annular structures on the levels of character, mimesis and diegesis as well as narrative. David Buchan, who devotes a long chapter of his *The Ballad and the Folk* to chiastic structuring, makes the following comment:

> At its most pronounced, framing becomes chiastic structuring. Chiasmus ... is used frequently by the oral mind where the literate mind, with its different habits, would use a straightforward linear arrangement. (...) Chiasmus is intrinsic to oral creation because of the basic, structural-mnemonic function of annular organization. Frames, however, serve a variety of functions: they enable the maker to break down his narrative into constituent units and impose a tight control on these units; to link and integrate these units; to express contemporaneous action; and, finally they enable him to keep to his narrative line while the binary and trinary rhythms allow him to expand dramatically. Annular structuring, especially in its chiastic form, shows how the oral mind operates spatially.[9]

As an example, Buchan analyses stanzas 4–12 of the ballad "Willie O Douglas Dale" (Child, 101A) which are organized by means of three superimposed chiastic frames:[10]

[7] Ibid., p. 252.
[8] Ibid., pp. 255–256.
[9] *The Ballad and the Folk* (London: Routledge and Kegan Paul, 1972), p. 100.
[10] See *The Ballad and the Folk*, p. 101 (H=He, S=She, n=narration, sp=speech).

a	4 He looted him low, by her did go, Wi his hat intill his hand: 'O what's your will wi me, Sir Knight? I pray keep your hat on.'	H + S	n + sp	Meeting of H + S
b	5 'O I am not a knight Madam, Nor ever thinks to be; For I am Willy o Douglassdale, An I serve for meat and fee.'	H	sp	H introduces himself to S
c	6 'O I'll gang to my bowr,' she says, 'An sigh baith even an moru That ever I saw your face, Willy, Or that ever ye was born.			S expresses her attraction
	7 'O I'll gang to my bowr,' she says, 'An I'll pray baith night an day, To keep me frae your tempting looks, An frae your great beauty.'	S	sp	to H
d	8 O in a little after that He keepit Dame Oliphant's bowr, An the love that passd between this twa, It was like paramour.	H + S	n	Act of love
c	9 'O narrow, narrow's my gown, Willy, That wont to be see wide; An short, short is my coats, Willy, That wont to be sae side; An gane is a' my fair colour, An low laid is my pride.			S laments her pregnancy
	10 'But an my father get word of this, He'll never drink again; An gin my nother get word of this, In her ain bowr she'll go brain; An gin my bold brothers get word o this I fear, Willy, you 'll be slain.'	S	sp	to H
b	11 'O will you leave your father's court, An go along wi me? I'll carry you unto fair Scotland, And mak you a lady free.'	H	sp	H proposes elopement to S
a	12 She pat her han in her pocket An gae him five bunder poun: 'An take you that now, Squire Willy, Till awa that we do won.'	H + S	n + sp	Elopement of H + S

Ornamental and Playful Uses

In a large number of literary texts chiasmus (especially on the sentence level) has no specific semantic function as a structure. In many of these texts chiasmus may be seen as a sort of oral or rhetorical residue whose original mnemonic or compositional task has become redundant.

Thus Pope's verse contains a number of frequently gratuitous chiastic patterns, as E. L. Epstein has demonstrated.[11] And in *A Portrait of the Artist as a Young Man* Joyce uses chiastic phrases which Hugh Kenner has described as stylistic showpieces of "a young man's copybook page" that leave "after-vibrations of sententiousness..."[12]

Two more recent poets have also used chiastic patterns for purely decorative or playful purposes. In his four-page "Author's Prologue" to the *Collected Poems 1934–1952* Dylan Thomas rhymes the first line with the last line (line 102), the second with the second last and so on until a couplet marks the exact middle.[13] This almost imperceptible chiastic rhyme-scheme[14] seems to have no other function than to make a show of Thomas's poetic virtuosity.

In his dramatic monologue "A Professor's Song" John Berryman makes a grammatically deviational use of chiasmus in order to reflect the puckish playfulness of young Mozart, who loved language-games, especially inverting word order or writing words backwards ("arschlings" he called it), for instance, signing his name backwards as "Gnagflow Trazom" (letter of 21 August, 1773) – a mannerism that may be due to the influence of musical composition in which chiastic sequences of notes are frequent:

A Professor's Song

(...rabid or dog-dull.) Let me tell you how
The Eighteenth Century couplet ended. Now
Tell me. Troll me the sources of that Song –
Assigned last week – by Blake. Come, come along.
Gentlemen. (Fidget and huddle, do. Squint soon.)
I want to end these fellows all by noon.

11 "The Self-Reflexive Artifact: The Function of Mimesis in an Approach to a Theory of Value for Literature," *Style and Structure in Literature*, ed. Roger Fowler (Ithaca, N. Y.: Cornell, 1975), pp. 40–78.

12 *Ulysses* (London: Allen and Unwin, 1980), p. 7.

13 *Collected Poems 1934–1952* (London: Dent, 1952), pp. ix–xii.

14 The reversed numbering of lines from line 52 onwards and the identity of rhyme words ("now," "end", "sun") in the first three and last three lines are the only clues to the chiastic pattern.

'That deep romantic chasm' – an early use,
The word is from the French, by our abuse
Fished out a bit. (Red all your eyes. O when?)
'A poet is a man speaking to men':
But I am then a poet, am I not? –
Ha ha. The radiator, please. Well, what?

Alive now – no – Blake would have written prose.
But movement following movement crisply flows,
So much the better, better the much so,
As burbleth Mozart. Twelve. The class can go.
Until I meet you, then, in Upper Hell
Convulsed, foaming immortal blood: farewell.[15]

Berryman's chiastic "So much the better, better the much so" of line 15 is an accurate translation of Mozart's "Desto besser, besser desto" which he used twice in a letter to Bäsle (5 November, 1777).

After this introductory consideration of primarily non-functional cases of chiastic patterning let me proceed to diverse literary uses of chiasmus in which the chiastic structure becomes part and parcel of the total meaning of a text. In other words, I shall now turn to examples of chiastic ordering of textual elements that are more functional by being of an iconic, mimetic or "emblematic" nature.

Reversal or Inversion

Seen in terms of a dynamic sequence, chiasmus reverses or inverts the order of its elements. Hence, the use of chiasmus as an iconic reinforcement of reversal or inversion is rather frequent in literary texts.

Laurence Sterne's famous "Ask my pen, – it governs me, – I govern not it." (*Tristram Shandy*, 6.6.416) expresses such a reversal chiastically and reinforces it by negation. The use of the rhetorical figure of antimetabole in this ironic phrase denies formally what it asserts semantically – a further element of opposition – for it demonstrates that the author is fully in command of his pen.

In "Autumn: The Third Pastoral" (ll.49–50) Alexander Pope suggests the reversal ("rebounds") or echoing of sounds by a chiasmus of nouns.

Thro' Rocks and Caves the Name of *Delia* sounds,
Delia, each Cave and ecchoing Rock rebounds.

[15] *The Norton Anthology of Modern Poetry* (New York: Norton, 1973), p. 896 (my italics).

Of course, echoes do not repeat in reverse but they are repetitions that return to their sources.

A reversal is also mimed in two chiastic lines – buttressed by antonyms – from William Wordsworth's "Resolution and Independence" (ll.24–25):

> As high as we have mounted in delight
> In our dejection do we sink as low...

Emily Dickinson uses chiasmus as an icon of reversal twice in poem 712:

> Because I could not stop for Death –
> He kindly stopped for me – (ll.1–2)

This initial chiasmus of reversal is strengthened by a further chiastic reversal in the very middle of the poem, a reversal that is further emphasized by the stanza-division between the two lines:

> We passed the Setting Sun –
>
> Or rather – He passed Us –[16]

At the very beginning of *Great Expectations* we are told that the protagonist's name is "Philip Pirrip", which is abbreviated to "Pip". Now both the family name "Pirrip" and the nickname "Pip" are palindromes, that is, names whose letters are chiastically arranged and, hence, sound the same when read backwards. In other words, the very same name may be read in two opposite ways, the normal reading being identical with its inversion. In my view, these two names are a "mise en abyme" of the plot: they are emblems of two possible "readings" of Pip's situation. For this is not due to the generous support of a gentlewoman, as he wrongly assumes, but of a criminal.

This reversal of Pip's "great expectations" is also foreshadowed in a passage at the begining of the novel. This passage shows the originator of the reversal first perform it physically and symbolically on Pip by turning him upside down, a passage, furthermore, which is itself chiastically structured:

> The man, after looking at me for a moment, turned me upside down, and emptied my pockets. There was nothing in them but a piece of bread. When the church came to itself – for he was so sudden and strong that he made it go head over heels before me, and I saw the steeple under my feet – when the

[16] *The Complete Poems of Emily Dickinson,* ed. Thomas H. Johnson (London: Faber, 1970), p. 350.

> church came to itself, I say, I was seated on a high tombstone, trembling, while he ate the bread ravenously.[17]

The chiastic sequence in this passage, partly hidden by synonymous expressions, is the following: "bread" – "When the church came to itself" – "he made it go head over heels" – "before me" = "I saw" – "the steeple under my feet" – "when the church came to itself" – "bread".

In "The Masque of the Red Death" E. A. Poe uses chiasmus to render not only the to and fro movement of the dancing dreams in the *seven* chambers of Prince Prospero's abbey but also to mime how the dance and the music come to a sudden stop at the striking of the ebony clock and how they begin again when the echoes of the chime die away:

> | *To and fro* in the seven chambers there stalked, in fact, a multitude of dreams. | And these – the dreams – *writhed* in and about, taking hue from the rooms, and causing the wild *music* of the orchestra to seem as the *echo* of their steps. | And, anon, there strikes the ebony *clock* which stands in the hall of the velvet. || And then, for a moment, *all* is *still,* and *all* is silent save the voice of the *clock.* || The dreams are stiff-frozen as they stand. | But the *echoes* of the chime die away – they have endured but an instant – and a light, half-subdued laughter floats after them as they depart. |And now again the *music* swells, and the dreams live, and *writhe to and fro* more merrily than ever, taking hue from the many-tinted windows through which stream the rays from the tripods.|[18]

In terms of its repeated key words this passage of *seven* sentences chiastically centres around the fourth or middle sentence which itself has its fulcrum in "all" – "still" – "all". Thus we get the following chiastic pattern of expressions: "To and fro" – "writhed" – "music" – "echo" – "clock" – "all" – "still" – "all" – "clock" – "echoes" – "music" – "writhe" – "to and fro." In addition, both sides of this chiastic symmetry are buttressed by four pairs of identical terms and one pair of synonyms (though not in perfect chiastic order): "dreams" (twice), "taking hue from", "stand(s)" and "a moment/an instant".

Ralf Norrman has convincingly and brilliantly demonstrated that chiastic inversion is the one pattern that permeates the entire fictional world of Henry James and dominates his thinking completely. "Chias-

[17] *Great Expectations,* ed. Angus Calder (Harmondsworth: Penguin, 1965), p. 36; it is noteworthy that the very title of this novel of inversions on the level of plot and character-relationships contains a chiastic sequence of sounds:
[greit ekspekteiʃnz]
ab c   c ba

[18] *The Portable Poe,* ed. Philip van Doren Stern (Harmondsworth: Penguin, 1979), p. 284 (my italics).

mus in James," Norrman writes, "is not only decorative or ornamental. It influences not only *how* James writes, but *what* he writes. Furthermore, it influences what he *thinks*, and even what he *perceives*."[19]

Thus the "hour-glass shape" (E. M. Forster) of *The Ambassadors* is due to a chiastic inversion of the narrative which also characterizes the story "The Real Thing," to name just two examples. However, James not only made a pervasive use of chiastic plotting but also of the inversion of sexual roles and of chiasmus on the sentence level. In short, Henry James was a habitual and compulsive chiasticist in his thought and fiction.

Circularity

The return of the chiastic sequence to its beginning may also be used as an emblem of circularity or a circular movement such as a dance.

Thus John Milton reinforces the circular dance of the angels, planets and stars in *Paradise Lost* (V,ll.618–624) by a chiastic antithesis that harmoniously combines regularity with irregularity itself:

> That day, as other solemn days, they spent
> In song and dance about the sacred hill,
> Mystical dance, which yonder starry sphere
> Of planets and of fixed in all her wheels
> Resembles nearest, mazes intricate,
> Eccentric, intervolved, yet regular
> Then most, when most irregular they seem...[20]

In a similar way Wordsworth strengthens the wheeling movement of skating by a chiasmus in his *Prelude* (1805; I, ll.455–458):

> I heeded not the summons: happy time
> It was indeed for all of us – to me
> It was a time of rapture! Clear and loud
> The village clock tolled six, – I wheeled about...[21]

19 *The Insecure World of Henry James's Fiction. Intensity and Ambiguity* (New York: St. Martin's Press, 1982), p. 185. See especially chapter 5, "Chiastic Inversion, Antithesis and Oxymoron," pp. 137–184.

20 *The Poems of John Milton*, ed. John Carey and Alastair Fowler (London: Longmans, 1968), p. 715. It is interesting to note that Book 3, which centres on the debate between God Father and his Son, "has more antimetabole than any other book" (Brian Vickers, *Classical Rhetoric in English Poetry*, London: Macmillan, 1970, p. 153).

21 *William Wordsworth. The Prelude. A Parallel Text*, ed. J. C. Maxwell (Harmondsworth: Penguin, 1972), p. 58.

The two similarly spelt phrases "I heeded" and "I wheeled" form the beginning and end of the chiastic sequence "happy" – "time" – "It was" – "for all of us" = "to me" – "It was" – "time" – "rapture", a sequence which syntactically indicates circularity.

Circularity is also expressed chiastically in George Herbert's "A Wreath":

A Wreath.

Wreathed garland of deserved praise,
Of praise deserved, unto thee I give,
I give to thee, who knowest all my wayes,
My crooked winding wayes, wherein I live,
Wherein I die, not live: for life is straight,
Straight as a line, and ever tends to thee,
To thee, who art more farre above deceit,
Then deceit seems above simplicitie.
Give me simplicitie, that I may live,
So live and like, that I may know, thy wayes,
Know them and practise them: then shall I give
For this poore wreath, give thee a crown of praise.[22]

By means of a "circular rhyme pattern" in the first and last four lines ("praise" – "give" – "wayes" – "live" = "live" – "wayes" – "give" – "praise"), the chiastic anadiplosis "of deserved praise/ Of praise deserved" (ll.1–2) and the use of "wreathed" in the first and of "wreath" in the last line, Herbert's poem offers a "formal hieroglyph" (Joseph H. Summers) of its circular subject.[23]

Non-Progression, Stasis, Deadlock

A chiastic sequence that leads back to its beginning may also suggest coming full circle or, more metaphorically, non-progression, stasis or a deadlock.

In "The Rime of the Ancient Mariner" (Part II,ll.107–108) S. T. Co-

[22] *The Works of George Herbert*, ed. F. E. Hutchinson (Oxford: Oxford University Press, 1941), p. 185

[23] Mary Ellen Rickey, *Utmost Art: Complexity in the Verse of George Herbert* (University of Kentucky Press, 1966), p. 122; see also Joseph H. Summers, *George Herbert: His Religion and Art* (London: Chatto and Windus, 1954), pp. 135–145. The banding of the text into quatrains and the frequent use of *anadiplosis*, which makes the lines weave in and out, overlap and intertwine, reinforce the hieroglyphic form of this poem on a wreath (see also Brian Vickers, op.cit., p. 165).

leridge seems to have reinforced the idea of a total lull – marginal note: "The ship hath been suddenly becalmed" – by the use of two chiastic patterns in sequence:

> Down dropt the breeze, the sails dropt down,
> 'Twas sad as sad could be...

The two expressions "the breeze" and "the sails" are synonyms in a metonymic relationship, whereas "'Twas" and "could be" are two conjugated forms of the verb "to be".

Ernest Hemingway also made repeated use of chiasmus in order to mirror or reinforce by means of narrative structure a deadlock or impasse in a person's situation from which there is no escape.

Thus in "The Killers" the ex-champion Ole Andreson, who is visited by Nick to warn him but remains lying on his bed and waits for the killers to get him, is tightly encapsulated by a series of chiastically arranged actions and conversations that seem to centre around the parallelism:

> 'Maybe it was just a bluff.'
> 'No. It ain't just a bluff."

The chiastic pattern of "The Killers" may be represented as follows:

[Inside Henry's lunch-room where Nick and George talk about the threat to Ole Andreson]
"Nick walked the street beside the car-tracks and turned at the next arc-light down a side-street." (p. 286)
"Three houses up the street was Hirsch's rooming-house. Nick walked up the two steps and pushed the bell. A woman came to the door." (p. 286)
"'Is Ole Andreson here?'" (p. 286)
"Nick followed the woman up a flight of stairs." (p. 286)
"Nick opened the door and went into the room, Ole Andreson was lying on the bed
with all his clothes. He did not look at Nick." (p. 287)
"'Come in!'" (p. 287)
"'There isn't anything I can do about it.'" (p. 287)
"'There ain't anything to do.'" (p. 287)
"'Maybe it was just a bluff.'"
"'No. It ain't just a bluff.'" (p. 287)
"'There ain't anything to do now.'" (p. 288)
"'There ain't anything to do.'" (p. 288)
"'Thanks for coming around.'" (p. 288)
"Nick went out. As he shut the door he saw Ole Andreson with all his clothes on,
lying on the bed looking at the wall." (p. 288)
"'He's been in his room all day,' the landlady said down-stairs." (p. 288)
"'I said to him: "Mr. Andreson, you ought to go out."'" (p. 288)
"They stood talking just inside the street door... 'Well, good-night, Mrs Hirsch,' Nick said. 'I'm not Mrs. Hirsch,' the woman said...I'm Mrs Bell.'" (p. 288)
"Nick walked up the dark street to the corner under the arc-light, and then along the car-tracks to Henry's eating house." (p. 288)
[Inside Henry's lunch room Nick and George talk about the threat to Ole Andreson.][24]

It is noteworthy that the introduction of the woman's name, "I'm Mrs. Bell" (p. 288) chiastically corresponds to "Nick...pushed the bell" (p. 286). I suggest that Hemingway's choice of the name "Bell" is chiastically motivated – probably the only such name in American literature.

A similar chiastic ordering of narrative elements to indicate a deadlock can also be found in Hemingway's "Cat in the Rain".[25] The part of the story that deals with the American wife's futile attempt to save a cat

[24] *The Short Stories of Ernest Hemingway* (New York: Scribners, 1966), pp. 286–288.
[25] Ibid., pp. 167–170.

from the rain is bracketed by a multiple pattern of narrative chiasmus. Apart from reinforcing the complete futility of the wife's action on the story-level, on the symbolic level Hemingway's narrative chiasmus signals that her displaced wish for more attention, tenderness and fulfilment in caring motherhood (which centres around the word "cat" or "kitty" – a pun on "kiddy" in American English) will find no satisfaction. The chiastic pattern of "Cat in the Rain" may be analysed in the following way:

Introduction		
hotel room	1-	"The American wife stood at the window looking out." (p. 167)
	2-	"'I'm going down and get that kitty'".
	3-	"The husband went on reading..."
stairs	4-	"The wife went downstairs
lobby	5-	and the hotel owner...bowed to her
	6-	as she passed the office." (p. 168)
going out		"As she stood in the doorway
	7-	an umbrella
	8-	opened behind her.
	9-	It was the maid..."
	10-	"...she walked along the gravel path"
	11-	"'There was
	12-	a cat,'
	13-	said
	14-	the American girl. 'A cat?' 'Si, il gatto.' 'A cat?'
outside	14-	the maid
	13-	laughed
	12-	'A cat
	11-	in the rain?'"
	10-	"They went back along the gravel path ..." (p. 169)
going in	9-	"The maid stayed outside
	8-	to close
	7-	the umbrella."
lobby	6-	"As the American girl passed the office,
	5-	the padrone bowed from his desk."
stairs	4-	"She went on up the stairs."
hotel room	3-	"George was on the bed, reading."
	2-	"I wanted that poor kitty."
	1-	"His wife looked out of the window." (p. 170)
coda		

It should be noted that the chiastic structuring even extends to the syntactical level. Thus the passage "...an umbrella opened behind her. It was the maid" (p. 168) is chiastically reversed by "The maid stayed outside to close the umbrella" (p. 169). The same holds for "...and the hotel owner... bowed to her as she passed the office" (p. 168) which is reversed by "As the American girl passed the office, the padrone bowed from his desk" (p. 169).

Symmetry

Seen in more spatial terms a chiastic arrangement of textual elements is an ideal emblem to indicate balance, symmetry or equality.

Thus I see the chiasmus of sounds and stresses [(ɪ) ǽ ə ú: ɪ ú: ə ǽ] in the first line of S. T. Coleridge's "Kubla Khan" ("Khan" rhymes with "ran" and "man" of lines 3 and 4)

> In Xanadu did Kubla Khan
> A stately pleasure dome decree

as an emblem of the perfect symmetry of the "stately pleasure-dome."

In John Keats's "Ode on a Grecian Urn" the chiasmus of the famous phrase "'Beauty is truth, truth beauty'" (l.49) may be also meant to mirror the perfect symmetry of the urn's "Attic shape" (l.41). But assuming that the Grecian urn is a burial urn, it may also function as an icon of enclosure: the beautifully shaped and decorated urn enclosing the truth that life and love ("for ever warm," l.26) turns to ashes preserved in a "Cold Pastoral" (l.45) of marble.

In her poem "Before I got my eye put out" (327) Emily Dickinson attempts to render the symmetrical arrangement of two eyes by a chiastic patterning of elements in the poem's text:

> Before I got my eye put out
> I liked as well to see –
> As other Creatures, that have Eyes
> And know no other way –
>
> But were it told to me – Today –
> That I might have the sky
> For mine – I tell you that my Heart
> Would split, for size of me –

The Meadows – mine –
The Mountains – mine –
All Forests – Stintless Stars –
As much of Noon as I could take
Between my finite eyes –

The Motions of the Dipping Birds –
The Morning's Amber Road –
For mine – to look at when I liked –
The News would strike me dead –

So safer – guess – with just my soul
Upon the Window pane –
Where other Creatures put their eyes –
Incautious – of the Sun –[26]

It is noteworthy that both the expression for midday, "Noon", and the phrase "Between my finite eyes" stand in mid-position in the text.

Symmetry was a key concept in E. A. Poe's poetics and cosmology. As he writes in *Eureka:*

> And, in fact, the sense of the symmetrical is an instinct which may be depended on with an almost blindfold reliance. It is the poetical essence of the Universe – *of the Universe* which, in the supremeness of its symmetry, is but the most sublime of poems. Now symmetry and consistency are convertible terms: – thus Poetry and Truth are one. A thing is consistent in the ratio of its truth – true in the ratio of its consistency...[27]

Apart from using a chiasmus in this very text about the importance of symmetry and its convertibility with consistency – "A thing is consistent in the ratio of its truth – true in the ratio of its consistency" – Poe's use of chiastic patterns to indicate symmetry of action or scene (e. g. mirroring, doubling) is pervasive in his work.

In "The Fall of the House of Usher," for instance, he uses chiasmus several times. Thus he uses it in his description of the mirroring of the House of Usher and of its bleak environs in the dark tarn:

[26] *The Complete Poems of Emily Dickinson*, p. 155.
[27] *The Science Fiction of Edgar Allan Poe*, ed. Harold Beaver (Harmondsworth: Penguin, 1976), p. 300.

"I looked upon the scene before me –
upon the mere house...
upon the vacant eye-like windows –
upon a few rank sedges – and upon a few white trunks of
decayed trees –
with an utter depression of soul..." (p. 245)

"I reined my horse to the precipitous brink of a black and
lurid tarn...and gazed down –
but with a shudder even more thrilling than before –
upon the remodelled and inverted images of the gray sedge,
and the ghastly tree-stems,
and the vacant and eye-like windows" (p. 245)
"Nevertheless, in this mansion of gloom..." (p. 246)[28]

The stages of the narrator's approach to the mansion at the beginning and of his flight from the foundering House of Usher at the end are also ordered in a chiastic manner.

As has been pointed out by critics before, Poe makes the most radical use of a chiastic narrative pattern in *The Narrative of Arthur Gordon Pym of Nantucket.* As Charles O'Donnell writes:

> I think Poe meant to give a clue to his intention in the way he ordered the book, dividing it roughly in half, making all events lead up to and away from Pym's rescue by the *Jane Guy* at the end of the central chapter, each event in the first half paralleling an event in the second half. At the beginning, the characters set sail in a small boat; there is a wreck from which they are rescued; Pym is confined in the hold; there is treachery in the form of a mutiny; they escape by killing treacherous men; and they sail in a disabled ship toward the equator and are rescued. In the second half they sail away from the equator toward an island; there is treachery; they are confined in the hills; they escape by killing treacherous men; they set sail in a small boat toward the pole; and... there is a wreck from which they are rescued, thus allowing Pym to get home. The general impression of parallel events is reinforced by other similar details in the two halves (some of them seemingly without other purpose than to call our attention to the order in the book)...[29]

But what is especially noteworthy about *Arthur Gordon Pym* is not just the parallel arrangement of its episodes but their chiastic order as can be seen from the following scheme of the plot:

[28] *The Portable Poe,* pp. 244–268.

[29] "From Earth to Ether: Poe's Flight into Space," *Twentieth Century Interpretations of Poe's Tales,* ed. William C. Howarth (Englewood Cliffs, N.J.: Prentice Hall, 1971), pp. 39–46; pp. 43–44.

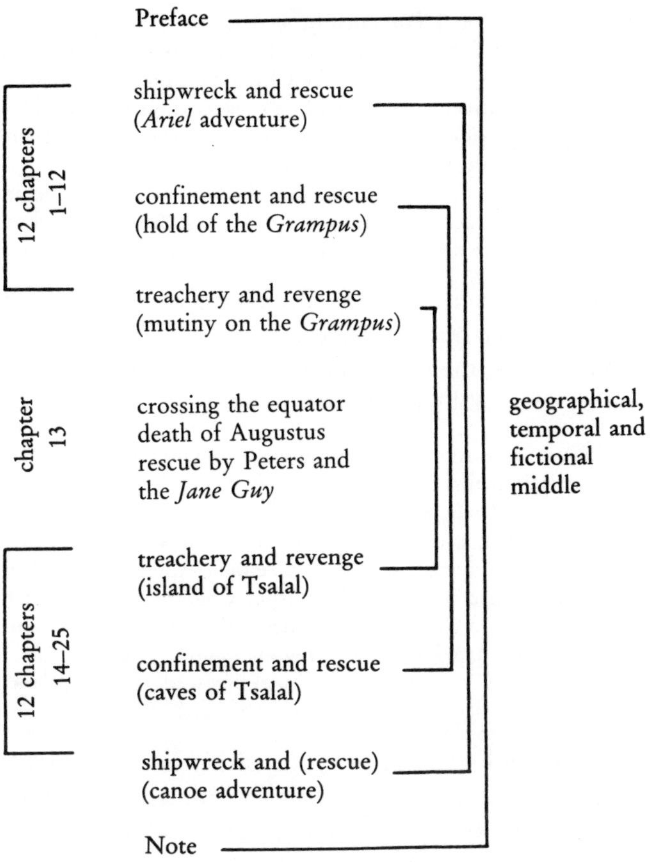

Framing, Centring and Enclosure

A chiastic pattern may also suggest framing, enclosure or centring, for the outer elements *a* frame, enclose or centre the inner elements *bb*.

James Joyce's *A Portrait of the Artist as a Young Man* uses a chiastic framing device that was discovered by Hans Walter Gabler sixty years after the publication of the novel.[30] For the three episodes and diary of the last chapter (Chapter V) chiastically reverse the overture and three episodes of Chapter I. As Gabler writes:

[30] "The Seven Lost Years of *A Portrait of the Artist as a Young Man*," *Approaches to Joyce's 'Portrait'*, eds. Thomas F. Staley and Bernard Benstock (University of Pittsburgh, 1976), pp. 25–60; the very first hint was given by Harry Levin, *James Joyce: A Critical Introduction* (1941; rpt. Norfolk, Conn.: New Directions, 1952), p. 53, who wrote that the novel is "symmetrically constructed."

> ...the fifth chapter of *A Portrait of the Artist as a Young Man* is the exact symmetrical counterpart to the first. The childhood overture and the two Clongowes episodes, separated by the Christmas dinner scene, are the mirror image of the two movements of Stephen's wanderings through Dublin, separated by the villanelle episode, and the diary finale.... Genetically, the novel's beginning and its end appear closely interdependent.
> It seems that it was a decision to abandon the sequential or cyclic narrative by episodes as used in *Stephen Hero* in favor of a chiastic centre design that broke the impasse in which Joyce found himself over *A Portrait*...[31]

Now, a chiastic frame is perfectly adequate to a literary "portrait". But as Gabler further demonstrates, the chiastic ordering of Joyce's novel is even more pervasive, the two hell sermons of the religious retreat marking its literal, structural and narrative centre:

> ...the chiastic disposition of the novel's beginning and end alters the functional relationships in the sections of the work which they encompass. Chapters II and IV take on a centripetal and a centrifugal direction, and the religious retreat becomes, literally and structurally, the dead center of the novel...the two hell sermons...emphasize the chapter's midpoint position in the chiastic structure of the book. Within Chapter III, divided by Joyce's familiar asterisks into three parts, the beginning in Nighttown and the close in Church Street chapel stand in obvious symmetrical contrast. From the close of chapter II, the Nighttown opening leads naturally into the hell sermon center.[32]

The text's thoroughly chiastic or spatial structure is also emblematic of what the painterly metaphor of the title – which is unique among Joyce's titles – implies. For this title, as Hugh Kenner comments, imposes "a pictorial and spatial analogy, an expectation of static repose, on a book in which nothing else except the spiritual life of Dublin stands still, a book of fluid transitions in which the central figure is growing older by the page. The book is a becoming which the title tells us to apprehend as a being."[33]

In *Ash-Wednesdey*, (V, ll. 1–3) T. S. Eliot disguises three similar chiastic word-patterns which put "word/Word" at their centre:

> If the lost word is lost, if the spent word is spent
> If the unheard, unspoken
> Word is unspoken, unheard;
> Still is the unspoken word, the Word unheard,

[31] Ibid., pp. 49–50.
[32] Ibid., p. 51.
[33] "The Cubist Portrait," *Approaches to James Joyce's 'Portrait'*, op.cit., pp. 171–184; p. 171.

The Word without a word, the Word within
The world and for the world;
And the light shone in darkness and
Against the Word the unstilled world still whirled
About *the centre* of the silent Word.[34]

The chiastic patterns hidden in the first three lines can be rendered as follows:

line 1: lost word lost
spent word spent
lines 2–3: unheard unspoken Word unspoken unheard

Although somewhat camouflaged by Eliot's free verse lineation, the chiastic word-patterns of the first three lines (and to a lesser extent in the succeeding lines) centre the "word/Word" and actually perform on the textual level what the whole passage is about.

Another example of chiastic enclosure is offered by Philip Larkin's short poem "Wires":

The widest prairies have electric fences,
For though old cattle know they must not stray,
Young steers are always scenting purer water
Not here but anywhere. Beyond the wires

Leads them to blunder up against the wires
Whose muscle-shredding violence give no quarter.
Young steers become old cattle from that day,
Electric limits to their widest senses.[35]

In this carefully crafted animal fable two chiastic patterns are superimposed in order to suggest the steers' imprisonment: namely the chiastic rhyme-scheme *abcddcba* and the chiastic sequence of key words (the only repeated expressions) which have been underlined in the text. This double chiasmus serves the further function of miming the reversal of the young steers blundering up against electric wires whose "muscle-shredding violence" (l.6) turns them into old cattle.

An effect of claustrophobic enclosure is also achieved by E. A. Poe's chiastic patterning of his description of Madeline's temporary entomb-

[34] *The Complete Poems and Plays of T. S. Eliot* (London: Faber, 1969), p. 96 (my italics).

[35] *The Less Deceived* (1955; London: The Marvell Press, 1973), p. 27. Some of the chiastic patterning has been described by David Timms, *Philip Larkin* (Edinburgh: Oliver and Boyd, 1973), pp. 70–71 and Simon Petch, *The Art of Philip Larkin* (Sydney University Press, 1981), p. 45.

ment in "The Fall of the House of Usher" – apart from testifying to his symmetry-addiction. Thus the scene is enclosed by an inner frame the two symmetrical parts of which are contained in the two parts of a single sentence: "A striking *similitude* between *the brother* and *the sister* now first arrested *my attention;* ‖ and Usher, divining, perhaps, *my thoughts,* murmured out some few words from which I learned that *the diseased* [sister] and *himself* [brother] had been *twins*" (pp. 259–260).[36] And this inner frame is encapsulated by an outer frame in which the following corresponding (not necessarily identical) expressions stand in chiastic opposition: "portion," "building/house", "appartment(s)", "door", "iron", "(un)screwed", "lid", and "face" (pp. 259, 260).

Conclusion

By way of summary, let me conclude with the best-known chiastic phrase in English literature, namely with the witches' "Fair is foul and foul is fair" in the first scene of *Macbeth* (I,i,11). For the perfect chiastic pattern *abcdcba* of this phrase does several of the things I have pointed out so far.

First, it enacts a reversal. "The main theme of the reversal of values is given out simply and clearly in the first scene," L. C. Knights comments, "...and with it are associated premonitions of the conflict, disorder and moral darkness into which Macbeth will plunge himself."[37] By indicating a conflict between being and seeming, by creating doubt about categories, the witches' chiastic inversion reflects a world of semantic chaos. And this anarchy of the witches' chiastic line in turn reflects the social, political and emotional chaos depicted in the play.

But in its static, formulaic symmetry and circularity of pattern this chiastic phrase is further expressive of both the atemporality of magic and of the circular dance movements of the witches' ritual. It is interesting to note that there are quite a number of chiastic patterns in the witches' scenes generally, thus conveying a more strongly ritual character to these scenes. To give but three examples: The very first line of *Macbeth* starts out with a vocalic chiasmus:

[36] *The Portable Poe,* op.cit., pp. 259–260 (my italics).

[37] "Some Contemporary Trends in Shakespeare Criticism," *Shakespeare: Macbeth. A. Casebook,* ed. John Wain (London: Macmillan, 1968), pp. 221–245; p. 227. See also Ralf Norrman's comment on this line in his *The Insecure World of Henry James's Fiction,* op.cit., p. 183.

1 *Witch.* "When shall we three meet again?"[38]

Or in the third scene of the first act (I,iii,68–69) we get another perfect chiastic sequence:

3 *Witch.* ...
So all hail, Macbeth and Banquo!
1 *Witch.* Banquo and Macbeth, all hail![39]

And a less perfect chiasmus is found at the beginning of the same scene (I,iii,1–3):

1 *Witch.* Where hast thou been, Sister?
2 *Witch.* Killing Swine
3 *Witch.* Sister, where thou?[40]

The chiastic sequence "Fair is foul, and foul is fair" may, however, also be considered as a kind of flow chart of the play. For the sequence of "fair" and "foul" and its inversion in the chiasmus mirror an equivalent order in the plot: the play starts out "fair" with the reign and the victorious campaign of good King Duncan, then proceeds with the two "foul" murders of Duncan and Banquo, and ends "fair" again with the triumphant campaign and the reign of good King Malcolm. In other words, the chiasmus of the witch's phrase is an icon of the symmetrical plot, serving a whole bundle of funtions. It may properly be regarded as a perfect "mise en abyme" of *Macbeth*.

[38] *Macbeth* (The Arden Shakespeare), ed. Harold Jenkins and Brian Morris (London: Methuen, 1982), p. 3: [e ə i: i: i: ə e].
[39] Ibid., p. 16.
[40] Ibid., p. 11.

The Labyrinth as a Structural Principle in Narrative Texts

Werner Senn

Critics seem increasingly fond of referring to texts metaphorically as labyrinths or mazes. Northrop Frye, in *The Anatomy of Criticism*, speaks of the mythical view of literature as giving a necessary centre without which archetypal criticism is "an endless labyrinth without an outlet."[1] Derrida's critique of the notion of centred structure, it has been noted, leads to an "interplay of signification *ad infinitum*" and urges us "to stay inside the labyrinth of discourse."[2] J. Hillis Miller, in an article entitled "Ariadne's Thread," explicates the critic's unavoidable entanglement in the text he analyses. David Lodge refers to texts like Pynchon's *Crying of Lot 49* or Fowles' *The Magus* as "labyrinths without exits." Angus Fletcher sees the narrative structure of *Tristram Shandy* informed by the labyrinth. The same has been said of *The Canterbury Tales.*[3] What is striking in many of these instances is the loose metaphorical use of the term "labyrinth," which makes it critically meaningless. Yet writ-

[1] Northrop Frye, *The Anatomy of Criticism* (Princeton: Princeton University Press, 1957), p. 118.

[2] Frank Lentricchia, *After the New Criticism* (Chicago: University of Chicago Press, 1980), p. 168.

[3] J. Hillis Miller, "Ariadne's Thread," *Critical Inquiry,* 3 (1976) p. 74; David Lodge, *The Modes of Modern Writing* (London: Edward Arnold, 1977), p. 226; Angus Fletcher, "The Image of Lost Direction," in *Centre and Labyrinth: Essays in Honour of Northrop Frye.* Ed. Eleanor Cook *et al.* (Toronto: University of Toronto Press, 1983), p. 329 (henceforth cited as Fletcher in the text). Donald R. Howard, *The Idea of the Canterbury Tales* (Berkeley: University of California Press, 1976), esp. pp. 327–332 (I am grateful to Professor Paul Taylor, Geneva, for drawing my attention to this book). Geoffrey Hartman, "The Maze of Modernism," in *Beyond Formalism* (New Haven: Yale University Press, 1970); Bernard Sharratt, *The Literary Labyrinth: Contemporary Critical Discourse* (Brighton: Harvester Press, 1984). For further recent examples, see Lentricchia, op. cit., chapter 5.

ers continue to be fascinated by the labyrinth as motif, metaphor and mythical symbol. Among contemporaries, the first that come to mind are Borges, Dürrenmatt, Robbe-Grillet, but there are many also in the English-speaking world.[4] A few contrastive examples, from the Elizabethan and the modern periods respectively, are going to be examined here.

This paper addresses itself to the question of how the labyrinth motif, widely current as an "image of lost direction" (Frye), as a metaphor denoting confusion, intricacy, or chaos, can be made to function as a structuring device or structural principle in narrative texts. How can a narrative structure be said to "imitate" a labyrinth design, how far can its intricacy, complexity and discontinuity be pushed for it to be still perceived as a structure, as a labyrinth rather than a chaos?

Independently of the labyrinth mythology, the labyrinth as motif primarily evokes a visual idea of some more or less intricate arrangement and division of space seen from above. If any analogy with the literary medium can be drawn, it can hardly be in the imitation of the vertical, synoptic view but only in the reader's horizontal, sequential experience of confusion. The story-line may well be tangled, "knotted, repetitive, doubled, broken, phantasmal," but the *narrative discourse* may be wholly linear, continuous, consistently focussed through a single narrating instance.[5] One might say, for example, that *Tristram Shandy,* for all its intricacy of structure, insofar as it is concerned with narration, is perfectly continuous, and that its single narrative voice constitutes the thread

[4] Among novels, see e. g. Helen Rose Hull, *Labyrinth* (New York: Macmillan, 1923); Cecil Roberts, *The Labyrinth* (New York: Doubleday, 1944); Lawrence Durrell, *The Dark Labyrinth* (London: Faber, 1958); Michael Ayrton, *The Maze Maker* (London: Longmans, 1967); Philip José Farmer, *The Magic Labyrinth* (New York: Berkley Publishing Corporation, 1980). For non-English examples see also: Ludmila Kapschutschenko, *El laberinto en la narrativa hispanoamericana contemporanea* (London: Tamesis Books, 1981); Anton Krättli, "Labyrinthe und Höhlen: Beobachtungen an der deutschschweizerischen Gegenwartsliteratur," *Neue Rundschau,* 4 (1984), 71–87. For criticism in addition to Fletcher's article, see: G. R. Hocke, *Die Welt als Labyrinth* (Reinbek: Rowohlt, 1957); Ernest H. Redekop, "Labyrinths in Time and Space," *Mosaic,* 13 (1980), 95–113; T. M. Evans, "The Vernacular Labyrinth: Mazes and Amazement in Shakespeare and Peele," *Shakespeare Jahrbuch West* (1980), 165–73; Joseph Leo Koerner, *Die Suche nach dem Labyrinth* (Frankfurt: Suhrkamp, 1983); Werner Senn, "Reading Melville's Mazes: An Aspect of the Short Stories," *English Studies,* 65 (1984), 27–35.

[5] Miller, loc. cit., p. 69.

of Ariadne through the labyrinth of its mimetic world.[6] On the other hand, as Hillis Miller has noted, the line of Ariadne's thread, in retracing a labyrinth already there, becomes itself a second labyrinth; copy and origin mingle to form a "tangled hierarchy" difficult to untwine.[7]

A different type of labyrinth structure emerges in the case of *Melmoth the Wanderer.* According to Fletcher, the labyrinth has given Maturin "the plan for the narrative form as a whole, [which] consists of nested subnarratives deliberately coiling in upon themselves, so that the form of the book projects the disorientation of the hero and narrator" (Fletcher, p. 333, 343). The technique of "nesting" produces a structure quite different from that of *Tristram Shandy,* and, for the reader, quite a different experience of disorientation. The proliferation of events is here combined with the multiplication of narrating instances, and the result is a complexity that may be read as a labyrinth by some but to others is evidence of sheer ineptitude.[8] Critical interest, then, must focus on the conditions under which what appears chaotic may in fact fall into a recognizable structure termed a labyrinth.

The experience of confusion and bafflement, basic as it is to the traveller moving horizontally in the literal labyrinth, cannot of course be a sufficient criterion. A sense of loss of direction necessarily provokes a state of mind, a conscious recognition, a "thinking into one's state of mind" (Fletcher, p. 330). This point is made neatly in W. H. Auden's poem "The Maze," which begins:

> Anthropos apteros for days
> Walked whistling round and round the maze,
> Relying happily upon
> His temperament for getting on.

[6] An original recent attempt to do justice to the "intricate structure" of *Tristram Shandy* as a work of narrative fiction that has "many open endings" but "a closed form" is Fritz Gysin's *Model as Motif in 'Tristram Shandy'* (Berne: Francke, 1983) p. 18.

[7] Cf. Fletcher, op. cit., p. 341; Linda Hutcheon remarks, in *Narcissistic Narrative: The Metafictional Paradox* (London: Methuen, 1984), that "no matter how diegetic, metafictions remain mimetic" insofar as they imitate their own fiction-making process (p. 47).

[8] See e. g. Douglas Grant, ed. *Melmoth the Wanderer* (London: OUP, 1968), p. x. The significance of the labyrinth for the gothic novel has been analysed by Jerrold E. Hogle in "The Restless Labyrinth: Cryptonymy in the Gothic Novel," *Arizona Quarterly,* 36 (1980), 330–358 (I owe this as well as many other useful references to my colleague Gustav Ungerer).

The hundredth time he sighted, though,
A bush he left an hour ago,
He halted where four alleys crossed
And recognized that he was lost.[9]

This recognition would seem to be the crucial point of the labyrinth experience: "it is not so much a trial of strength as a kind of perceptual skill... To a degree the labyrinth leaves the traveller with nothing much but state of mind" (Fletcher, p. 330). The writer who, without necessarily using the labyrinth as setting, wants to exploit the labyrinth experience, has to place such perceptual clues. Readers more apt than anthropos apteros may not need a hundred of them, but the principle of repetition is a basic means of provoking this consciousness of loss of direction.

Before pursuing the analogies of labyrinth and narrative structure, a typological distinction needs to be made: art historians and archaeologists distinguish sharply between two basic types of labyrinths. The unicursal, Daedalian or Cretan-type labyrinth as represented pictorially since the second millenium B. C. is a type which has no intersections and no blind alleys but leads inevitably, though in an endlessly roundabout way, to the centre, and from which the way out is an exact duplication of the way in.[10] While in this type the ultimate goal is never in danger of being missed, the frequent reversals of direction nevertheless result "in a vertiginous loss of clarity as to what 'forward' means" (Fletcher, p. 336).

The other type, the multicursal maze of popular lore – like the Hampton Court Maze – is best defined by the *OED* entry for "labyrinth:" "A structure consisting of a number of intercommunicating passages arranged in bewildering complexity...". This is obviously the type envisaged in Auden's poem. Every traveller through the first, the Cretan type, retraces exactly the same path, repeats a single structure, whereas in the second, the choice of path traced is entirely arbitrary, determined by the law of chance and hence a kind of game of trial and error. It is tempting though premature to attribute the first type of structural analogy to texts of the pre-modern era, the second to those of the modern and postmodern. We may recall here the fact that Joyce, when he was writing the "Wandering Rocks" section of *Ulysses,* to which he explicitly assigned a labyrinth technique, bought a game called "Labyrinth-Spiel", which "he played every evening for a time with his

[9] W. H. Auden, *Collected Poems.* Ed. Edward Mendelson (London: Faber & Faber, 1976), p. 236.

[10] See Hermann Kern, "Labyrinth Cities – City Labyrinths", *Daidalos,* 3 (1982), p. 10. Cf. also Kern's monumental *Labyrinthe: Erscheinungsformen und Deutungen* (Munich: Prestel Verlag, 1982).

daughter [to find out and] to catalogue six main errors of judgement into which one might fall in choosing a right, left or centre way out of the maze."[11]

The archetypal experience of loss of direction is exemplified by Spenser's Redcross Knight as he enters the Maze of Error which is placed at the beginning of *The Faerie Queene.* Spenser's first point is that entering the maze is an unavoidable but unintentional act: Redcross and the veiled lady, who is Una, the Truth, seek shelter from a sudden shower in a nearby grove, which they find suitable for purpose:

> And all within were pathes and alleies wide,
> With footing worne, and leading inward farre:
> Faire harbour that them seemes; so in they entred arre.[12]

The grammatical ambiguity of tense and voice here suggests that the transition from outside to inside has been made unwittingly. Once inside, they proceed blithely, unawares, "led with delight,"

> Vntill the blustring storme is ouerblowne;
> When weening to returne, whence they did stray,
> They cannot finde that path, which first was showne,
> But wander too and fro in wayes vnknowne,
> Furthest from end then, when they neerest weene,
> That makes them doubt, their wits be not their owne:
> So many paths, so many turnings seene
> That which of them to take, in diuerse doubt they been.
> (I.i.10)

This is the thinking oneself into one's state of mind that the labyrinth experience characteristically induces, an experience "of thought experiencing itself" (Fletcher, p. 330). There is a degree of self-consciousness and self-reflectiveness inherent in the labyrinth motif that distinguishes it from other geometrical motifs which have also become basic human symbols, such as the circle or the cross. It is this quality, too, that seems to make the labyrinth an ideal figure for the technique of *mise en abyme,* i. e. for thematizing mimetic as well as diegetic concerns.[13]

[11] Frank Budgen, *James Joyce and the Making of 'Ulysses'.* 1934 (London: OUP, 1972), p. 125. Cf. also Koerner, op. cit., pp. 171–72. Budgen's account suggests that Joyce was here interested in the structuring as much as in the symbolic or mythical functions of the labyrinth.

[12] *The Faerie Queene.* Ed. Thomas P. Roche (Harmondsworth: Penguin, 1978), I.i.7. All references in the text are to this edition.

[13] Hutcheon, op. cit. p. 53.

Spenser uses the motif here to establish a concrete visual image in the first place, to bring home fully its perplexing and paradoxical nature:[14]

> At last resoluing forward still to fare,
> Till that some end they finde or in or out,
> That path they take, that beaten seemd most bare,
> And like to lead the labyrinth about;
> Which when by tract they hunted had throughout,
> At length it brought them to a hollow cave,
> Amid the thickest woods. (I.i.11)

The broad beaten path paradoxically leads not outward but inward, to further entanglement, to "Errors den." The well-trodden path suggests that Redcross' experience is representative. Spenser could draw on a rich iconographic tradition of the labyrinth as a symbol of the world or of human life, but also on contemporary critical discussion of the labyrinth as a principle of narrative design and structure, a point relevant to my discussion.

When Philip Sidney revised his original *Arcadia*, he increased its bulk, diversity and complexity not merely by adding a few "new stories dovetailed into the principal one, after the manner of Spanish romances," but by changing a simple action involving only a few characters and told in a straightforward manner, into "a Chinese puzzle of enormous intricacy," a vast design of manifold actions and multiplied characters held together in an intricate structural network of corresponding exemplary stories.[15] The complex and involved narration, in which narrating instances keep changing – the "over-seer of the print" (probably Fulke Greville) in his chapter headings often draws attention to these "interruptions" – is given coherence neither in the mimetic nor the diegetic mode but through the fact that all the stories are "parts in an emblematic moral spectrum."[16]

It seems that in revising his text, Sidney was modelling it on the pattern of Heliodorus' romance *Aethiopica*, published in an English

[14] One of those "enigmatic images whose main purpose is to tease the reader into thought," as Maurice Evans writes (quoted in *The Faerie Queene: A Selection of Critical Essays.* Ed. Peter Bayley (London: Macmillan, 1977), p. 109).

[15] See Walter R. Davis and Richard A. Lanham, *Sydney's Arcadia* (New Haven: Yale University Press, 1965), p. 55. The two quotes are from: Albert Feuillerat, ed. *Arcadia* (Cambridge: CUP, 1922), p. viii; Mona Wilson, *Sir Philip Sidney* (London: Duckworth, 1931), p. 140. References to the *New Arcadia* are to Feuillerat's edition.

[16] Jon S. Lawry, *Sidney's Two 'Arcadias': Pattern and Proceeding* (Ithaca: Cornell University Press, 1972), p. 155. Cf. also Nancy Lindheim, *The Structures of Sidney's Arcadia* (Toronto: University of Toronto Press, 1982).

translation about 1577 and praised by John Harington in the following terms:

> The delicacy of the invention and variety of accidents, strange yet possible, leads the curious reader, by a baited appetite, with a methodical intricateness, through a labyrinth of labours, entertaining his expectation till he come unto an end, which he must seek that he may understand the beginning.[17]

The methodical intricateness of the *New Arcadia* is certainly no less deliberate than that of the *Aethiopica*, its complexity and apparently chaotic proliferation of incident no less informed by a moral aim. The narration subjects the reader to what has been called a "processional principle of action," digressive and diversionary in practice.[18] Like Spenser, Sidney placed an emblematic labyrinth, in the form of a garden maze, at the beginning of his story; it is evoked through the experience of the characters traversing it:

> ...the backeside of the house was neyther field, garden, nor orchard; or rather it was both fielde, garden, and orcharde: for as soon as the descending of the stayres had delivered them downe, they came into a place cunninglie set with trees of the moste tast-pleasing fruites: but scarcelie they had taken that into their consideration, but that they were suddainely stept into a delicate greene, of each side of the greene a thicket bend, behinde the thickets againe newe beddes of flowers, which being under the trees, the trees were to them a Pavilion, and they to the trees a mosaical floore: so that it seemed that arte therein would needes be delightfull by counterfaiting his enemie error, and making order in confusion (p. 17).

This emblematic image displays the characteristic of the literary labyrinth: its equivocal nature as a signifier. It is none of several things and yet all of them together, it is discrete and yet unified, conceals order by imitating disorder and hints at order in apparent confusion, drawing attention to itself as a locus which provokes recognition and insight.[19]

Fulke Greville made an interesting point about structure: in commenting on the multiplicity of events in the *New Arcadia* he said that "[Sidney's] end in them was not vanishing pleasure alone, but morall images, and Examples (as directing threds) to guide every man through the confused *Labyrinth* of his own desires, and life."[20] The moral pur-

[17] Quoted in Wilson, op. cit., p. 140.
[18] Lawry, op. cit., p. 163.
[19] According to Koerner, op. cit., p. 35, the image of the labyrinth embodies both chaos and order, confusion and knowledge.
[20] Quoted in Joan Rees, *Fulke Greville, Lord Brooke, 1554–1628* (London: Routledge & Kegan Paul, 1971), p. 52.

pose, and the referential nature, of the work of art are clearly hinted at in the centre of Sidney's own labyrinth image, as he continues:

> In the middest of all the place, was a faire ponde, whose shaking christall was a perfect mirrour to all the other beauties, so that it bare shewe of two gardens: one in deede, the other in shaddowes (p. 17).

This is an icon, as it were, conveying the notion that the entire fiction "shadows forth," to use Spenser's term, an ulterior truth: the labyrinth of life through which Christians have to wander as a necessary condition of their salvation.

Spenser's image of the labyrinth, placed strategically like Sidney's, at the beginning of the narrative, serves much the same purpose of producing that insight, recognition of loss of direction, thus initiating the reader into the art of reading the work – the literary maze – he has imaginatively entered. It "foreshadows emblematically" the later development of the narrative, with Redcross soon lost "all in amaze" (I.ii.5) in the false trail of Archimago.[21] It anticipates the whole multiplex structure with its endless doubling and permutation of characters and events, its "entrelacement" of stories from canto to canto and from book to book.[22] The labyrinth image, thus foregrounded or "mis en abyme," attracts sufficient attention to itself to induce an awareness of the labyrinth structure of the whole text, to suggest to the reader an awareness of order in apparent confusion. While to William Hazlitt, e. g., *The Faerie Queene* was "a labyrinth of sweet sounds [whose] undulations are infinite" and tend to make us forget the moral purpose, the modern critic, looking deeper, perceives the purposeful labyrinthine structure and recognizes the labyrinth as the "imaginative source" and the basic structural image of the work.[23]

While the specifically Christian connotations of the labyrinth motif in *The Faerie Queene* and the *New Arcadia* have lost their significance in our time, its mythical and symbolic potential continues to be explored and exploited in modern narrative texts. We can deal here with only two examples. In both Michael Ayrton's sadly neglected novel *The Maze*

[21] A. C. Hamilton, *The Structure of Allegory in 'The Faerie Queene'* (Oxford: Clarendon Press, 1961), p. 40.

[22] The term "entrelacement" is used by Rosemond Tuve, quoted in Bayley, op. cit., p. 79.

[23] Angus Fletcher, *The Prophetic Moment: An Essay on Spenser* (Chicago: University of Chicago Press, 1971), p. 31; Koerner thinks that for Spenser the labyrinth is *the* symbol of the experience of the world (op. cit., p. 74). Hazlitt's view is quoted in Bayley, op. cit., p. 40.

Maker (1967) and John Hawkes' *Virginie* (1981) the protagonists tell their own life stories, both novels are evidently concerned with the fictitiousness of their narratives, and in both, the labyrinth motif serves to structure the fiction and thematize the fiction-making process.

The professional maze maker, Daedalus, who modestly calls himself "technician" (p. 4), asserts at the beginning that in telling his story he is trying to understand "the pattern of [his] life," through which he has blundered as "in a maze" (p. 3):

> I did not know until now that in places the walls of this maze were cunningly polished so that the perils I have endured, my fears and hopes and the joy I have taken in my tasks have time and again been reflected in one another ... In all my life I never learned from one experience how to encounter its reflected twin (p. 3).

Not surprisingly,the labyrinth appears to Daedalus to be the adequate metaphor of his life (e. g. pp. 4, 64, 217, 282), but then, as he knows, "a maze is a map of ironies, a pattern of paradox" (p. 253), and thus retracing his life by writing it produces another labyrinth of his own making, full of ironies and paradoxes not this time under his control. In an attempt to create order and impose control, he tries to find out how the events of his life reflect one another, not as shadow and reality, but as repetitions of homological structures.[24] Even a relationship of binary opposition is preferable to chaos, but if the resulting labyrinth serves to create or reveal order in confusion, it also emphasizes the relationship between its elements and de-emphasizes their individual significance, their reference: the self-reflectiveness of the labyrinth seems inescapable.

Daedalus' concern with structuring and ordering is part of a wider concern with the processes of artistic creation, with fiction-making and myth-making. This covert diegetic narcissism is in evidence throughout and takes various characteristic forms.[25] Thus over a time gap of more than 3000 years, Daedalus frequently addresses us, his readers, to dismiss with impatience some of the more absurd myths we have fashioned around his person (e. g. pp. 102, 210). The favourite device of *mise en abyme* is also repeatedly employed in a variety of ways, e. g. when Daedalus describes how, in the bronze doors he made for the temple of Apollo at Cumae, he pictured the main episodes of his life, including the

[24] Cf. Simone Oettli, "The Maze Maker," *Kenyon Review*, N. S. 5 (1983), 67–84. In Oettli's view, the labyrinth provides not only the matrix for the relationships between characters but also "the organic pattern of the novel" as a whole (p. 79).

[25] See Hutcheon, op. cit., p. 23.

maze he had built at Knossos. Extended structural analogies with a labyrinth which we are induced to create ourselves rather than to perceive in the given product are evoked throughout in covertly diegetic passages:

> The labyrinth is not merely a dancing floor, nor a complex of passages nor a web of air; it is a field of force. Its architect, as I have learned, embarks upon the construction of a maze, believing that its force lies within his control only to discover that the field is held in equilibrium by opposed forces, at once containing and excluding, and his life's labyrinth has the laugh on him (pp. 253–54).

We even find overt, direct thematizing of the story-telling concern:

> How entangled the memories of memories can become! I write them down, in an effort to establish some sort of sequence of events and my recollections proliferate and intertwine so that they bind me like a net ... it seems I am so skilled in making mazes that I block the true paths through my own past and wander down false trails. They are trails I planned myself but I lose my way in them (pp. 217–218).

As one who, by his own admission, "prefer[s] cognition to revelation" (p. 117), Daedalus must content himself with a final insight into the paradox of the maze he built, which is also that of his life and his story:

> All this long burrowing and building, to protect or to imprison, this flight through the sky and tunnelling in the earth, seems to me now to add up to no more than the parts of a single great maze which is my life ... Its shape identifies me. It has been my goal and my sanctuary, my journey and its destination ... Toy, trial and torment, the topology of my labyrinth remains ambiguous. Its materials are at once dense, impenetrable, translucent and illusory (p. 282).

For the narrator, structure and experience, product and process have become interchangeable. Re-tracing the way through the maze, the reader can appreciate both in their dialectical relationship, without being able to disentangle them. Like Daedalus, ultimately, the reader finds it easier to note a correspondence between discrete events than to assess their individual significance.

Even more radically than Ayrton, Hawkes, in *Virginie Her Two Lives,* makes repetition, reflection of signifiers, a principle of his narration. The novel consists of the two journals which the 11-year-old Virginie kept in her two lives, one in 1740, when she lives in Seigneur's château called "Dédale" (French for labyrinth of the Cretan type), the other in 1945, when she lives in a rather run-down Parisian flat owned by Bocage, a taxidriver. The phallocratic Seigneur, whose noble vocation is to train five young women in the art of true womanhood, bears a faint resemblance to the Marquis de Sade (1740 is the year of Sade's birth). Bocage, a goodnatured giant of a man, has surrounded himself with five Parisian girls and some male friends who stage what they call charades of love. In both lives Virginie witnesses a large amount of erotic display pandering to male fantasies. Spectator and willing stagehand, she describes it with perfect, uncanny innocence in beautifully transparent prose. The episodes from the two journals alternate and are obviously made to reflect each other. Virginie, however, betrays only the faintest awareness of the identity of the two narrating instances, which the reader assumes as a matter of course despite its logical impossibility.

Although the journal form makes for one of the most authenticating narrative situations, its fictitiousness is openly declared here at the very beginning, with the diegetic self-consciousness characteristic of postmodern fiction.[26] The novel opens with an anticipation of its own end, as Virginie records how at this moment, while she is being made love to by Bocage, the house, her dress, her journals are burning; "thus I am as impossible a child as the story I tell" (p. 9). It ends with her account of how she throws herself into the fire in which Seigneur has been condemned to die. With the conventions of story-telling thus undermined and made unreal, we are left with two signifying chains made to reflect one another in an elaborate network of correspondences, in which the clarity of the fictional design is as evident as the enigmatic ambiguity of reference.

Hawkes thematizes this ambiguity by using the labyrinth motif as a metaphor, an extended structural image, and a *mise en abyme* in all possible variants.[27] Virginie, the author of the unreal journals, admits finding comfort in reading her own journal, and in both narratives she teases us with hints of an awareness of her other existence, as the subject of another life and author of another journal. Musing on the labyrinth that is "Dédale," she is able to see it both from within and without (p. 51), combining vertical synopsis with horizontal sequence, present desire with memory (p. 59).

The most striking *mise en abyme* occurs in Seigneur's extended allegory of the Land of Love, in which the Citadel of the Desire to Please is situated, with the Labyrinth of Surrender All at its centre:

[26] Hutcheon, p. 53. Cf. also David Lodge, "Mimesis and Diegesis in Modern Fiction," in *Contemporary Approaches to Narrative, SPELL* 1. Ed. Anthony Mortimer (Tübingen: Gunter Narr, 1984); pp. 89–108. All references to *Virginie* are to the Arena edition (London: Arrow Books, 1984).

[27] Hutcheon, op. cit., pp. 54–55.

> Obviously there can be no pleasing without surrender, no surrender that does not please. The labyrinth is to the citadel as the fountain is to the park. The garden of green confusion, which it initially appears to be, is in fact as orderly as the citadel itself; the greenness of the labyrinth determines all. Everything in the citadel is held in its proper place, attains its balance and hence its meaning (p. 100).

Although this occurs in a discourse on sexual love, it is difficult not to read it as a metafictional statement, and not to relate it to the narrative itself, in which events are made to reflect each other in correlated structures (labyrinth to citadel as fountain to park!), where every element derives its meaning only from its place and its relation to others and *not* through external reference: as a labyrinth, the text is self-referential and self-reflective.

To conclude: in both the Elizabethan and the modern texts, the inherent dual nature of the labyrinth – as perceived, for instance, by Sidney – allows for generating complex response. We note a kind of dialectic of vertical synopsis (emphasizing, through structure, the product, the signified, the significance), and of horizontal sequence (emphasizing, through experience, the writing and reading process, the signifier). It is fair to say that the Elizabethan texts favour the former mode and are hence associated structurally with the Cretan type of labyrinth figuring in the Renaissance emblem books, with its firm *arche* and *telos*, whereas the modern texts have structural affinities with the confusing, discontinuous and multicursal maze of random intersections and dead ends, where choices are entirely arbitrary and the way itself, not the goal (centre, exit) to be reached, provides the focus of interest. While these distinctions are general enough to hold true for the examples discussed here, it should nevertheless have become clear that the dialectic of outside/inside, horizontal/vertical, and sequential/synoptic prevents any rigid taxonomy and reductive closure but offers rich possibilities of complex narrative structuring.

Namings for the Hero and the Structure of *Beowulf*

Pierre E. Monnin

"Naming is basic to all poetry, but perhaps most so to Germanic alliterative verse, which has its presumed origins in magic and ritual." Introducing *Beowulf*, Howell D. Chickering, Jr., further remarks that "the heavy nominalism of the poetic lexicon was doubtless inherited. However, the poet utilized it more fully than other Old English poets."[1] Indeed, for Beowulf alone, some one hundred and twenty terms or phrases have been recorded, with occurrences totalling well over two hundred. These figures are based on the lists provided by William Whallon in three successive publications where the "epithets" of Homeric diction are contrasted with the "kennings" of Old English poetry.[2] Ranging from single terms such as *cyning* or *hlaford* to phrases that may be longer than a half-line, e. g., *wilgeofa Wedra leoda,* not to mention such vocatives as *wine min Beowulf,* where the actual name of the hero is uttered, these appellations may not all be regarded as "kennings". Neither R. Meissner's definition, "any two membered substitution for a substantive of common speech," nor A. Heusler's, "a metaphor with an associating link,"[3] can always be appropriate; the items recorded by Whallon, which will be used in the present analysis,[4] are therefore more suitably referred to as "namings" for Beowulf.

[1] *"Beowulf": A Dual-Language Edition* (Garden City, New York: Doubleday, 1977), p. 6.

[2] "The Diction of *Beowulf,*" *PMLA,* 76 (1961) 309–19, "Formulas for Heroes in the *Iliad* and in *Beowulf,*" *MPh,* 63 (1965), 95–104, and *Formula, Character, and Context: Studies in Homeric, Old English, and Old Testament Poetry* (Washington, D. C.: Harvard Univ. Press, 1969).

[3] Meissner (1921) and Heusler (1922) are quoted by Thomas Gardner in "The Application of the Term 'Kenning'," *Neoph.,* 56 (1972), 464 and 465.

[4] The convenient, but decidedly too broad definition of "kenning" used by James W. Rankin in "A Study of the Kennings in Anglo-Saxon Poetry,"

Alliterating sound, length, position within the line, and frequency are objective features that have enabled clear classification in Whallon's publications. More subjective is the relationships that each of these namings establishes with the hero himself; here is a feature that suggests another, more progressive, type of grouping.

As a "center of attraction," an expression found in Joan Blomfield's analysis of the structure of *Beowulf*,[5] the hero is surrounded by namings in concentric circles. Closest to the center, since they could not possibly apply to any other character, are repetitions of the name itself with further specification, such as *Beowulf Geata* or *wine min Beowulf*. Next are patronymic epithets, with *bearn, maga* or *sunu* repeatedly followed by the genitive *Ecgþeowes* (twelve occurrences altogether). As for *mæg Higelaces,* which is potentially applicable to other members of the Geat dynasty, its five occurrences apply to Beowulf; the "king's nephew", a regal version of the "sister's son" relationship, is made prominent in *Beowulf* as it is privileged in the context of several other early societies.[6]

Higelaces þegn, which first introduces Beowulf in the epic (l. 194b) and is once repeated for him just before the beheading of Grendel (1574b), also applies to Eofor (2977b), the son of Wonred, who has distinguished himself among the Geats by killing Ongentheow the Swedish king, for which deed of valour he is given in marriage Hygelac's only daughter as a pledge of friendship. This naming, through its application to a character other than Beowulf, introduces another group revolving around the hero; its circle, if one elaborates on the metaphor of elements gravitating around a central unit, is now wide enough to come into contact with the circle it also draws around another character.

While the shift from namings that shut out other characters to those that may admit them is hard to define, distinction within this second group is made clear through respective occurrences. Among all the different namings recorded for Beowulf – some one hundred and twenty according to Whallon's listing – about two thirds do not occur for any other character. When used exclusively for Beowulf, namings that do not repeat his name or refer to a family tie set off various particularities

JEGP, 8 (1909), 357–422, could include all of Whallon's listings, which, though most useful, have not always proved utterly reliable, as will be mentioned occasionally below.

5 "The Style and Structure of *Beowulf*," *RES* 14 (1938), 396–403.

6 Mentioned by Tacitus (*Germania,* ch. 20), male kinship through the wombs of mother and sister is indeed venerated outside Germanic tribes and therefore cross-cultural – see for instance early Hebrew, Slavic, even South-American societies.

of his: warlike dispositions, for instance, are magnified through such terms and expressions as *se hearda, mære cempa, guþrinc goldwlanc,* or the superlatives *secg betsta* and *wigena strengest,* whereas *freodryhten, þioden þristhydig,* or *wigena strengel* exemplify the exaltation of leadership, and more precisely that of a Geat, as proclaimed with *goldwine Geata* or *Wedra þeoden.* Such a pool of namings has led Whallon to conclude that "The kennings for Beowulf rank high in relevance to context, but low in economy ..."[7] The second half of that assertion may be questioned when namings used not exclusively for Beowulf are examined; the case of *Higelaces þegn,* introduced above, would rather hint at economy: through its mere repetition for another character, is not the poet comparing Eofor with Beowulf, implying that through similar valiance both deserve in turn to be called "the follower of Hygelac"?

In fact the forty or so namings that Beowulf shares with other characters in the epic do establish connections; terms or phrases heard for more than one character "ring a bell" and thus make the audience aware of links between different parts of the epic. The structure of *Beowulf* – which has now been so beautifully evidenced by the scholarship of half a century – is underlined by these repetitions; they condition the listener, leading him to draw parallels between characters, hence between various passages in the poem. Shared namings, as they may be called, unify the work through the implicit ties that they establish; they allude to otherwise unworded similarities or contrasts around the central figure of Beowulf.

The namings shared with Hrothgar are not few, as will be shown through the following list:

	for Beowulf, ll.	for Hrothgar, ll.
– *æþeling ærgod*	2342a	130a
– *eald eþelweard*	2210a	1702a
– *eorla dryhten*	2338b	1050b
– *har hilderinc*	3136a	1307a
– *hildfruma*	2649a, 2835a	1678a
– *hlaford*	2375, 2634b, 2642b, 3142b, 3179b	267b
– *hordweard haeleþa*	1852a	1047a
– *mære þeoden*	797a, 2572a, 2788b, 3141b	129b, 201a, 345a, 1046b, 1598a, 1992a
– *rices hyrde*	3080a	2027a

[7] *Formula, Character, and Context,* p. 71.

	for Beowulf, ll.	for Hrothgar, ll.
– *se wisa*	2329a	1698b
– *þeoden mære*	2721a	353a
– *wigendra hleo*	1972b, 2337b	429b
– *winedrihten*	1604b, 2722a	360b, 862a.[8]

For Beowulf, a large majority of them occur after line 2200, whereas all those recorded for Hrothgar are before. The accumulation of repeated namings, besides linking the two characters with each other, sets off the binary architecture of the poem, as first revealed by J. R. R. Tolkien.[9] Part A, which ends at line 2199, is echoed by Part B through the portraying of an aging king; yet symmetry does not exclude contrast, since Hrothgar's impotence is succeeded by Beowulf's valiant, though fated, efficiency. Wrenn asserts: "A Germanic hero ... shows his highest greatness not alone in winning glory by victory, but rather by finding his supremely noble qualities especially in the moment of death in battle."[10] Similar trying circumstances do not produce similar responses; Beowulf's heroism is found to be of a higher order.

Four of the namings listed above are also shared by other characters. Heremod, the Danish king who is traditionally opposed to Hrothgar for his infamous ruling after a promising youth, is equally called *mære þeoden* (1715a); put in the mouth of Hrothgar panegyrizing Beowulf, this is a phrase that links a digression (the second concerning Heremod) with the main story while contrasting characters. "Heremod is made to serve as a foil to the exemplary Beowulf," Klaeber wrote,[11] and the digression is meant to make the young and promising Geat feel that, in Adrien Bonjour's words, "he has yet to show greater moral qualities than Heremod to escape a similar disastrous reversal."[12]

Onela is also called *mære þeoden* (2384a), which may be surprising; why should a Swedish king, an enemy, be graced with a naming so

[8] Whenever recorded for more than one occurrence, namings are given uninflected, with the spellings of lemmas in the Glossary of Klaeber's edition; emendations suggested by standard editions are tacitly accepted. Among the namings shared by Beowulf and Hrothgar, *rices hyrde,* at line 2027a, has been erroneously ascribed to Ingeld by Whallon, both in "Formulas for *Beowulf,*" (p. 97) and in *Formula, Character, and Context* (p. 99).

[9] "*Beowulf*: The Monsters and the Critics," *PBA* 22 (1936), 245–95.

[10] *Beowulf With the Finnesburg Fragment,* 2nd ed. (London: Harrap, 1958), p. 41.

[11] In the Notes of *Beowulf and the Fight at Finnsburg,* 3rd ed. (Boston: D. C. Heath, 1950), p. 164.

[12] *The Digressions in "Beowulf"* (Oxford: Blackwell, 1950), p. 49.

characteristic – ten occurrences for the two of them – of both Hrothgar and Beowulf? Perhaps this is a reminder of Beowulf's family link with the Swedes, through the Wægmundings, a relationship that must have been important enough for Onela to favour his accession to the Geatish throne (and yet not close enough for Beowulf to be prevented from avenging his kinsman Heardred through the death of Onela).[13]

The inverted form *þeoden mære,* which enables alliteration with thorn, applies once to Hrothgar, later once to Beowulf, and, as a plural, also to the former owners of the treasure kept by the dragon (3070a). Besides establishing a connection with Beowulf, whose involvement with the maleficent heirloom has proved fatal, this repetition of the naming may allude to the lordly origin of those who had their treasure buried, and consequently to the great wealth at stake.

Wigendra hleo (899b), too, is shared by another character, here Sigemund. The bard who improvises the tale of Beowulf's exploits at the Danish court appropriately compares the victorious opponent of Grendel with a traditionally famous killer of giants, who are other descendants of Cain. His digression further mentions Sigemund's reputation as a dragon-slayer, which is ominous of Beowulf's last fight and therefore tightens the link between Part A and Part B of the poem.

As for *winedrihten,* its occurrence at line 3175a refers to Beowulf, but also applies to any 'beloved lord' mourned over by his *heorðgeneatas* (3179b), a generalization that befits the solemn, even religious, close of the poem.

There are, furthermore, namings for Beowulf and for Hrothgar that are used for Hygelac as well. They are listed as follows:

	Beowulf	Hrothgar	Hygelac
– *eorla hleo*	791a	1035a, 1866a, 2142a	1967a, 2190a
– *folces hyrde*	2644b	610a	1832a, 1849a
– *guþcyning*	2563a, 2677b, 3036b	199b	1969a
– *mondryhten*	1229b, 1249b, 2604b, 2647a, 2849a, 2865a, 3149b	1229b	436a, 1978b
– *se goda*	205a, 675a 758a	355a	2944b, 2949a
– *se rica*	399a	310b	1975b.

[13] See Norman E. Eliason, "Beowulf, Wiglaf and the Wægmundings," *Anglo-Saxon England,* 7 (1978), 95–105, esp. 100–01.

A triangular pattern is thus developed between Beowulf and two other major characters. With *eorla hleo* and *se rica*, this pattern is circumscribed in Part A of the poem, which means that the young Beowulf is readily raised to the stature of his elders. It is the case too with *se goda*, although the two occurrences for Hygelac are in Part B, and more precisely in the digression of the Battle at Ravenswood, where the victorious behaviour of the Geat leading a body of retainers recalls that of his nephew at the Danish court; the triangle of a shared naming here bridges the two parts and, moreover, tightens the bond between a significant digression and the whole.

Folces hyrde, also used once for the Swedish king Ongentheow (2891a),[14] and *guþcyning* specifically evoke kingly virtues; it is therefore not surprising to hear them applied to Beowulf in Part B only, after his accession to the throne of the Geats. King Beowulf recalls both King Hrothgar and King Hygelac, in a threefold structure that complements the binary composition of the poem.

Parallelism between the two Geatish rulers is further evidenced with:

	Beowulf	Hygelac
– *Geata dryhten*	2560b, 2576a	1484b, 1831a, 2991b.

This is again a naming found only in Part B for Beowulf, where he is also twice called *dryhten Geata*, a reversal that introduces an alliteration on "d" (2402a, 2901a). All these occurrences, which echo those heard for Hygelac in Part A, as well as in the Ravenswood digression, and for Hygelac's elder brother Hæthcyn (2483a), duly relate Beowulf to the royal house of the Geats and repeatedly present him as the legitimate successor of his maternal uncle.

As for *mondryhten*, it is a naming that may apply indiscriminately to Beowulf and to Hrothgar at line 1229b and, in that respect, is shared in the most literal sense of the word. Both are indeed implied in Wealhtheow's self-reassuring, and therefore sweeping, statement about each nobleman at Heorot being faithful to his liege. Yet it must be acknowledged that the compound, with its strikingly unbalanced distribution (seven occurrences for Beowulf, against two for Hygelac and one, even a shared one, for Hrothgar), becomes much more characteristic of the main hero than of the two others.

Though applied to two, and not to three characters, *hlaford* is distrib-

[14] Ibid. As Onela's father, Ongentheow may be accepted to share a naming with Beowulf, whose family ties with the Swedes are irrefutable.

uted with a similar lack of balance: one single occurrence for Hrothgar is followed, in Part B of the poem, by five consecutive references to Beowulf (see listing above), and the only compounded form, *ealdhlaford* (2778b), also refers to the Geat. Here is again a naming that is less shared than essentially ascribed to one individual.

In retrospect, then, since they occur earlier in Part B, both *mondryhten* (2281b) and, only three half-lines below, *hlaford* (2283a), may be likewise ascribed to Beowulf; the two namings, through their repeated, and in Part B otherwise exclusive, use for him, make it possible to identify with some confidence Beowulf as the lord of the slave who rifled the dragon's hoard. Because he is answerable for his servant, who may indeed have been prompted by his master's lust for wealth when he stole the cursed cup,[15] Beowulf does not show ignorance, as Joseph L. Baird contends,[16] but rather a due sense of responsibility, upon hearing about the disaster; his guilty feelings need no other explanation than his own involvement in the matter of angering God *ofer ealde riht* (2330a).

Also related to *hlaford*, and consequently to Beowulf, is the adjective *hlafordleas*, with its single occurrence, at line 2935b. In the relation of the Battle at Ravenswood, the killing of the Geatish prince Hæthcyn occasions its use for the Geats, yet this adjective may be heard as an echo of their even greater destitution through the recent death of their lord Beowulf. Calling the Geats *hlafordleas*, the poet establishes another link between a digression and the main plot.

Shared namings, besides establishing a parallel with his elders Hrothgar and Hygelac, also compare Beowulf with his young retainer Wiglaf. Three are heard in turn for the two characters:

	Beowulf	Wiglaf
– *feþecempa*	1544[17]	2853a
– *hæle hildedeor*	1646a, 1816a	3111a
– *secg on searwum*	249a	2700a.

[15] Bernard F. Huppé, in *The Hero in the Earthly City: A Reading of Beowulf* (Binghamton: Medieval and Renaissance Texts and Studies, 1984), esp. pp. 38–39, holds the view that the hero is no longer truly heroic in Part B, where he is led to his fate through his pursuit of gold and glory.

[16] "The Uses of Ignorance: 'Beowulf' 435, 2330," *Notes and Queries*, n. s. 14 (1967), 6–8, esp. 7–8.

[17] Whallon suggests that "it might have been slightly handsomer for him [Beowulf] here to be named *folces hyrde* (as he is in line 2644), since *feþecempa* [typographical error not reproduced] is in line 2853 used for Wiglaf" ("The Diction of *Beowulf*," 318), which seems irrelevant, perhaps all the more so since the two occurrences are collocated with cognates in the preceding lines: *werigmod* (1543a), for Beowulf, is echoed by *gewergad* (2852b) for Wiglaf,

All of them first describe Beowulf in his youth and are then repeated for the youthful Wægmunding whose behaviour during the last fight recalls that of his lord fifty years earlier. They are neatly distributed, in Part A for Beowulf, and in Part B for Wiglaf; their function in building up the symmetry of the poem could hardly be questioned.

The fact that it is also uttered by Beowulf addressing all his close retainers before his heroic challenge of the dragon, at line 2530a, does not lessen the value of *secg on searwum* as a link between the two warriors: after the fight has begun, Wiglaf alone proves worthy of sharing this naming with his lord.

The parallelism between the two noblemen in their youth could be expected to extend to their relationship with their respective lords, with Hygelac for the young Beowulf and, symmetrically enough, with the old Beowulf for Wiglaf. Is *mæg Ælfheres* (2604a) to be understood then as equivalent, for Wiglaf, to *mæg Higelaces* for Beowulf? In Part A of the epic, as seen above, this naming characterizes the hero and, furthermore, stresses the privileged position of "sister's son". Eliason has postulated the existence of Beowulf's sister as a mother for Wiglaf, "a logical necessity," it seems, to make out family links that the poet would have deliberately obscured in consideration of the artistic design of his work.[18] Forms of *mæg*, in *Beowulf*, essentially express close, even blood relationships; besides, when alliterating and connected with the genitive of a proper name, they are limited to the parallel namings mentioned above, with the inclusion of *Higelaces/ mæg and magoðegn* (407b–8a), which also designates Beowulf.[19] Since six out of seven occurrences undoubtedly refer to a blood tie with a maternal uncle, will not the seventh, and last, too? But, as Ælfhere's nephew, could Wiglaf also be Beowulf's? A most satisfactory solution is provided through the identification of the two uncles as one single character. Kemp Malone thought it possible that Ælfhere would be "an isolated survival of the hero's true name, which elsewhere had been completely driven out by the nick-

which confers similar "weariness" on the two "foot-warriors". Another similarity of mood is expressed by *collenferhð,* wrongly ascribed twice to Beowulf by Whallon (ibid., 316), and deliberately left out here since "bold of spirit, excited," that qualifies successively Beowulf (1806a) and Wiglaf (2785a) is adjectival and therefore ruled out as a "naming" (or "kenning" in Whallon's terminology).

18 "Beowulf, Wiglaf and the Wægmundings," esp. 104.

19 Though the exact nature of his blood tie with Beowulf is not revealed before line 1485a, "It looks as if . . . Hygelac was meant to be familiar already." T. A. Shippey, *Beowulf* (London: Arnold, 1978), p. 31.

name,"[20] and sound arguments in favour of that hypothesis, which explains away the apparent lack of alliteration between father and son, have been set forth by Henry B. Woolf.[21] Instead of *mæg Beowulfes,* a predictably modified echo of the naming *mæg Higelaces,* what is heard must have been most palatable to an initiate audience, who would know both Beowulf's true identity and the nature of his kinship with Wiglaf, and could therefore appreciate the poet's mastery. With *mæg Ælfheres,* a symmetry is kept, while the family link between Beowulf and Wiglaf, though identical to the one between Hygelac and Beowulf, is toned down, both through a limitation to one occurrence as a match for the often repeated *mæg Hygelaces* and through a subtle substitution of names. Wiglaf is indeed introduced as a "sister's son", but in such a subdued way that he never stands as a potential successor to the throne, so that "the epic sweep and grandeur imparted to the poem by the realization that the death of Bewoulf spelled the doom of the Geatish nation"[22] is skilfully maintained.

Among other shared namings that appear to be used as a function of a general structure, worth mentioning is

	Beowulf	Scyld
– *leof þeoden*	3079b	34b.

The poem opens and closes with a funeral. A reference to the two deceased leaders of their people through the repetition of the same naming enhances the circularity that bestows upon the work a unifying elegiac quality.

An exhaustive presentation of shared kennings should also include terms like *æþeling, cyning, dryhten, frea, rinc,* or *þeoden.* Yet, when heard neither in compounds nor with attributives, they sound far less specific than merely generic and, unless their distribution is noticeable enough to make them the appanage of individuals – as with *hlaford,* for instance –, they fail to hint at important relationships. Resorting again to the metaphor of circles drawn around names, one may consider the radius, or more precisely its length, as a function of specificity. The less distinctive a naming is, the longer its radius will be, and wide circles touching each other revolve around centers, that is to say characters, that are too far from each other to establish meaningful connections.

If Beowulf were connected with Grendel merely through the sharing

[20] *The Literary History of Hamlet* (Heidelberg, 1923), I, 236.

[21] "The Name of Beowulf," *Englische Studien,* 72 (1937–38), 7–9.

[22] Eliason, p. 105.

of *rinc*, which occurs also for other characters, the relevance of such a link might be questioned. It is reinforced, however, with the repetition of the compounded form

	Beowulf	Grendel
– *hilderinc*	1495a, 1576a	986b,

which is also used once for a group of retainers headed by Wiglaf (3124a) and, as seen above, parallels Beowulf with Hrothgar in the formulaic *har hilderinc*. Stanley B. Greenfield, refuting Whallon's suggestion that the work should be "explained from the limited resources of the traditional poetic wordhoard,"[23] demonstrates that *hilderinc* 'battle-warrior,' used for Grendel when his severed claw is described as a formidable weapon, belongs to terms that are judiciously selected by the poet and "contribute effectively to the emotional impact of his scenes."[24] And is not this impact further heightened by his use of identical namings for opponents? Bringing them together through the repetition of terms applied to both may increase the dramatic power of the tension developed between characters who are engaged in a fight against each other.

Though no naming is shared between the opponents during the second fight, it is worth mentioning that the two occurrences of *hilderinc* for Beowulf are actually heard then. Is a link that has been established between the hero and Grendel extended, then, to Grendel's dam? It must be conceded, moreover, that connections may be suggested between characters with the use of elements of speech other than proper namings.

Thus the relationship between Beowulf and the dragon is not only expressed through *bealohycgendra* (2565a) and *þa aglæcean* (2592a), two namings that refer to both at the same time and stress shared fierceness,[25] but also through the adjectival *stearcheort* qualifying successively *se wyrm* (2287a), at line 2288b, and *Weder-Geata leod* (2551a), at line 2552a. As for *hordweard*, a naming heard four times for the dragon (2293b, 2302b, 2554b, 2593a), if not shared as such, it recalls, with a significant omission, the full formula *hordweard hæleþa* heard previously for Hrothgar and for Beowulf (see listing above).

Repetitions with omissions, or with substitutions within formulaic systems – e. g. *fyrena hyrde* (750b) contrasting Grendel with *folces hyr-*

[23] "Formulas for *Beowulf*," 100.

[24] "The Canons of Old English Criticism," *ELH*, 34 (1967), 148.

[25] See the elaborate analysis of the second of these shared namings by Doreen M. Gillam in "The Use of the Term 'Æglaeca' in *Beowulf* at lines 893 and 2592," *SGG*, 3 (1961), 145–69.

de, applied to no less than four kings (see listing above) – would provide a subject for research far beyond the scope of the present analysis of namings for Beowulf.[26] Yet through their mere distribution and repetition, these namings happen to 'ring bells' in rather subtle ways for the appreciative ears of an experienced audience and furthermore develop around the central character patterns that show the structure of the poem as reflected in its very texture.

[26] Concluding on the digressions concerning episodes of Beowulf's life and Geatish history, Bonjour had already stated that "the poet succeeds in reaching an artistic effect that generally transcends their immediate and tangible contents, and this by creating subtle links of relevance which are mostly suggested by means of delicate hints and very light touches rather than fully expressed and explicit statements," in *Digressions,* p. 43.

Wife of Bath, Pardoner and *Sir Thopas*: Pre-Texts and Para-Texts

Paul B. Taylor

The *Canterbury Tales* are neither a miscellany of medieval narratives nor a concatenated roadside drama of a group of pilgrims. The meaning of each tale interacts with the sense of the work as a whole, and it is the context of a telling that informs it with purpose and directs reading. A reading directed by the conventions of genre constrains and deforms interpretation, for the constant refiguring of ideas in the tales dupes generic expectations and frees possibilities of narrative form that carry well beyond convention. Chaucer's own term for freeing of form to carry new sense is "conjoining" (fragment VIII, 951),[1] by which he means a refraction of a term or form to refigure sense.[2] The refigured form I call a para-text, a word borrowed from my colleague Gregory Polletta,[3] and the text it refigures is its pretext. A good many of the Canterbury Tales are para-texts in the manner in which they counter, or oppose another text. A para-text *answers* another text by its imitative

[1] All references to the *Canterbury Tales* are to the edition of F. N. Robinson, *The Complete Works of Geoffrey Chaucer*, 2nd edition (London: Oxford U. Press, 1957).

[2] R. M. Jordan, "The Question of Genre: Five Chaucerian Romances," *Chaucer at Albany*, ed. Rossell Hope Robbins (New York: Burt Franklin, 1975), 77–103, uses the French *conjointure* to describe the process by which Chaucer, like Crétien de Troyes, elaborates traditional forms for philosphic, moral and comic purposes.

[3] *Paratextualité* is the term that Gérard Genette uses for all that which *surrounds* a text, including title, book-jacket, and so forth (*Palimpsestes*, Paris: Seuil, 1982, p. 8 ff). For what I call *pre-text* and *para-text*, Genette uses *hypertexte* and *hypotexte;* that is, one text united to an anterieur text by reflecting its form, or alluding to its structure, as Joyce's *Ulysses* to Homer's *Odyssey*. Much of the critical terminology I use derives from my colleague G. T. Polletta, though responsibility for imprecision in its use is wholly mine.

form and style, and in doing so lends to the original text, or pre-text, ideas not retrievable in its own style or form until revealed by the para-text. A paratext, then, is a *refraction* (a term I prefer in this context to "deconstruction") of another text or texts, conjoining a narrative form with ideas typical of other narrative forms, or genres. Joyce's para-text of Homer, for an example, conjoins epic conceptions with a Dublin narrative. The relationship between Homer's and Joyce's works is transitive, so that a reading of the first through the form of the second allows the second to be read as well through the first.

In the *Canterbury Tales*, the complex relationship between the performances of the Wife of Bath, the Pardoner, and Chaucer the Pilgrim exemplifies the para-textual structure of the work as a whole. The Wife establishes her tale as an illustration of those preoccupations with *maistrie* revealed auto-biographically in her prologue, and that self-revelation provides a text through which her Breton *lai* must be read; that is, as a public and universal figure of a private and personal argument. That personal argument lends sense to her tale beyond its generic conventions. So too the Pardoner uses a "moral" tale to exemplify his confessed intent to spew out "venym under hewe/of hoolynesse, to semen hooly and trewe" (VI, 421–22), and thus he opens his text to both read and be read through its prologue pre-text. In both cases, however, the task of reading is complicated by the teller's display of self. Wife and Pardoner alike strain interpretive access to their tales by drawing much of their audience's attention to themselves. Of course, the challenge to reading is precisely here; and the audience is forced to read both parts of performance as a single text, and the pilgrim's reaction to those performances reveals failures of reading, which, in each case, join the text.

The argument I propose in the remainder of this paper is that the performance of the Wife of Bath comprises a pre-text for the Pardoner's performance, and that the Pardoner's performance of reading and re-figuring the Wife's is Chaucer's pre-text for performing. His *Sir Thopas* is a refraction of both texts and invites a reading through them.

The canon of criticism on *Sir Thopas* emphasizes the tale's reflection of both its own occasion for performance and its context in the order of telling, but denies it *sentence*, or a serious purpose and idea. It is variously seen as a joke on the Host's aversion to homosexuals (Lumiansky, 1951), a burlesque of bourgeois knighthood (Scheps, 1966), a satire of the literary tastes of his audience (Gaylord, 1967, and Whittock, 1968), inane nonsense serving to contrast with the sober truth of *Melibee* (Howard, 1976), a figuring of idle *solaas* (Allen and Moritz, 1981), and a purposely-constructed "worst" tale to serve as a joke on an audience expecting to hear the "best" tale from Chaucer himself (Kooper, 1984).[4] I would argue, to the contrary, that Chaucer's literary purpose in *Sir Thopas* is so serious that it establishes a criticism of not only Wife and Pardoner, but of pilgrimage itself.[5] A seriousness of purpose despite however one may respond to his form is made clear in Chaucer's reaction to the Host's interruption of *Sir Thopas* and his request for another tale. "Ye woot that every Evaungilist," Chaucer explains patiently to the Host,

> "That telleth us the peyne of Jhesu Crist,
> Ne seith nat alle thyng as his felawe dooth;
> But nathelees hir sentence is al sooth,
> And alle acorden as in hire sentence,
> Al be ther in hir tellyng difference.
> For somme of hem seyn moore, and somme seyn lesse,
> Whan they his pitous passioun expresse –
> I meene of Mark, Mathew, Luc and John –
> But doutelees hir sentence is al oon."
>
> (VII, 943–52)

(Proving his point in the act of making it, Chaucer forces two different stress structures on *sentence* in lines 945 and 946 without altering the word's semantic force.)

This remark has little relevance to *Melibee,* which is a slavish parroting of a source well-known to Chaucer's audience, but it does retrieve *Sir Thopas,* the tale just told. The comparison with Scriptural versions of

[4] R. M. Lumiansky, *Of Sondry Folk* (Austin: U. of Texas Press, 1955), 87–8; Walter Scheps, "Sir Thopas: The Bourgeois Knight, the Minstrel and the Critics," *TSL,* 11 (1966), 35–43; Alan Gaylord, "Sentence and Solaas in Fragment VII of the *Canterbury Tales:* Harry Bailly as Horseback Editor," *PMLA* 82:2 (1967), 226–35; Trevor Whittock, *A Reading of the Canterbury Tales* (Cambridge: Cambridge U. Press, 1968), 213; Donald R. Howard, *The Idea of the Canterbury Tales* (Berkeley: U. of California Press, 1976), 309 ff.; Judson Boyce Allen and Theresa Anne Moritz, *A Distinction of Stories* (Columbus: Ohio State U. Press, 1981), 215; E. S. Kooper, "Inverted Images in Chaucer's *Tale of Sir Thopas,*" *Studia Neophilologica,* 56:2 (1984), 147–54. Jordan, *op. cit.*, p. 81, labels *Sir Thopas* a self-parodic form of "conjointure". Jonathan Culler, *Structuralist Poetics* (London: Routledge and Kegan Paul, 1975), p. 152, reminds us that "in calling something a parody we are ... freeing ourselves from the demands of poetic seriousness."

[5] Urs Dürmüller, *Narrative Possibilities of the Tail-Rime Romance* (Bern: Francke, 1975), p. 221, shares Jordan's appreciation of Chaucer's mastery of the form, and denies any intent on Chaucer's part to deride the genre, but he does not consider to what effects Chaucer's mastery attains.

the Passion of Christ invests *Sir Thopas* with a *sentence* that has escaped the Host, and can even suggest that the "tellyng difference" of the form of *Sir Thopas* does not disqualify it as a para-textual gloss to the Gospels.[6] Chaucer had made a comparable alignment of his own with scriptural style in the General Prologue (I, 739), noting that "Crist spak hymself ful brode in hooly writ," where *ful brode* means "figuratively." By paratactic implication, then, *Sir Thopas* contains *in sondry wise*, a meaning comparable to the Passion. As such, as well as in form and style, the tale *corrects* the Wife's and the Pardoner's readings of quests; or rather, the readings that can be generated out of their performances. The refraction of those performances is effected by a mimetic structure and style.

The Wife's tale is of a quest in which a knight saves his life by finding the answer to a question about women's desires. Such a quest figures pilgrimage, even though the act of devotion that incites it is *fin amor.* Both plot and theme reach well beyond the Wife's avowed concern for domestic *maistrie,* so that the tale deceives the intent of the teller. The Hag's exchange of a body-saving reply for a marriage-promise places the knight's body in another peril. She saves him from this threat with moral instruction on the topic of *gentilesse.* Her success secures for them both a marriage that promises common profit. The marriage-bed lesson is a refiguring of the original riddle, a converting of its superficial triviality into an issue of soul-saving import. So, without having to realize what she is doing, the Wife of Bath conjoins the Breton *lai* to a range of ideas alien to the historical possibilities of the genre.

The Pardoner seizes upon the Wife's style and upon what he reads in the form of her tale, and sets up her performance as a pre-text for his own. He imitates her display of self in a private revelation, followed by a quest-tale that reads hers in a way that raises its possibilities of interpretation to another critical context.[7] In his display of self he shortens and intensifies a self-portrait, avoiding the Wife's lengthy autobiographical form. He abstracts himself as a figure of cupidity, answering the implications of the Wife's self-portrait as one of concupiscence. He exhibits self-avowed viciousness of character to screen the implications of his tale, so that his listeners are seduced into mistaking a reading of the figure of the Pardoner for a reading of his tale. Having set up a misread-

[6] Cf. Augustine, *De Doctrina* II, 10–11, where he argues that different understandings and different expressions of Scripture complement one another.

[7] The Pardoner's interruption of the Wife's *Prologue,* to thank her for exposing women's vicious methods of mastery, trivializes her narrative sense by a calculated misreading that both masks and marks his reading of her.

ing of his tale, he proceeds to tell a story which turns on a number of misreadings: Death misread as person, an old man misread as Death, and a heap of gold, a figure of the death the rioters seek, misread as a commodity. A quest to kill Death reads quite naturally as a salvific quest for eternal life, for which gold is an apt emblem. Thus, the quest of the three rioters figures pilgrimage to the shrine of Thomas Becket, a rehearsal of the passing of the soul from this world to the next whose penitential process comprises contrition, confession, and satisfaction – thought, word and deed, if you will. The Pardoner's prologue deforms that process and progress to grace into viciousness of intent, hypocrisy of word and selfishness of deed; and the Pardoner vaunts his success. The quest in his tale is a success. Gold causes the death which it figures, but the death of the rioters does not liberate saved souls to eternal life.[8] All of this sketches a reading of the Wife's tale and a refiguring of its theme into a criticism of pilgrimage. The knight's quest to save his life in the Wife's tale is refigured by the rioters' quest to kill Death, and the questers in each tale misunderstand the necessary moral and spiritual implications of their search. The shape-shifting Hag instructs the knight, and when he responds correctly she accords him a gift of beauty and fidelity which figure the grace accorded to those who submit their wills to Divine instruction. The rioters' fatal misreading of the Old Man's instruction counters the optimism of the Wife's ending. The rioters' obtuseness concerning the nature and goal of their quest mirrors the Pardoner's own view of his audience. The Host's scurrilous attack on him at the close of his performance only confirms the Pardoner's implication that the pilgrims cannot read the truth behind either his posture, his tale, or their holiday excursion to Canterbury. The Wife's self-serving propaganda for the acts of love, though they issue no fruits, makes of her a figure of wasted quest; the Pardoner's wry boast that he will have a jolly wench in every town invites his audience to speculate on the issue of *his* love-acts. Now, while the Pardoner's tale refigures the Wife's performance as a reading of it, his own challenges his audience's reading. Whether or not he feels that his audience is incapable of reading him, it can be argued that the Parson and the Nun's Priest respond later in their tales to the Pardoner's challenge. Before them, however, Chaucer uses the occasion for tale-telling to refigure, in erotic comedy to match the Pardoner's tragedy of spirit, the Pardoner's quest-tale and, by associa-

[8] Cf. The Wife's figuring of the perfection of virginity as gold (III, 100) and the Prioress's golden "A" which figures *Amor,* and finally, the *Nun's Priest's Tale* (VII, 3021) where gold figures death.

tion, the Wife's as well. If the Pardoner had prefaced his tale with an abstracted self-portrait, Chaucer does him one better by allowing the Host's portrait to stand as pretext for his narrative. Appreciating the Pardoner's challenge to read figures, Chaucer generates a tale out of the Host's reading of his own person as figure:

> "... What man artow?" quod he;
> "Thou lookest as thou woldest fynde an hare,
> For evere upon the ground I se thee stare."
> (VII, 695–97)

Then, turning to the pilgrims, Harry exhibits Chaucer:

> "This were a popet in an arm t'enbrace
> For any womman, smal and fair of face.
> He semeth elvyssh by his contenaunce,
> For unto no wight dooth he daliaunce."
> (VII, 701–4)

This bit of verbal dalliance of Harry's part contains a number of elements which inform Chaucer's tale that follows. I need point out only two of these to make my point. The first is the allusion to venery, in both its modern senses, in the image of the hare. Though Sir Thopas will ride soon through a forest full "of bukke and hare" (VII, 756) on his pursuit of the elf-queen, the image of the hare engages a number of texts and contexts in the *Canterbury Tales.* Appropriately, the image always binds together religious and sexual preoccupations. Of the Monk it is said in the General Prologue that "of prikyng and of hunting for the hare/Was al his lust..." (I, 191–92). The Pardoner's features that signal an unnatural sexual character include the detail that "swiche glarynge eyen hadde he as an hare" (I, 684). The Friar's tale links the Summoner's harlotry to the fact that he "wood were as an hare" (III, 1327–28). Finally, in the Shipman's tale, the lecherous monk characterizes wedded men in leporine terms, sleeping long in the *fourme* because of their sexual weariness (VII, 104).[9]

A second image which serves Chaucer in the designing of his tale is contained in the adjectival form "elvyssh", used to poke fun at Chaucer's facial expression. Elsewhere in Middle English, *elf* and *elfish* regularly link sexual with magical powers.[10] The "marriage" of metals and the

[9] Beryl Rowland, *Blind Beasts* (Kent, Ohio: Kent U. Press 1971), 87–102, elaborates on the implications of concupiscence in the hare image.

[10] R. W. V. Elliott, *Chaucer's English* (London: André Deutsch, 1974), 325, notes that, since elves are malign beings, the use by the Host of this adjective

process of "multiplying" in alchemy are described as "*elvyshhe craft* and *elvysshe nyce lore* in the Canon's Yeoman's tale (VIII, 751 and 842). Constance is accused of being an elf by Donegild in the Man of Law's tale (II, 754) to explain the monstrous son she is accused of having issued. The Wife of Bath contrasts the present with a magical pre-Christian past: "... ther as wont to walken was an elf,/ Ther walketh now the lymytour himself.../ Ther is noon oother incubus but he" (III, 873–80). The Wife reclaims that past in her tale whose heroine is an elf-queen (III, 860) who shifts in and out of hag-shape. As fas as I can discern, this is the first elf-queen in English literature. Indeed, female elves are rare before Chaucer's day.[11] The switching of sexual identity for a figure of sexual power is what we might expect from the Wife, recalling her own pursuit of husbands. So, when the Host calls Chaucer "elvish" because he lacks dalliance (a term with certain sexual overtones), he means ironically to chide him for a lack of sexual vitality (one recalls that he misjudges the sexual nature of both the Monk and the Nun's Priest).

"Hare" and "elf" nucleate a text for Chaucer; that is, the two words and their contextual associations throughout the Canterbury tale-telling sessions, if not throughout the Middle English literary corpus, establish a kernel of thematic suggestions, and inform the text that can contain them. To Harry Bailly's display of him, Chaucer responds with a tale whose form is a quest for a love-object endowed with magical powers. Like the knight of the Wife's tale and the rioters of the Pardoner's tale, Sir Thopas seeks something he has never seen. The Wife's knight finds an elf-queen without being able to realize her significance to his quest; Sir Thopas has a signification for quest without ever seeing its object. As if to underline the comedy implicit in such a quest, Chaucer performs his tale as an irregular metrical romance adroitly conjoining that form with ideas figured more cleverly than either Wife or Pardoner did, or might have done.[12]

Sir Thopas is only the third quest tale told on the Canterbury road, and so sets itself up to be read through as well as a comment upon the

is "ironic". The *MED* defines *elf* as a "supernatural being having powers for good and evil, a spirit, fairy, goblin, incubus, succubus, or the like." It cites the *Medulla* gloss: *satirus: an helfe.*

11 The Middle English romances and ballads seem to feature only male elves, such as those in Child's ballads, 1 and 4, and the king of fairy in *Sir Orfeo,* etc.

12 Northrop Frye, *The Secular Scripture* (Cambridge, Mass.: Harvard U. Press, 1976), 24, notes that the romance genre "appears to be designed mainly to encourage irregular or excessive sexual activity."

other two.[13] Its allusive and mimetic style links its form to a number of other tales, but particularly to the Wife's and Pardoner's performances. Allusions to the Pardoner and his tale are especially critical. Where the Pardoner swears to have "licour of the vyne" (VI, 452), while his mouth is full of beer (VI, 456), Sir Thopas swears on ale and bread (VII, 872) while he is drinking wine (VII, 851). The three rioters meet the Old Man as they are about to tread over a stile on their hunt for Death (VI, 712), and Sir Thopas pricks over "stile and stone/An elf-queene for t'espye" (VII, 798–99). This sort of directed aping aligns the two texts, the latter drawing attention to particular features of the former. The plot of *Sir Thopas* is both comic and erotic in its mirroring of the other quest tales. All three are directed to objects never seen, but which some authority establishes the existence of. For Thopas, that authority is but a dream, but dreams, as the Nun's Priest's Chantecler discovers, are likely to be reified by experience. The elf-queen, like the goals of the other quests, figures the goal of pilgrimage, *grace,* a word comically insisted upon in the text by the forced rhyme of *Thopas* with *grace (gras)* (VII, 830–31).

The plots of all three tales turn on a particularly significant structural element, that of the opposer or diverter of quest. Each of the quests is diverted or retarded by a screening force which doubles as an instructor to the quester on the nature of his quest. The Hag instructs the knight happily and converts his quest from a trivial domestic quibble to a spiritual understanding of marriage. The Old Man instructs the rioters tragically, since they misread his directions and misdirect their quest. Hag and Old Man stand in pertinent contrast, since the success of her instruction allows her to retrieve youth and beauty, while the Old Man's wasted counsel matches his wasted age. Thopas's quest is temporarily blocked by a three-headed giant named Olifaunt, whose instruction is in his figure rather than in his words. The Parson explains that many-headedness is a figure of a woman, such as the Wife herself, who marries often: "... If a womman hadde mo men than oon, thanne sholde she have moo hevedes than oon" (X, 922). Olifaunt also figures the Pardoner's cupidity, for Chaucer uses the term elsewhere in a context which

[13] Larry D. Benson, "The Order of the *Canterbury Tales,*" *Studies in the Age of Chaucer,* 3 (1981), 77–120, argues convincingly that the Ellesmere order of the tales represents Chaucer's final intention, and this would place *Thopas* after the *Pardoner's Tale,* which follows long after the Wife's. Be it as it may, the ordering is not essential to my argument, for the para-textual relationships between the three tales is independent of their order of performance, though the dramatic interplay between the tellers is heightened by a reading of *Sir Thopas* as the last of the three.

reflects the imagery of the Pardoner's tale. In his translation of Boethius, Book III, Prose 8, line 27, *olifaunt* "elephant" figures the weight of earthly goods which counters man's attraction to heavenly goods. In the following Meter, Lady Philosophy extends the idea as she chides Boethius for his cupidity: "Certes ye ne seke no gold in grene trees, ne ye gadere nat precyous stones in the vynes... But folk suffren hemselve to ben so blynde, that hem ne reccheth nat to knowe where thilke goodes ben yhidd whiche that thei coveyten, but ploungen hem in erthe, and seken there thilke good that surmounteth the hevene that bereth the sterris." Sir Thopas is as undaunted by figure and as unenlightened by sense as the three rioters are undaunted by Death and unenlightened by the Old Man's identification of it as gold.

The quest in the Wife's tale is achieved happily in an embrace of beauty and wisdom. The quest in the Pardoner's tale ends bitterly in a death which was not the death sought. Sir Thopas's quest is unachieved because disrupted, not by Olifaunt (whom Thopas does not read as either gaoler or protector of the value he seeks), but by a Harry Bailly who stops the tale at the point where Thopas is armed for the decisive encounter. So, as if aping his own hero, Chaucer re-arms himself with instruction to the Host on reading texts, and then continues with the tale of *Melibee.*

However comic or even absurd we are tempted to think this stepping of character out of story is, it contains the kernel of Chaucer's serious *sententia.* Chaucer casts the Host in the role of Olifaunt in order to dramatize a moral implicit in his tale. Neither espousing the Wife's fantasy optimism, nor condoning the Pardoner's caustic pessimism, Chaucer figures the Host's interruption as blocked or failed pilgrimage; disruption ends a quest, but not questing. Even the subversive narrative of the Pardoner cannot prevent continued renewal of the journey of the human soul toward grace.[14] One foppish knight may indeed figure those whose purpose on the road to Canterbury is seasonal rather than festival, but the feast remains, unspoiled and available.

If Sir Thopas is retrievable as *sentence,* it is because of its para-textual refraction and correction of the Wife's and the Pardoner's opposing meanings. The apparent bare and idle *solace* of *Sir Topas* is as much a challenge to reading as the apparent waste of character of the Pardoner. Chaucer's reading converts that waste to fruit in a form which challenges

[14] Cf. Corinthian 6.8: "God's grace can be received by honour and dishonour, by evil report and good report, as deceivers and yet true" *(ut seductores et veraces).*

his audience to see profit in his "drasty speche". That the challenge can be met is proved by Edmund Spenser's reading of *Sir Thopas* which informs his own Chaucerian para-text, *Faerie Queene.*

Word and Image Clusters in Shakespeare

Barbara Sträuli

In the course of the fifth act of *Othello*, Iago stabs Roderigo with the words

> O murd'rous slave! O villain!

Roderigo, dying, answers:

> O damned Iago! O inhuman *dog*! (V.1.61–62)[1]

Othello, about to commit suicide, camouflages his preparations by telling an anecdote:

> And say besides that in Aleppo once
> Where a malignant and a turbaned Turk
> Beat a Venetian and traduced the state,
> I took by the *throat* the *circumcised dog*
> and *smote* him – thus. (Stabs himself) (V.2.352–56)

And Cleopatra, finally, prevented in her attempt at suicide after Octavian's soldiers have taken her palace, has the following exchange with Proculeius:

> Quick, quick, good hands! [Draws a dagger]
> *Proculeius:* Hold, worthy lady, hold! [Disarms her]
> Do not yourself such wrong, who are in this
> Relieved, but not betrayed.
> *Cleopatra:* What, of *death* too,
> That rids our *dogs* of languish?
> (*Antony and Cleopatra*, V.2.39–42)

In all three passages the setting for murder or suicide on stage produces the word *dog* in the text. What we have here is a Shakespearean image

[1] Quotations are from *The Complete Pelican Shakespeare*, ed. Alfred Harbage (Baltimore: Penguin Books, 1969); the italics are mine throughout.

cluster with the components 'violent death' – 'knife' – 'dog' as central images. A further example shows that the murder or suicide need not even be enacted on stage, but may simply be referred to in the text:

> *Shylock:*
> ...
> You call me misbeliever, *cutthroat dog,*
> And spit upon my Jewish gaberdine,
> And all for use of that which is mine own.
> Well then, it now appears you need my help.
> Go to then. You come to me and you say,
> 'Shylock, we would have moneys' – you say so,
> You that did void your rheum upon my beard
> And foot me as you *spurn* a *stranger cur*
> Over your threshold! ...
> (*The Merchant of Venice,* I.3.107–115)

Another passage, presumably written about a year before the *Merchant of Venice,* shows the cluster in a similar context. Its subject matter is again hatred of strangers:

> You'll put down *strangers,*
> *Kill* them, *cut their throats,* possess their houses,
> And lead the majesty of law in lyam
> To slip him like a *hound;* alas, alas, say now the King,
> As he is clement if th'offender mourn,
> Should so much come too short of your great trespass
> As but to banish you, whither would you go?
> What country by the nature of your error
> Should give you harbor? Go you to France or Flanders,
> To any German province, Spain or Portigal,
> Nay, any where that not adheres to England,
> Why, you must needs be *strangers;* would you be pleas'd
> To find a nation of such barbarous temper
> That breaking out in hideous violence
> Would not afford you an abode on earth,
> Whet their detested *knives* against your *throats,*
> *Spurn* you like *dogs,* and like as if that God
> Owed not nor made not you, nor that the elements
> Were not all appropriate to your comforts,
> But charter'd unto them? What would you think
> To be thus us'd? This is the *strangers'* case
> And this your [mountainish] inhumanity.
> (*Sir Thomas More,* Addition II,120–140)[2]

[2] Cf. G. Blakemore Evans' edition of the Shakespearean additions to the play in *The Riverside Shakespeare* (Boston: Houghton Mifflin Company, 1974), pp. 1693–94.

The associated words 'stranger', 'cut', 'throat', 'dog/hound/cur', which are common to both texts, not only support the assumption that the above passage is really by Shakespeare, but also that it was written in the early or mid-nineties, around the time when the *Merchant* was produced, and not, as some critics have maintained, after 1600.[3]

Further research reveals that the death-dog cluster is not only linked to the element of knifing or stabbing but also to the equally violent death by hanging. The connecting word seems to be *throat*, the part of the body that is affected in both cases (cf. *cut-throat*):

> *Pistol* [who is trying to save Bardolph's life]:
> Fortune is Bardolph's foe, and frowns on him;
> For he hath stol'n a pax, and *hanged* must 'a be
> A damnèd *death!*
> Let *gallows* gape for *dog;* let man go free,
> And let not hemp his *windpipe suffocate.*
> (*Henry V,* III.5.38–42)

Pistol is referring to the fact that it was still customary in the sixteenth century to punish animals for crimes (e.g. dogs for sheep-biting).[4] The following passage from the *Merchant* is quite explicit:

> *Gratiano:* [to Shylock]
> O be thou damned, inexecrable *dog,*
> ...
> Thy currish spirit
> Governed a wolf who, hanged for human slaughter,
> Even from the gallows did his fell soul fleet, ...
> (*The Merchant of Venice,* IV.1.128,133–35)

There remains little doubt now that in the following well-known lines spoken by Lear, the use of the word *dog* is not accidental but induced by association:

> And my poor fool is *hanged:* no, no, no life?
> Why should a *dog,* a horse, a rat have life,
> And thou no breath at all?
> (*King Lear,* V.3.306–308)

As hunting to the dogs was one of the more important Elizabethan pastimes and a popular source for metaphors in Elizabethan love lyrics,

[3] The different propositions that have been made concerning the date of the play are discussed by G. Blakemore Evans in *The Riverside Shakespeare,* p. 1684. *Sir Thomas More* is generally dated 1594–95, *The Merchant of Venice* 1596–97.

[4] Cf. John Russell Brown's introduction to the New Arden edition of *The Merchant of Venice,* p. xxxiii.

it is quite natural that dogs in the Shakespearean text should occasionally be accompanied by the word *hart:*

> *Orsino:*
> That instant was I turned into a *hart,*
> And my desires, like fell and cruel *hounds,*
> E'er since pursue me.
>
> (*Twelfth Night,* I.1.22–24)

In associative thinking, the sound of a word may be more influential than its content. Thus, in the succeeding passage, *hart* is replaced by its homonym:

> *Cassio:*
> This [i. e. Othello's suicide] did I fear,
> but thought he had no weapon;
> For he was great of *heart.*
> *Lodovico* [to Iago]: O Spartan *dog,*
> More fell than anguish, hunger, or the sea!
>
> (*Othello,* V.2.360–62)

However conscious Shakespeare may have been in other places of this well-worn pun, he certainly did not use it intentionally here, while in the throes of composing the complex finale of *Othello.*

The dog-death cluster has not, to my knowledge, been described before. It occurs at least sixteen times,[5] allowing us to draw a tentative model of the associative field connected with the central elements *dog* and *death* in Shakespeare's memory:

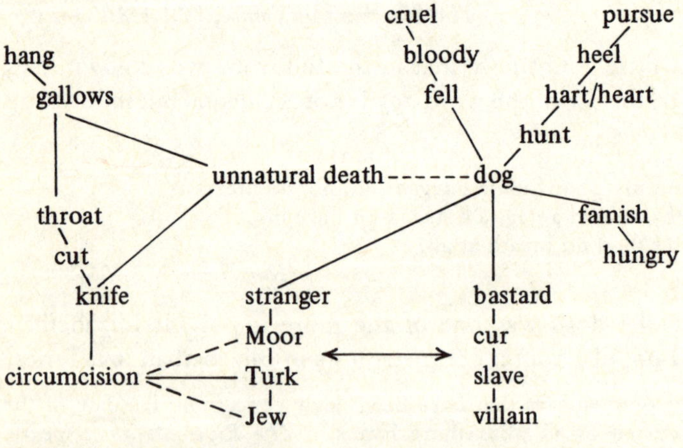

[5] *Tit.A.* II.3.281, V.3.14; *Rich.III* IV.1.39, V.5.2; *Merch.V.* I.3.111, IV.1.128–138; *Sir Thomas More,* addition II, 119–140; *Hen.V,* Prol. 5–8, III.6.38–42; *Twel.N.* I.1.22–24 *Oth.* V.1.61–62, V.2.351–356, V.2.360–62; *Lear* V.3.306–08; *Anth.and Cl.* V.2.39–42; *Timon* II.2.80–85.

The same material arranged according to plays yields the following table:

Play	death (on stage or mentioned in the text)	dog	knife (on stage or mentioned in the text)	gallows throat	hunt	presence of, or reference to person of base behaviour or origin
Tit. A., II.3	murder	whelps	dagger			Tamora's sons
		curs				
Rich. III, IV.1	death	dogs			heels	Richard III
More	–	hound	cut	throat	slip	foreigners
(Add. II)		dogs	knives	throats		
Merch. V., I.3	–	dog	cut	throat		Jew
Merch. V., IV.1	murder	dog	slaughter	hanged		Jew
		currish		gallows		Jew
		wolf				
Henry V, III.6	hanging	dog		hanged		thief
				gallows		
Twel. N., I.1	love/death	hounds			hart	
					pursue	
Oth., V.1	murder	dog	dagger			Iago
Oth., V.2	suicide	dog	circumcised	throat		Turk
			dagger			
Oth., V.2	suicide	dog	dagger		Spartan	Iago
					dog	
Lear, V.3	suicide	dog		hanging		'my poor fool'
A. and Cl., V.2	suicide	dog	dagger			
Timon, II.2	death	whelped		hanged		servant
		dog				

Whenever the cluster appears, two conditions are fulfilled:

a) Someone is killed on stage, or death is mentioned by one of the characters.

b) Someone is abused, a person of low or discriminated origin (servant, foreigner, Turk, Jew, thief, villain) is present on stage or mentioned by one of the characters.

A convincing explanation for the associative connection between the words *dog* and *knife* cannot be produced. Quite possibly, it has its origins in a personal experience of the dramatist. The presence of persons of low rank, their abuse, their bad reputation or scape-goat functions, on the other hand, can be related to the double meaning of the word *dog*, which is frequently used by Shakespeare as an epithet for baseness or a term of abuse.

The first to discover that certain words and images in Shakespeare's works are frequently connected beyond the 'natural' (as he called it) level of syntax, was Walter Whiter. Convinced that he had made a significant discovery, he published an essay (in 1794) with the title

> An Attempt to explain and illustrate various passages of Shakespeare on a New Principle of Criticism, derived from Mr. Locke's doctrine of the Association of Ideas.[6]

However, those of his contemporaries who did react were less than enthusiastic.[7] The phenomenon of associated words in Shakespeare was described a second time in 1923, by E. E. Kellett, who obviously had not read Whiter's essay, and who did not pursue the idea beyond the publication of his one article.[8] After the Second World War, the British ornithologist E. A. Armstrong took the matter up again, and this time it received thorough treatment.[9] Unlike his predecessors, Armstrong was armed with concordances and, by that time, considerably advanced knowledge in the field of memory processes. He succeeded in isolating large groups of associated images or word-chains in the text, and in demonstrating the re-occurrence of individual clusters in the Shakespearean plays over a time-span of up to twenty years. In nume-

[6] In: *A Specimen of a Commentary on Shakespeare. Being the text of the first (1794) edition revised by the author and never previously published,* ed. Alan Over, completed by Mary Bell (London: Methuen, 1967), pp. 59–207.

[7] Cf. the introduction to Whiter's *Specimen* by Mary Bell, pp. xxix–xxxix.

[8] E. E. Kellett, "Notes on a Feature of Shakespeare's Style," in *Suggestions. Literary Essays.* (1923; rpt. London: R. West, 1979), pp. 57–78.

[9] E. A. Armstrong, *Shakespeare's Imagination. A Study of the Psychology of Association and Inspiration* (London, 1946; rpt. with revisions Lincoln/London: University of Nebraska Press, 1963).

rous cases, he furnished explanations for apparently random associations.[10]

The reaction to Armstrong's book was reserved. He was taxed with showing rather more interest in the workings of the mind than in the qualities of the Shakespearean text, but in the fifties, such criticism may still have been infused by a latent fear that a method as dangerously near psychoanalysis as Armstrong's might unearth something of Shakespeare's dirty mind. One point, however, which had already been discussed by Whiter, could not be ignored: image clusters can be used as supportive evidence in the ascription of doubtful passages. Thus, with convincing argumentation based exclusively on the play's image clusters, Karl Wentersdorf was able to refute the hypothesis that *The Taming of the Shrew* had been written in collaboration.[11] Another method of putting clusters to practical use was developed by Ernst Leisi, who restored several corrupt passages by means of word collocations, using the new knowledge of Shakespeare's associative habits in the procedure. This method invalidates the older emendation practice, which consisted in choosing words with the appropriate number of syllables and a content that was in keeping with the general trend of the passage concerned. Leisi rightly maintains that a word is likely to be the original expression if it is 'cluster-prone', i. e. if it is found elsewhere in Shakespeare, in a similar collocation with the surrounding words of the crux.[12]

The fact that association processes can be observed with such clarity in a great author's literary output has far-reaching implications. It seems that we are given insight into areas of the creative process that are gener-

[10] Thus Armstrong found an explanation for the frequent alliance of birds of prey, especially the kite, with bed vocabulary such as *sheets, linen* etc. The kites, which circled in large numbers over the city of London, living on offal, had the habit of padding their nests with little pieces of linen hung out to dry. The key to this association is, among others, Autolycus' line "My traffic is sheets, when the kite builds, look to lesser linen". (*Wint.T.* IV.3.23–24).

[11] Karl Wentersdorf, "The Authenticity of *The Taming of the Shrew,*" *Shakespeare Quarterly,* V (1964), 11–32, and "Imagery as a Criterion of Authenticity: A Reconsideration of the Problem," *Shakespeare Quarterly,* XXIII (1972), 231–259.

[12] Ernst Leisi, "A Possible Emendation of Shakespeare's Sonnet 146," *English Studies,* 47 (1966), 271–285; "Die Töchter von Harfleur: Zu einer Emendation in *Henry V* III.3.35," in: *Festschrift für E. Mertner* (München: Wilhelm Fink Verlag, 1968), 169–171; "Some New Readings in *As You Like It,*" *Shakespeare Jahrbuch 1969,* 143–151 (together with Christine Trautvetter); "'Now entertain conjecture of a time'. Sprachliche Probleme in *Henry V,* Chorus IV," in: *Festschrift Rudolf Stamm* (Bern/München: Francke Verlag, 1969), 117–124.

ally hidden from view, and that the discoveries to be made here may also be pertinent to the workings of other writers and to other art forms.[13] Research will consequently have to be extended to the question of artistic creation and thinking processes, besides investigating what the clusters tell us about how Shakespeare functioned as a writer. How much can be gleaned about Shakespeare's biography is, perhaps, of secondary importance here.

I should like to address myself to the following questions: How many more clusters are there besides those discovered by Armstrong? How many of those are of literary origin and what are their sources? Which collocations or parts of clusters are general knowledge and may also be found in the classical authors or in the works of Shakespeare's contemporaries?[14] Since the scope of this article does not permit a comprehensive treatment of the problem, I shall try to shed more light on it by discussing one cluster not yet described by Armstrong. A brief elucidation of the laws of association ruling the formation of a cluster will be helpful here.

The features of an image cluster

For Armstrong the image cluster is defined

> as a group of unconsciously associated words (or pictures) which has accumulated in the writer's mind and which may be called up by reference to any of its component units.[15]

Whiter speaks of

> words and ideas which have been suggested to the mind by a principle of union unperceived by himself [i. e. the poet], and independent of the subject to which they are applied.[16]

[13] Very revealing in this context is H.-G. Clouzot's documentary film *Le mystère Picasso* (1956). In it, the painter is seen to produce a series of pictures within a very short time-span, using a limited number of motifs in an apparently unlimited number of variations. The conditions for this style of production are obviously a thorough mastery of the craft as well as a large catalogue of motifs stored in the artist's memory. These motifs he produces at will, without paying special attention to them, while his conscious effort is directed towards the problem of the composition as a whole.

[14] Cf. also the programme for future imagery and cluster research outlined by Kenneth Muir in "Shakespeare's Imagery – Then and Now," *Sh. Survey 18* (1965), p. 55.

[15] Walter Whiter, *Specimen,* p. lx.

[16] Walter Whiter, *Specimen,* pp. 62–63.

As opposed to the single associative link or collocation the cluster consists of a larger group of words or images which occurs several times (in fact, up to 20 times) in Shakespeare's plays and poems. The arrangement of the words in such a cluster could be pictured as a net or three-dimensional structure in which each word or image represents a node connected to several others by association. These associative links occur neither in fixed numbers nor in definite order. The description de Saussure gave of the paradigmatic relations in language can easily be extended to the associative field constituted by an image cluster:

> A particular word is like the center of a constellation; it is the point of convergence of an indefinite number of coordinated terms.[17]

Thus, the net of associations in the text is a continuum without beginning or end, and the isolation and description of a cluster is, in fact, arbitrary. This does not quite coincide with the findings of Armstrong and Wentersdorf, who propose a hierarchic order of the cluster images, with some strong key images at the centre attracting weaker, subordinate images.[18] However, de Saussure speaks of all the potential associations a word may have whereas Armstrong describes the actual realization, where some images are more emotionally 'loaded' or richer in accompanying elements than others, because of their content.

In a modification of de Saussure's model of the associative family (as he called the paradigmatic relations)[19], cluster associations could be represented as follows:

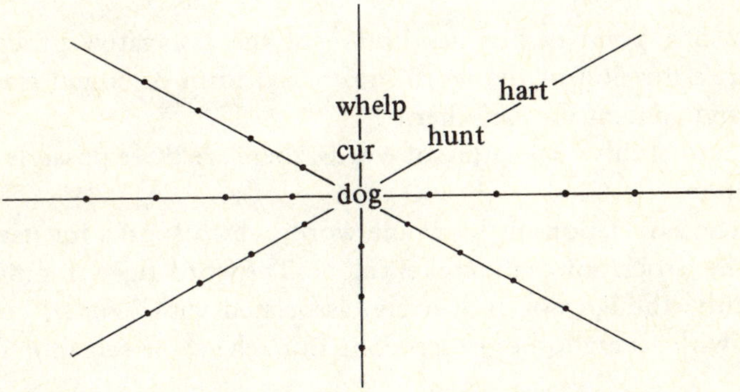

[17] F. de Saussure, *Course in General Linguistics,* trans. Wade Baskin, ed. Charles Bally and Albert Sechehaye (New York: McGraw-Hill, 1966), p. 126.

[18] Karl Wentersdorf, "Imagery as a Criterion of Authenticity: A Reconsideration of the Problem," p. 241.

[19] F. de Saussure, *Course in General Linguistics,* p. 126.

However, this model is not quite adequate, since each word may be linked to more than just one other word, as shown below:

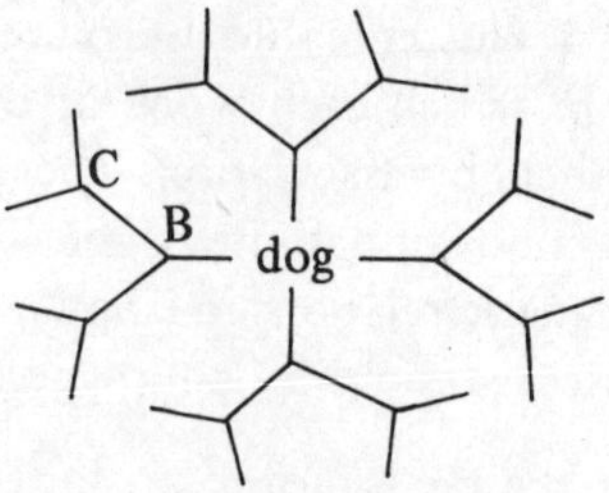

And finally, if we take into account that the words of the C-generation may be linked to both A and B generation words, we arrive at the following diagram to illustrate the connections in a cluster.

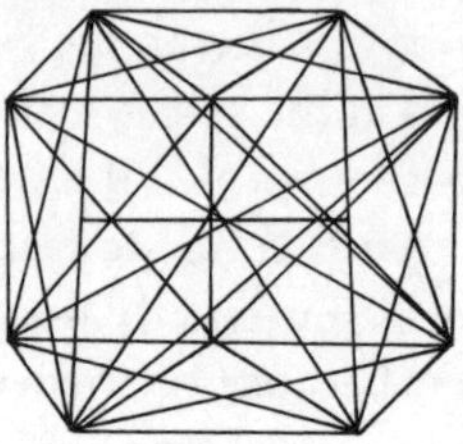

Types of association

The starting point in our description of the associative process is de Saussure's division of the word into visual form or sound on the one hand, and content on the other.

Because of this dual nature of words, there are three possible types of association:

1) The association of the whole word, which speaks for itself.

2) The association of the content alone. The word 'tiger', for instance, is frequently, though not exclusively, associated with *hunger,* but it also occurs with several other expressions from the same semantic field:

Play	*key image*	*associated element 1*	*associated element 2*
Tit. A.	tiger	ravenous	(Lavinia enters)
Son. 19	"	devouring	– – –
King J.	"	fasting	woman
Rom. & J.	"	empty	lady
3 Hen. VI	"	hungry	queen
etc.			

We can imagine the cluster as a batch of empty association slots ('hunger' being one in our example, 'woman of high standing' another) which can at each materialization of the cluster be filled with any word from the field concerned. It is this mobility on the selection axis which makes the recognition of clusters difficult, and a collection of cluster data by means of a computer almost impossible. The associative chain *tiger-queen-face (3 Henry VI)*, for instance, contains the same cluster elements as *Hyrcanian beast-complexion-Hecuba (Hamlet)*, only the tokens differ.

3) The association of the *form* (visual or sound) alone. Here, the meaning is ignored by the writer, only the visual or acoustic form of the word is associated. The word *tear*, e.g., is very frequent in the tiger cluster, it occurs for the first time in *3 Henry VI:*

> But you are more inhuman, more inexorable –
> O, ten times more! – than *tigers of Hyrcania.*
> See, ruthless queen, a hapless father's *tears.* (I.4.154–56)

In *The Rape of Lucrece*, it is the homonym that appears in a similar context. Lucrece is cursing Tarquin:

> Stone him with hard'ned hearts harder than stones,
> And let mild women to him lose their mildness,
> Wilder to him than *tigers* in their wildness.
> Let him have time to *tear* his curled hair,
> Let him have time against himself to rave,... (978–82)

4) There is a fourth type of association as well. Not only a word in the text, but also an object on stage can belong to the cluster. We have already established that a dagger on stage sometimes draws the word *dog* in its wake. Another example is the figure of the warrior covered in blood, who seems to be part of the tiger-cluster. In *Macbeth*, the appearance of Banquo's ghost at the king's banquet soon brings the word *tiger* to Macbeth's lips:

> What man dare, I dare.
> Approach thou like the rugged Russian bear,
> The armed rhinoceros, or th'*Hyrcan tiger;*
> Take any shape but that, and my firm nerves
> Shall never tremble. (III.4.99–103)

The black box

The image cluster is composed partly of associations that are general knowledge – in the case of the tiger words like 'claws' and 'teeth' or literary commonplaces such as 'swift' and 'fierce'. But there are also those whose origin cannot be detected unless luck comes to our aid. They may stem from an author's personal experience (as the bed-kite cluster does), in which case their unveiling is purely accidental; or they may be of literary origin, which means that a source can be found. Caroline Spurgeon and E. A. Armstrong were perhaps somewhat led astray by the idea that Shakespeare's image clusters had their sources primarily in his biography or in Elizabethan everyday life. Our improved knowledge of the rhetorical tradition and the grammar-school system of the period now leads us to the assumption that literary influences were far more significant than was held possible in the thirties and forties. Unfortunately, we lack the Elizabethans' knowledge of the ancient authors that would enable us to retrieve immediately the associative links stored in the black box of the author's memory; more often than not they remain a puzzle. What connects the dog and the knife, the tiger and the queen, the ship and the idea of rivalry?

There are two different procedures which, combined, guarantee a certain amount of success:

A thorough survey of all the passages containing a certain cluster very often brings to light the key to its main association – generally it is to be found in the early plays. If a cluster element is suspected to be of literary, i. e. classical origin, it usually pays to check it carefully in the concordances of the more important Latin authors such as Virgil, Ovid and Seneca. However, if the expression chosen is neither rare nor conspicuous, the search will be extremely time-consuming.

Triggering off the cluster

Armstrong describes the cluster as being tied to memory and emotion. Feelings like repulsion, fear or pleasure arising during the act of writing, whether they are the emotions of the author or those expressed by his characters, are often accompanied by a specific image cluster. Thus, the goose-cluster is linked to feelings of revulsion, the dog-candy-cluster to disgust at abject servility, and the contemplation of murder or suicide may, as we have seen, produce the dog-knife cluster.

According to Armstrong, either the emotion present in the mind of the author or the chance appearance of a cluster word will suffice to trigger off the whole cluster concerned. I should like to take the problem a step further. A closer look reveals that it is neither a single word nor an isolated emotion that makes a cluster appear, but rather a whole complex of conditions on stage and in the text. Thus, although the cluster is organized sequentially in time (when spoken) or space (when written), we have to assume the simultaneous presence of associated words, emotions and images. Underlying the cluster is a remembered *situation*, the ghost-like reenactment of a recurrent scene by faceless protagonists. Special attention shall be paid to this phenomenon in the following chapter.

The tiger-cluster

The tiger is, to my knowledge, one of the few animals which has not yet been treated in cluster-research. Its cluster can be traced through sixteen plays, the two longer poems and the sonnets, appearing for the first time in *3 Henry VI* and for the last, in a somewhat weakened state, but still recognizable, in *The Two Noble Kinsmen* (V.1, a scene firmly attributed to Shakespeare).[20] Regrettably, the lack of space does not allow for the presentation of the full textual evidence or for a portrayal of the individual cluster elements. The cluster's most important associative links are: the tiger, a reference to a child-parent relationship (i. e. mother, father, son, daughter, child), a reference to a wild animal or monster (lion, bear, wolf, but also phoenix, dragon, leviathan), a reference to a noblewoman (queen, lady), the words *eyes, tears, weep, wind, blow, stone, marble, hard, pity,* and many others. The three passages quoted below, composed by Shakespeare over an extended period of time, shall serve as introductory examples:

3 Henry VI,

York:
Thou art as opposite to every good
As the Antipodes are unto us
Or as the South to the Septentrion.
O *tiger*'s heart wrapped in a *woman*'s hide!
How couldst thou drain the lifeblood of the *child,*
To bid the *father* wipe his *eyes* withal,
And yet be seen to bear a *woman's face?*
Women are soft, mild, *pitiful* and flexible;
Thou stern, obdurate, *flinty*, rough, remorseless.

[20] Spevack lists 31 instances of the word *tiger* in his concordance. Only three of those are not accompanied by any of the associated elements that constitute this large cluster. They are: *Com. Err.* III.1.95, *Tr. and Cr.* I.3.49 and *TNK* IV.2.131, the latter belonging to a part of the play generally ascribed to Fletcher.

Bid'st thou me rage? Why, now thou hast thy wish.
Wouldst have me *weep?* Why now thou hast thy will.
For raging *wind blows* up incessant showers,
And when the rage allays the rain begins.
These *tears* are my sweet Rutland's obsequies,
And every *drop* cries vengeance for his death...
...
That *face* of his the *hungry* cannibals
Would not have touched, would not have stained with blood;
But you are more inhuman, more inexorable –
O, ten times more! – than *tigers of Hyrcania.*
See, ruthless *queen,* a hapless *father's tears.*

(I.4.134–148, 152–56)

The Rape of Lucrece

'To show the *beldame daughters* of her daughter,
To make the *child* a man, the man a child,
To slay the *tiger* that doth live by slaughter,
To *tame* the *unicorn* and *lion wild,*
To mock the subtle in themselves beguiled,
To cheer the ploughman with increaseful crops
And *waste* huge *stones* with little *water-drops.*
...
'Disturb his hours of rest with restless trances;
Afflict him in his bed with bedrid groans;
Let there bechance him *pitiful* mischances
To make him moan, but *pity* not his moans.
Stone him with *hard'ned* hearts *harder* than *stones,*
And let *mild women* to him lose their *mildness,*
Wilder to him than *tigers* in their *wildness.*
'Let him have time to *tear* his curled hair,
Let him have time against himself to rave,...

(953–59, 974–82)

King Lear, IV.2.29–53

Albany: O *Goneril,*
You are not worth the dust which the rude *wind*
Blows in your *face.* I fear your disposition:
That nature which contemns its origin
Cannot be bordered certain in itself.
She that herself will sliver and disbranch
From her material sap, perforce must wither
And come to deadly use.

Goneril:
No more; the text is foolish.

Albany:
Wisdom and goodness to the vile seem vile;
Filths savor but themselves. What have you done?
Tigers not *daughters,* what have you performed?
A *father,* and a gracious aged man,
Whose reverence even the head-lugged *bear* would lick,
Most *barbarous,* mosts *degenerate,* have you madded.
Could my good brother suffer you to do it?
A man, a prince, by him so benefited!
If that the heavens do not their visible spirits
Send quickly down to *tame* these vile offenses,
It will come,
Humanity must perforce *prey* on itself,
Like *monsters* of the *deep.*
Goneril: *Milk*-livered man,
That bear'st a cheek for *blows,* a head for wrongs;
Who hast not in thy *brows* an eye discerning
Thine honour from thy suffering;...

(IV.2.29–53; the Pelican text here follows Q_1. In F_1 lines 30–50 are missing).

In all three passages, a lady or queen is speaking or addressed on the subject of pity, there is talk of a child-parent relationship and of monsters, and the words *hard, mild, tears, blow, face* occur in various combinations, but we are given no explanation for this strange assembly of elements.

The clue to the cluster's origin is provided by the word *Hyrcania (3 Henry VI),* which, like 'Tartar', 'Phrygian', 'Scythian' and all the other exotic ethnica so popular among early Elizabethan dramatists, must have been borrowed from classical literature. The concordance to Virgil furnishes us with the source text: Shakespeare's tiger-cluster is the reworking of a well-known passage from the fourth book of the *Aeneid.* Aeneas has just told Dido that he is forced to leave her, obeying the gods who have ordered him to set sail for Italy. Dido's response is bitter:

"nec tibi diva parens, generis nec Dardanus *auctor,*
perfide, sed *duris genuit* te *cautibus* horrens
Caucasus, *Hyrcanae*que admorunt *ubera tigres.*
nam quid dissimulo aut quae me ad maiora reservo?
num *fletu ingemuit* nostro? num *lumina* flexit?
num *lacrimas* victus dedit aut *miseratus* amantem est?

[False one! no goddess was thy mother nor was Dardanus founder of thy line, but rugged Caucasus on his flinty rocks begat thee, and Hyrcanian tigresses gave thee

suck. For why hide my feelings? Or for what greater
wrongs do I hold me back? Did he sigh while I wept?
Did he turn on me a glance! Did he yield and shed
tears or pity her who loved him?][21]

The cluster elements 'mother', 'father', 'hard', 'rock', 'weep', 'tears', 'pity' are all there, as well as the queen (who does not appear in the text, but is the person speaking).

The fourth book of the *Aeneid* is probably the one translated most frequently in Latin classes, be it in the 16th or the 20th century. After Chaucer had used the material in his *Legend of Dido,* the story gained special importance in England and became detached from the Virgilian epic. Chaucer was greatly influenced by Ovid, who, in his *Heroides,* presents the events through the eyes of the unhappy queen, his main interest lying in the artistically successful description of her extreme emotional state.[22] Ovid's influence can be measured by the fact that in Elizabethan grammar schools Dido's lament was one of the textbook examples. The pupils were asked to create free speeches in the imagined persona of a famous figure from ancient literature.[23] The baroque content of Virgil's lines could not have been better suited to the taste prevailing in the drama of the early nineties. 'How that beast, the tiger,' Harry Levin writes in *The Question of Hamlet,* 'goes ramping through Elizabethan drama, as the proverbial embodiment of hardness of heart, a glance at any concordance will show.'[24] Two passages from non-Shakespearean plays may serve to illustrate this remark. One is from Marlowe's *Dido, Queene of Carthage,* the other from the anonymous atrocity play *Selimus.* They were, incidentally, printed in the same year (1594) as *3 Henry VI,* Shakespeare's first play which contained the tiger cluster.

[21] Virgil, *Aeneid,* IV. 365–370; trans. H. Rushton Fairclough (Cambridge, Mass.: Harvard University Press, 1934).

[22] Cf. Rudolf Sühnel, "Vergil in England," in: *Festschrift für Walter Hübner,* ed. Dieter Riesner and Helmut Gneuss (Berlin: Erich Schmidt Verlag, 1963), pp. 123–24.

[23] "One of the schoolroom exercises familiar to the Elizabethan school-child (and based on antique school exercises) was the imaginary speech: the histrionic monologue in the imagined persona of a famous figure from ancient literature. The textbook example of such a speech was Dido's lament for the departed Aeneas; second to this came Hecuba's outpouring of grief for the fallen Priam. Both are based on episodes from the Aeneid and both are familiar reference points in Elizabethan literature to invoke intense and majestic female suffering." Lisa Jardine, *Still Harping on Daughters. Women and Drama in the Age of Shakespeare.* (London: The Harvester Press, 1983), p. 192.

[24] Harry Levin, *The Question of Hamlet* (1959; Oxford University Press, 1970), p. 149.

Dido:
And wilt thou not be mov'd with Dido's words?
Thy mother was no Goddesse perjurd man,
Nor Dardanus the author of thy stocke:
But thou art sprung from Scythian Caucasus,
And Tygers of Hircania gave thee sucke:
Ah foolish Dido did forbear this long!
(*Dido, Queene of Carthage,* V.1.155–60)[25]

Zonara:
Thou art not false groome son to Baiazet,
He would relent to heare a woman weepe,
But thou wast born in desart Caucasus,
And the Hircanian tygres gave thee sucke,
Knowing thou wert a monster like themselves.
Acomat:
Let you her thus to rate us? Strangle her.
(They strangle her)
(*Selimus,* 1234–1239)[26]

Marlowe and the anonymous author of *Selimus* quote the passage practically verbatim, while Shakespeare breaks up its syntax, reduces its vocabulary to significant elements and rearranges the whole in various combinations. In addition, he not only remembers the Virgilian key words, but the circumstances accompanying them as well. In his 'adaptation' the situation 'wronged queen complaining' is no longer tied to the original character involved, but split up into the smaller situational elements 'presence of queen', 'wrong committed' and 'accusation raised against someone'. These situational elements assume, in the three texts quoted, the nature of slots that can be filled ad libitum. Thus York accusing queen Margaret of having killed his son, Albany accusing Goneril of treating her father badly and Lucrece lamenting the rape committed by Tarquin are all instances of the same. In each case the conditions of 'queen/lady present', 'wrong committed' and 'accusation being raised against someone' are fulfilled and the cluster appears.

An inventory of the instances when the tiger-cluster emerges in Shakespeare's works reveals that the visualizations or situational 'stills' underlying the cluster are not limited to that of the wronged queen. Especially in the later plays, the cluster is often accompanied by the

[25] Christopher Marlowe and Thomas Nashe; *Dido, Queene of Carthage.* in Vol. I of *The Complete Works of Christopher Marlowe* (Ed. Fredson Bowers, Cambridge University Press 1971).

[26] *The Tragical Reign of Selimus* (1594). Ed. W. Bang (The Malone Society Reprints, 1908, rpt. Oxford University Press, 1964).

description or appearance on stage of a warrior-figure steeped in blood and sometimes endowed with almost ghostly or robot-like features. In addition, there is frequently talk of the siege, fall or burning of a city.

Let me list a few examples:

1) Henry V encourages his soldiers in a fierce harangue to storm the walls of the besieged city of Harfleur. In peace, he says, 'modest stillness and humility' becomes a man

> But when the blast of war *blows* in our ears,
> Then imitate the action of the *tiger:*
> Stiffen the sinews, summon up the blood,
> Disguise fair nature with *hard-favoured* rage;
> Then lend the *eye* a terrible aspect;
> Let it pry through the portage of the head
> Like the brass cannon; let the *brow* o'erwhelm it
> As fearfully as doth the galled *rock*
> O'erhang and jutty his confounded base,
> Swilled with the *wild* and *wasteful ocean.*
> Now set the teeth and stretch the nostril wide,
> Hold *hard* the breath and bend up every spirit
> To his full height! On, on, you noble English,
> Whose blood is fet from *fathers* of war-proof,
> *Fathers* that like so many Alexanders
> Have in these parts from morn till even fought...
>
> (*Henry V*, III.1.5–20)

The cluster here is inscribed into a text in which man is seen to transform himself into a war-engine of curious rigidity, half beast, half weapon. Significantly, it emerges at the moment when Henry's soldiers are about to break into a city.

2) As has already been mentioned, the appearance of Banquo's ghost in the banquet scene in *Macbeth* evokes the tiger cluster:

> *Macbeth:*
> What man dare, I dare.
> Approach thou like the rugged Russian *bear,*
> The armed *rhinoceros,* or th' Hyrcan *tiger;*
> Take any shape but that, and my firm nerves
> Shall never tremble. Or be alive again
> And dare me to the *desert* with thy sword.
> If trembling I inhabit then, protest me
> The *baby* of a *girl....*
>
> (*Macbeth*, III.4.99–106)

Here, too, we are dealing with the intrusion of a soldier figure into a round, as the ghost is sitting down among the guests seated around the table. Banquo is covered in blood (l.50) and would, on stage, show certain dehumanized features that mark him as no longer living.

3) Menenius has failed in his mission, which was to persuade Coriolanus not to attack the city of Rome. The fall of the city seems imminent. Menenius describes how he found Coriolanus:

This Marcius is grown from man to dragon. He has wings; he's more than a creeping thing.
Sicinius: He loved his *mother* dearly.
Menenius: So did he me; and he no more remembers his *mother* now than an eight year old horse. The tartness of his *face* sours ripe grapes. When he walks, he moves like an engine, and the ground shrinks before his treading. He is able to pierce a corslet with his *eye;* talks like a knell and his hum is a battery. He sits in his state, as a thing made for Alexander. What he bids be done is finished with his bidding. He wants nothing of a god but eternity, and a heaven to throne in.
Sicinius: Yes, *mercy,* if you report him truly.
Menenius: I paint him in the character. Mark what *mercy* his *mother* shall bring from him. There is no more *mercy* in him than there is *milk* in a male *tiger.*

(*Coriolanus,* V.4.12–28)

4) The key passage explaining the presence of the warrior in the tiger-cluster is one of the intertextually more complex passages in Shakespeare: it is the player's speech in *Hamlet.* Hamlet is searching his memory for the speech he 'chiefly loved':

'Twas *Aeneas*' tale to *Dido* and thereabouts of it especially
where he speaks of Priam's slaughter. If it lives in
your memory, begin at this line – let me see, let me
see:
'The rugged Pyrrhus like th'*Hyrcanian beast*',...

(II.2.434–37)

No doubt, the Hyrcanian beast occured to the writer after Dido had been mentioned. The fact that, according to Hamlet, the line is the wrong opening in no way prevents the cluster from unfolding in the sequel:

'Tis not so; it begins with Pyrrhus:
'The rugged Pyrrhus, he whose sable arms,
Black as his purpose, did the night resemble
When he lay couchèd in the ominous horse,
Hath now this dread and black *complexion* smeared
With heraldry more dismal. Head to foot
Now is he total gules, horridly tricked
With blood of *fathers, mothers, daughters, sons,*
Baked and impasted with the parching streets,
That lend a tyrannous and a damnèd light

To their lords's murder. Roasted in wrath and fire,
And thus o'ersizèd with coagulate gore,
With *eyes* like carbuncles, the hellish Pyrrhus
Old grandsire Priam seeks.'
So, proceed you.

Player
'Anon he finds him,
Striking too short at Greeks. His antique sword,
Rebellious to his arms, lies where if falls,
Repugnant to command. Unequal matched,
Pyrrhus at Priam drives, in rage strikes wide,
But with the whiff and *wind* of his fell sword
Th'unnervèd *father* falls. Then senseless Ilium,
Seeming to feel this *blow,* with flaming top
Stoops to his base, and with a hideous crash
Takes prisoner Pyrrhus'ear. For lo! his sword,
Which was declining on the *milky* head
Of reverend Priam, seemed i'th'air to stick.
So as a painted tyrant Pyrrhus stood,
And like a neutral to his will and matter
Did nothing.
But as we often see, against some storm,
A silence in the heavens, the rack stand still,
The bold *winds* speechless, and the orb below
As hush as death, anon the dreadful thunder
Doth rend the region, so after Pyrrhus'pause,
Arousèd vengeance sets him new a work,
And never did the Cyclops' hammers fall
On Mars' armor, forged for proof eterne,
With less remorse than Pyrrhus' bleeding sword
Now falls on Priam.
Out, out, thou strumpet Fortune! All you gods,
In general synod take away her power,
Break all the spokes and fellies from her wheel,
And bowl the round nave down the hill of heaven,
As low as to the fiends.'
Polonius This is too long.
Hamlet It shall to the barber's, with your beard. –
Prithee say on. He's for a jig or a tale of bawdry, or he
sleeps. Say on; come to *Hecuba*.
Player
'But who (ah woe!) had seen the mobled *queen* –'
(*Hamlet*, II.2.439–490)

The full chain of associations runs from Aeneas to Dido and the tiger, from there to the burning of Troy and the death of Priam through the hands of the ghastly warrior Pyrrhus. The logic behind this ordering of events in Shakespeare's memory is that it corresponds more or less to the organization of the first four books of the *Aeneid*.

Arrival in Carthage. Aeneas meets Dido	Aeneas' tale: the destruction of Troy	Aeneas' tale: his wanderings	Dido's love Tiger-passage A. leaves by ship Dido's death
Bk. I	Bk. II	Bk. III	Bk. IV

The story opens with the landing of Aeneas' ships in Carthage. Its sequel is, in imitation of the Homeric hysteron-proteron, a flash-back: Aeneas tells Dido of the events accompanying the destruction of Troy. We can assume that Virgil's tale was present in the minds of Shakespeare's more educated contemporaries and that it was reproduced in a variety of texts, shorter versions and as exercise pieces. Shakespeare himself tells us, in the most abbreviated form of the story imaginable, how its elements were placed in his memory.

> Speak, Rome's dear friend, as erst our ancestor,
> When with his solemn tongue he did discourse
> To lovesick Dido's sad-attending ear
> The story of that baleful burning night
> When subtle Greeks surprised King Priam's Troy.
> (*Titus Andronicus*, V.3.80–84)

The same order can also be found in other passages. Pieces of rhetorical lament or the mention of a tiger sometimes evoke the burning city in the writer's mind. Lucrece, who, after being raped, bitterly laments her fate, twice mentions the tiger in connection with Tarquin's pitilessness, only to turn her attention in the end to a tapestry depicting the taking of Troy by treason. 'Rome is a wilderness of tigers,' cries out Titus Andronicus. When, immediately afterwards, his raped and mutilated daughter Lavinia enters, he refuses to lament (which means, in terms of cluster-thinking, that the idea of lament has been expressed) and continues thus:

> Speak, Lavinia, what accursed hand
> Hath made thee handless in thy father's sight?
> What fool hath added water to the sea
> Or brought a fagot to *bright burning Troy?*
> (III.1.66–69)

In as late a play as *Coriolanus,* the city and the tiger are still mentioned together. Menenius opposes the tribunes who want to put Coriolanus to death because killing him would mean for all 'a brand to th'end of the world' (III.1.303). When the tribunes insist, Menenius says that they are driven by *tiger-footed rage*.

The identification of Dido with Hecuba in the memory of the dramatist is probably responsible for the tenacious link between the tiger and the fall of Troy. At the same time, certain of the original circumstances accompanying the passage in the Virgilian text are suppressed. Aeneas' disreputable behaviour, the fact that he leaves Dido, has never formed part of the cluster.

Thus, it can be said that the tiger-cluster is attached not only to the circumstances of its source text (i. e. Dido lamenting) but also to an array of situational elements from the first four books of the *Aeneid.* Like the individual words of the cluster, these elements give the impression of being involved in a game of musical chairs, as their number varies each time the cluster appears.

The mechanics of fantasy

Obviously, Shakespeare commands a vast multitude of associations on the preconscious level, which are activated as soon as the corresponding memories, emotions and situations come into play. As if by magnetic attraction, the cluster elements rise to the surface and arrange themselves into patterns dictated by the surrounding text. This phenomenon has much in common with the mechanics of dreaming or day-dreaming. Had Armstrong's attitude towards Freud been less defensive, he might have developed a more comprehensive model of the organization of clusters. Unfortunately, he firmly believed that Freud's concerns were strictly pathological and not applicable to the creative side of human thought and emotions. Accordingly, he tried somewhat desperately to keep the two apart in his essay, so that Shakespeare's character should not be sullied with the suspicion of pathological tendencies.[27] I need not discuss the artificiality of such a distinction, as a great deal has since been written on the subject of art and madness, which have long been known to spring from the same source. I shall, instead, try to show briefly that the Freudian model applies to the emergence of clusters as much as to dreams and day-dreams.

Language into image

As far as can be ascertained, a cluster includes words and also a kind of underlying vision of an action or event. I will start from the assumption that language is first and the visualization second, and that there are no

[27] Cf. E. A. Armstrong, *Shakespeare's Imagination*, pp. 148–49, 174–180.

archetypal patterns involved. As Freud remarked, in dreams and related processes, language has to be translated back into pictures, as they are the material basically used in the process:

> There is no need to be astonished at the part played by words in dream-formation. Words, since they are the nodal points of numerous ideas, may be regarded as predestined to ambiguity; and the neuroses (...), no less than dreams, make unashamed use of the advantages thus offered by words for purposes of condensation and disguise.[28]

The situational elements underlying the cluster, e. g. the image of the queen, the warrior, the burning city, can be compared to the visualizations in dreams, the only difference being that they are of literary rather than biographical origin. Like dream images, they are detached from their original surroundings and linked to the memory and the cluster only by emotional and associative bonds. It would follow that they are subject to the same changes as are our ideas in dreams, namely to condensation and displacement, and in fact, examples of both processes abound in the context of the tiger-cluster.

Displacement

In the earlier plays the tiger is several times connected with a wronged woman, in the later plays with a warrior breaking into a city. These two situations actually have the same source. What happened in the course of Shakespeare's writing career was that the tiger moved along the chain of associations rooted in the landscape of the *Aeneid*, from Dido to Pyrrhus, from the victim to the aggressor, the raped to the raper. The transition was facilitated by the fact that Shakespeare related both situations to the great field of metaphors taken from love and war. Thus, the body of Lucrece is compared to a besieged city, whereas in *Henry V*, the French cities spared by the English king are described as being "girdled with maiden walls that war hath never entered' (V.2.308–9).

Condensation

Cluster images, like dream images, are usually concocted of various elements, the main condition being that there are points of resemblance.

[28] Sigmund Freud, *The Interpretation of Dreams* (Second Part). Vol. V of *The Standard Edition of the Complete Psychological Works of Sigmund Freud*, gen. ed. James Strachey (London: Hogarth Press, 1958), pp. 340–41.

Dido and Hecuba, for instance, who according to Elizabethan rhetorical tradition share the same characteristics, are frequently merged into one. It is more difficult to explain, however, why Shakespeare's cruel queens such as Tamora, Margaret and Goneril, who have precious little in common with their tearful counterpart, also elicit the tiger-cluster. The answer may be found in a second source text, the legend of Tereus and Procne from Ovid's metamorphoses, which Shakespeare used in *Titus Andronicus.* Here, a queen behaves 'like a tigress', when she kills her own son in an act of revenge:

> Without more words she dragged Itys away, as a tigress drags a suckling fawn through the dark woods on Ganges' banks. And when they reached a remote part of the great house, while the boy stretched out pleading hands as he saw his fate, and screamed 'Mother, mother!' and sought to throw his arms around her neck, Procne smote him with a knife between breast and side – and with no change of face.[29]

Several elements in this passage coincide with the tiger-cluster engendered by the Virgilian text: the tigress, the mother-child relationship, the queen. New are the motif of the murder and the word *face.* Especially the immutable or mask-like face becomes one of the most frequent cluster-satellites. The very first tiger-cluster in Shakespeare *(3 Henry VI)* also seems to be indebted to these two sources; Virgil provides the vocabulary and Ovid the situational elements: child-murder and a cruel queen.

Although the processes of displacement and condensation are features of all human thinking and imagining, Shakespeare's habit of cluster-forming appears to be rather unusual, its peculiarities being due not only to his outstanding ability, but to the nature of his schooling as well. As the study of the clusters clearly shows, the poet produces them without conscious effort, in an act akin to day-dreaming, while consciously concentrating on other parts of his composition. Like all skilled workers, he no longer has to grapple with the basic form. The cluster elements must have been internalized at an earlier stage of his career by means of much

[29] "Nec mora, traxit Ityn veluti Gangetica cervae
lactentem fetum per silvas *tigris* opacas,
utque domus altae partem tenuere remotam,
tendentque *manus* et iam sua fata videntem
et "mater! mater!" clamantem et colla petentem
ense ferit Procne, lateri qua pectus adhaeret
nec *vultum* vertit."
Metamorphoses, VI, 636–642; ed. and trans. Frank Justus Miller (Cambridge, Mass: Harvard University Press, 1971).

training and repetition. The two institutions that could provide this type of training were the grammar school and the theatre. As research done on Elizabethan education has established, the knowledge provided by the grammar schools was extremely formulaic;[30] the ancient texts, the *Aeneid* and Ovid's *Heroides* among them, were learnt by heart, translated into English, backtranslated, dissected into their grammatical and rhetorical parts, reassembled, and finally used as models by the students to compose their own speeches in the same style. On leaving school, the pupil had acquired a considerable store of texts, lines, turns of phrase and commonplaces which could be recalled at wish and which certainly also influenced his associations.[31] At the theatre Shakespeare must have heard his own texts repeated innumerable times, without even actively listening. Thus, the auditive transmission may have played a role in fixing first the cluster elements and later his own clusters in his memory, whereas the training at grammar school may have reinforced the (natural) tendency to associate a certain set of words with an emotionally defined situation.

[30] On techniques employed in assimilating the classical texts see, for instance, R. R. Bolgar, *The Classical Heritage and Its Beneficiaries* (Cambridge: Cambridge University Press, 1958), pp. 271–275, 295–301. The formulaic nature of the knowledge transmitted in the grammar schools and the strong share oral reproduction had in Elizabethan teaching are discussed by Walter J. Ong in his article "Oral Residue in Tudor Prose Style," *PMLA* LXXX (1965), 145–154.

[31] On Shakespeare's grammar school studies of Virgil and Ovid cf. T. W. Baldwin, *Shakespere's Small Latine and Lesse Greek* (Urbana: University of Illinois Press, 1944), II, pp. 417–95. Baldwin comes to the conclusion that Shakespeare had a firm knowledge only of the second, fourth and sixth book of the *Aeneid,* which include the fall of Troy, the grief of the forsaken Dido and the 'infernal machinery of Hades'.

Full of Doubt I Stand: The Structure of *Paradise Lost*

Neil Forsyth

Paradise Lost was published in two different editions during Milton's life. The first edition of 1667 *(Ed. I)* appeared in ten books, the second of 1674 *(Ed. II)* in twelve. Apart from some fifteen new lines, there were no other important changes between the two editions, yet the alteration of its external form shifts the way in which one perceives the poem's informing structure, what Aristotle called the *mythos*.

The longest books of the first edition were the last four. These were divided into six for *Ed. II*. Most of the extra lines also occur in the second half of the poem, changes which had the effect of moving the formal centre of the poem. This fact has troubled the numerologists, whose spectacular successes with other Renaissance poets[1] have not been repeated in Milton's case. By counting the lines of *Paradise Lost* as part of more ambitious numerological enterprises, Gunnar Qvarnström and Alastair Fowler found that the exact middle of the poem fell between lines 761 and 762 of Book VI. There the Son

> . . . in celestial panoply all armed
> Of radiant urim, work divinely wrought, 761
> Ascended, at his right hand victory 762
> Sat, eagle-winged, beside him hung his bow.[2]

[1] See especially A. Kent Hieatt, *Short Time's Endless Monument: The Symbolism of Numbers in Edmund Spenser's Epithalamion* (New York: Columbia University Press, 1960); also Maren-Sofie Røstvig, "Ars Aeterna: Renaissance Poetics and Theories of Divine Creation," *Mosaic* 3 (1970) 40–61, Alastair Fowler, ed., *Silent Poetry: Essays in Numerological Analysis* (London: Routledge and Kegan Paul, 1970), and his own book *Triumphal Forms: Structural Patterns in Elizabethan Poetry* (Cambridge: Cambridge University Press, 1970).

[2] Citations of Milton's poetry are from the Longman edition, *John Milton:* Paradise Lost, ed. Alastair Fowler (London 1971). For Fowler's discussion of the numerological centre, see pp. 22–28, 345–47 and 379–80; also Gunnar

That is, the hero of the cosmic battle climbs up into his chariot wearing the mysterious "urim," the stone on Aaron's breastplate of judgment that had taken on alchemical overtones. The action is seen to have various symbolic implications, including an anticipation of the event commemorated in the liturgical year by Ascension Day.

Now a poet as conscious of structural organization as Milton may well have intended this minor felicity, but if so he seems to have abandoned or deconstructed it himself. It is the first edition only in which this figural ascension is exactly placed at the centre: in *Ed. II,* the one we all read, the new centre, as Fowler was honest enough to admit, comes 4½ lines later. Fowler did not, however, feel obliged to quote the new line at the middle, which announces that from about the Son rolled a fierce effusion "Of smoke and bickering flame and sparkles dire" (766). That is, in words which adapt Psalm 18, the Son is so angry that he gives off smoke and flames.

The question now poses itself: what led Milton so to decentre his own poem that the exact middle became "bickering flame" rather than the neat and satisfying moment of the archetypal ascension? No critic who has paid attention to the problem offers a positive reason. W. B. Hunter, indeed, decided it was the printer's fault. The lines of the first edition had been misnumbered, so Milton was unaware that, in adding lines for *Ed. II,* he shifted the numerical centre. This may be true, but the argument smacks of the notorious insistence of Bentley that the blind Milton was at the mercy of an incompetent friend who saw the book through the press.[3] What is more, Hunter's suggestion unfortunately implies that Milton did not pay as much attention to line-counting as this particular kind of formalism would require, or perhaps that the structure of the poem, conceived in this way, is, like its main characters, finally in the hands of Providence. Yet one is forced to wonder whether other more

Qvarnström, *Poetry and Numbers* (Lund: Gleerup 1966) 93 and *The Enchanted Palace: Some Structural Aspects of Paradise Lost* (Stockholm: Almqvist and Wiksell, 1967); Christopher Butler, *Number Symbolism* (London: Routledge and Kegan Paul, 1970) 140–58.

[3] William B. Hunter, Jr., "The Center of *Paradise Lost,*" *English Language Notes* 7 (1969) 32–34. For discussion of Richard Bentley, whose edition appeared in 1732, see William Empson, *Some Versions of Pastoral* (London: Chatto and Windus, 1935), Robert M. Adams, *Ikon: John Milton and the Modern Critics* (Ithaca: Cornell University Press, 1955), Christopher Ricks, *Milton's Grand Style* (Oxford: Clarendon Press, 1963), and Frank Kermode, "Adam Unparadised," in *The Living Milton,* ed. Kermode (London: Routledge and Kegan Paul, 1960) 85–123.

important considerations than line-counting were at work in the restructuring of the second edition.

A persuasive approach to this question has been that of Arthur Barker.[4] He argued that the ten-book structure still suggested too much of Milton's original intention, recorded in the Trinity manuscript, to write a five-act tragedy, whereas the twelve-book structure, echoing Virgil, subsumed the tragedy within the larger encyclopedic possibilities of epic. The new shape was achieved very simply, by dividing the two longest books of *Ed. I* into what are now Books VII, VIII, and XI, XII. The accompanying diagram, based on Barker's essay, shows how the ten-book structure of *Ed. I* (what Barker saw as five two-book acts) was broken and converted by the various new designs discernible in the twelve-book second edition. I have added several suggestions of my own, in order to show how *Ed. II* makes clear what was only implicit in *Ed. I,* that conversion, regeneration, the bringing of good from evil, are structural as well as doctrinal principles of *Paradise Lost.* The reorganization of the second edition is, I suggest, Milton's final illustration of this principle.

Not only was Milton aware, as the preface to *Samson Agonistes* makes clear, of the basic Aristotelian dictum that a poet is more the maker of plots than of metres, but in writing the first version of *Paradise Lost* he had perhaps followed too closely the Renaissance understanding of Aristotle. Although the *Poetics* contains many remarks about epic poetry, its focus on tragic form had led to a Renaissance fashion for ten book epics according to what the period took to be Aristotelian precepts. The crisis, the major turn of events, for example, should come in the equivalent of the fourth act. What we read as Book IX of *Paradise Lost* was originally Book 8, and thus the Fall of Man had its obvious and rightful place as the tragic *peripeteia.*[5] Each of the first three acts moves toward anticipations of this crisis: in Book II Satan conceives the plan to subvert mankind and begins his journey to the new world; in Book IV he makes a preliminary attempt and the book ends with a face-off between Gabriel and Satan, the scales dangling enigmatically in God's sky; the third act,

[4] Arthur E. Barker, "Structural Pattern in *Paradise Lost,*" *Philological Quarterly* 28 (1949) 17–30, reprinted in *Milton: Modern Essays in Criticism,* ed. Barker (New York: Oxford University Press, 1965) 142–55.

[5] See Barker, p. 148; Jeffrey P. Ford, "*Paradise Lost* and the Five-Act Epic," Diss., Columbia University, 1966; and especially the authoritative discussion by John M. Steadman, *Epic and Tragic Structure in Paradise Lost* (Chicago: University of Chicago Press, 1976) 29–59.

Act	Total lines (1667, Ed I, First edition)	Book	Content	Note	Book (1674, Ed II, Second edition)	Total lines	Ed II note	Group
I	798	1	Satan revives in Hell		I	798	Hell ↓	Satan B10
I	1055	2	Plot against man; Satan's voyage through Chaos		II	1055		Satan B10
II	742	3	Heaven discusses Satan's plot, countermeasures		III	742	(birth of Eve)	Satan B10
II	1015	4	Satan in Paradise; first attempt		IV	1015	scales in Heaven	(Raphael)
III	904	5	Rebellion in Heaven	Abdiel ↓ Christ	V	907	Rebellion ↓	(Raphael)
III (=)	912	6	War and Satan's defeat		VI	912		(Raphael)
IV	1290	7	Creation		VII	640		(Raphael)
IV		7	Dialogue on astronomy, love for Eve		VIII	653	(birth of Eve) precarious balance	(Raphael)
IV	1189	8	Fall, Satan's success		IX	1189	Fall ↓	Adam
	1104	9	Consequences: Satan's triumph, A. and E. penitent		X	1104		Adam
	1541	10	Vision of future misery till Flood		XI	901		Adam
		10	Narration from 'world restored' to Redemption		XII	649	(birth of Christ) doubt: repent/rejoice	Adam
	10550					10565		

Structural Divisions in the two editions of Paradise Lost

Books V and VI, contains the Rebellion and War, dramatic image of divine discord, and although it ends with Satan's defeat, we know this to be the immediate occasion for the revenge he is planning. By the end of the fourth act he has succeeded and can retire from the scene. Act Five, all of what is now the last three books, presented the consequences of his success: as a well known passage near the end of the poem puts it, "so shall the world go on,/ To good malignant, to bad men benign,/ Under her own weight groaning" (XII 537–39). Satan and his plot thus dominated the first edition in a way that appeared to confirm the Romantic view of the poem's hero. It looked very much as if Blake was right, and Milton was of the devil's party.

This *Paradise Lost*, we may add, had something like the structure, not simply of tragedy *tout court*, but of that peculiar and largely indefinable Renaissance type that we have learned to call revenge tragedy. Satan's real model, then, would not be the motiveless malignancy of Iago proposed by C. S. Lewis, or the Faustus suggested in an influential essay by Helen Gardner,[6] nor even, though they come closer, Macbeth, Beatrice-Joanna in *The Changeling*, or Ferdinand in *Malfi*, but Hamlet himself. The sympathy we are invited to feel for each has a similar occasion – their magnificent and tormented soliloquies, and in each case they are eventual victims of parallel revenge plots against themselves, but worked out in secret and so without their knowledge. In Hamlet's case, the patent villainy of Claudius's counterplot intensifies our fearful sympathy with the hero, while Shelley, Empson and other accomplished if partial readers have testified that they have similar reactions to Milton's Satan and his villainous God. At least we can say that Milton squarely faced the possibility that God might not be good. We should add that Satan uses or is linked with the word "revenge" many times,[7] and that the action of *Paradise Lost* is touched off by the same kind of action which, in a revenge tragedy, often initiates the chain of events – some irrational and wilful decision of an absolute monarch,[8] in this case God's

[6] C. S. Lewis, *A Preface to Paradise Lost* (London: Oxford University Press, 1942) 98; Helen Gardner, "Milton's Satan and the Theme of Damnation in Elizabethan Tragedy," *English Studies* 1 (1948) 46–66, reprinted in her *A Reading of Paradise Lost* (Oxford: Clarendon Press, 1965) 99–120.

[7] I 35, 107, 148, 170, II 107, 330, etc., ten times in Books I and II, twenty-one times in the poem as a whole; see O. B. Hardison, Jr., "In Medias Res in *Paradise Lost*," *Milton Studies XVII*, ed. James D. Simmonds (Pittsburgh: University of Pittsburgh Press, 1983) 27–41.

[8] Franco Moretti, "Tragic Form as the Deconsecration of Sovereignty," in his *Signs Taken For Wonders* (London: Verso, 1983) 42–82.

announcement of the exaltation of his son, and that Milton has done his best to make reasonable Satan's response to this absolutist act. Most obviously, the action of *Paradise Lost* is controlled by the plot which drives the poem into motion – Satan's effort to colonize the newly created earth in revenge for the defeat he has suffered in heaven. The question must soon be faced, of course, whether Milton, as Dame Helen put it, was "creating the last great tragic figure in our literature and destroying the unity of his poem in so doing."[9]

The plot of *Paradise Lost* thus defined was what Milton was constructing from the time when he first conceived the idea of a tragedy, at some point in the late 1630's according to the jottings in the Trinity manuscript, until *Ed. I* was published in 1667.[10] This is the version of the poem's *mythos* which makes it begin in Hell, so that Heaven appears as a parody of what the reader has already seen; which makes the War in Heaven precede the Creation, an unusual though not unprecedented choice of sequence, so that the Creation appears to be God's reaction to the depopulation of Heaven; and which makes Satan's success in the garden the cause of the Redemption, a structural connection whose inplications many critics have tried to minimize by allusion to the doctrine of the Fortunate Fall.[11] In sum, this is a plot which makes good and evil balanced opponents, and which shows God's goodness as required by Satan's badness.

Since the shift of the second edition involved little more than renumbering the books of the poem, however, it is clear that the second plot emphasized by this new division was already present in the first edition. Milton's tinkering with the poem's structure served merely to draw out in an explicit way what was already written into *Ed. I*, the secret and usually silent plot with which God and Milton had informed their creations, but which the power and dominance accorded, by their permissive wills, to Satan, had threatened to obscure. Good emerges from evil in the divine, benign scheme of things and in Milton's imitation and justification of that scheme.

[9] Gardner, p. 120. She had changed her mind about this by the time she reprinted the essay in her book (note 6 above), adding a note to say that "the strength of Milton's design holds together the cosmic and the human theme" (ibid.). This change of mind corresponds, I think, to Milton's, as my argument will suggest.

[10] See Fowler, ed. *Paradise Lost* (note 2 above), pp. 3–5.

[11] Arthur O. Lovejoy, "Milton and the Paradox of the Fortunate Fall," *English Literary History* 4 (1937) 161–79, and widely reprinted since. For further discussion see below.

Several objections might be raised to this account of the poem's growth. The first edition, after all, is not a tragedy but an epic. Renaissance practice had usually produced epics in multiples of ten books – Camões' was in ten, Tasso's in twenty, for example – and Milton's *Ed. I* simply followed suit. Helen Gardner, indeed, in the essay cited previously, pays no attention to the difference between the two editions but argues instead that it was the decision to write an epic that loosed Satan from the chains in which a classical tragedy would have confined him. One could reply, however, that this argument appears to contradict the main point of the rest of her essay about the tragic and dramatic power of Satan. More generally, we should remember that Italian neoclassical theory had, in the course of adapting Aristotle, closely associated tragic and epic genres, and that this had led among Milton's predecessors to several experiments in five-act epics, from Sidney to Davenant's *Gondibert.*[12] So ten books was current epic practice, yes, but in Milton's mind the practice may still have born a close association with his original conception of a tragedy on the Fall of Man.

A more serious objection would be that none of the plans for the tragedy preserved in the Trinity manuscript bears much resemblance to the structure of the ten-book first edition. Milton's nephew, Edward Phillips, it is true, tells us he first saw Satan's Niphates speech as the opening of a drama, perhaps during the 1650's, and this does suggest the idea of an Elizabethan revenge tragedy.[13] Yet the plans of the Trinity manuscript and Phillips's version are quite different, and, in any case, what Phillips says, always supposing it is true, itself suggests how far the epic form had modified the tragic idea, since the Niphates speech now occurs at the opening of Book IV, what in Barker's scheme would be the middle of the second act. Against this objection one could reply that Milton still kept the essential idea of a plot which opens with powerful scenes for Satan, even when the epic scope allowed him to expand Satan's role and set scenes in Heaven and in Hell. Thus the tragic figure of the "lost Archangel" as well as the tragic five-act form persisted when "Milton changed his mind... and set himself a problem of extraordinary difficulty in choosing to treat this particular subject in epic form."[14]

12 R.H. Perkinson, "The Epic in Five Acts," *Studies in Philology* 43 (1946) 465–81; see also Barker (note 4 above), Steadman and Ford (note 5), and especially Hardison (note 7), p. 31.

13 Helen Darbishire, ed., *The Early Lives of Milton* (London: Constable, 1932) 13, 72–3.

14 Gardner (note 6 above) p. 119. Hardison (note 7) developes Gardner's ideas but ends by suggesting that, far from allowing Satan to escape his conscious

A further objection to Barker's hypothesis has recently been put forward by John Shawcross.[15] He claims that he fails to see the dramatic unity of Barker's Act IV, for example, what is now Books VII, VIII and IX. He points out that the "act" was broken in two by an invocation even in *Ed. I.* But this objection may be turned on its head. For one thing, the claim is not that *Ed. I* showed "unity" in its acts, certainly not in the fourth act, which was often in Elizabethan tragedy (like *Hamlet*) packed and diverse, but rather that *Ed. I* had something about it which Milton felt obliged to change: the traces of an earlier tragic design still clung too noticeably to it. For another thing, that "invocation," unlike the three previous ones (which do introduce "acts" in Barker's scheme) is not a direct address to the Muse but rather a meditation on the mixed form of the poem: it is here that the narrator says he "now must change/ These notes to tragic," a "sad task," as he calls it, "yet argument/ Not less but more heroic" than those of classical epics. It is here too that he stresses the process of composition rather than the finished product:

> If answerable style I can obtain
> Of my celestial patroness, who deigns
> Her nightly visitation unimplored,
> And dictates to me slumbering, or inspires
> Easy my unpremeditated verse:
> Since first this subject for heroic song
> Pleased me long choosing and beginning late.[16]

The Muse remains here "unimplored" in the third person, and this personal aside or digression both insists on how recently epic form and subject have come together and goes on to cite the tragic rather than epic virtues of "patience and heroic martyrdom" as the proper but unsung subject of this new and unprecedented genre.[17]

control, Milton's difficulty was in creating a credible symbol of evil in a poem dominated by an omnipotent God. Once again, it is revealing to find different critics reacting differently to the same evidence. Hardison cites as precedents *The Jew of Malta* and *Richard III,* which both open with soliloquies for the villain.

15 John T. Shawcross, *with Mortal Voice: The Creation of Paradise Lost* (Lexington: University of Kentucky Press, 1982) 64.

16 IX 20–26. See the extensive discussion by Steadman, op. cit., pp. 29–38. Hardison, op. cit., p. 34, makes the interesting point that the dramatic action of "Adam Unparadised," one of the projects for a tragedy, is focused on the material which appears in Books IX to XII of *Paradise Lost.*

17 Dennis Burden, *The Logical Epic* (London: Routledge and Kegan Paul, 1967) 59. Burden also develops the parallels with Elizabethan tragedy along the lines proposed by Gardner.

Shawcross's own list of structural symmetries is heavily dependent on the ten-book edition, so he is obliged to argue that Milton bowed only to external pressure, the neo-classical requirements of the age of Dryden, in publishing the second edition in twelve books. Yet since he groups his symmetries in two columns, the first of which comprises the first six books, the second the last four, of *Ed. I,* it would seem that the second edition would have been more appropriate, so that six would have been the number of books in each of his columns. And since he occasionally violates the sequence of events, whether in *Ed. I* or *Ed. II,* to produce his often fascinating list of correspondences between the two halves of the poem, the second edition would surely have done as well as the first. Shawcross appears to wish that Milton had not changed the form of the poem simply in order that the reader might have had more work to do.

> The drawing of good out of evil is seen also in terms of drawing order out of disorder (such as God's creation of light), of harmony out of disharmony, of proportion out of disproportion. Much more is thus achieved by a metaphor of structure where the seeming disorder, disharmony, and disproportion which the ten-book version allows disappear as the full structure is recognized. But man's finite perception has frequently failed to let him see that structure.[18]

Although he disapproves, then, Shawcross's version of Milton's reason for the change agrees with Barker's, that Milton wanted God's plot to emerge more clearly.

Actually Barker's explanation for the shift between the two editions implied something more interesting. It was not only a desire to emulate the *Aeneid* that he stressed, but Milton's sense of what he saw in his own creation. Although he did not say so, Barker makes his Milton sound a lot like Milton's God, at least as Empson read him. Having made his point that the Virgilian twelve-book structure corrects the excessive emphasis on Satan, Barker continues:

> Milton, it is clear, was by no means unaware of what has been called 'the unconscious meaning' of *Paradise Lost.* It may be that in 1667 he was not quite aware of it, or that for some reason or other he was then inclined towards it; it is certainly emphasized by his having written in ten books. But the 1674 renumbering indicates his consciousness of Satan's power over the poem, and (it if was not simply a trivial toying) the new disposition was meant to strengthen Satan's chains. Its motive was to shift the poem's emphasis and its centre in a way that would point more clearly to its stated intention.[19]

[18] Shawcross (note 15 above), pp. 46, 64.
[19] Barker (note 4), p. 28.

Barker's parenthetical proviso allows for the absence of external evidence to suggest why Milton made the changes, but what he implies is that Milton noticed something as a reader of his poem of which, as its writer, he had not been "quite aware."

Although he does not cite Barker, Joseph Summers's argument might seem to confirm him. He made a similar point, more extensively, about the poem's centre. In the twelve-book version, the centre, in book numbering, not lines, has shifted from the division between Books V and VI, the rebellion and consequent war, to that between Books VI and VII, the war and subsequent creation. Thus it is no longer Abdiel who appears on each side of the central divide, the "angelic exemplum of man's ways at their most heroic," the one just man, the saving remnant, he who undergoes and, alone of the poem's angelic or human characters, resists temptation; now it is Christ who bestrides the central books, "the divine image of God's ways at their most providential."[20] So the larger activity of Christ, not just his clambering into the chariot, becomes the true centre of the poem. Yet whereas Barker suggested that it was the Satanic power of which Milton became fully conscious on a second reading, Summers implies the opposite. In his view, it may have been the other plot, God's, of which Milton was not quite aware in the writing of the first edition. Summers seems to imply this when he notes something "oddly touching" about a Milton who, "in humility before his own creation," perceives afresh the structural implications, which are "larger and other than his conscious intention."[21]

In practice it may not matter whether Satan's or the providential plot were not quite conscious as Milton wrote the first edition. One can see how important the question would be if we were arguing about the source of poetic inspiration, whether it be demonic, as Blake thought, or divine, as Milton's Muse and the classical tradition required. What matters to my argument here is that both are conceivable.[22] As we have pursued the ideas of various critics, we have found a Milton who fully discovers one or the other side of his poem only on re-reading it, who shifts the balance between them for *Ed. II*, and who finds that his own act of writing corresponds to the major movement he inscribed within it

20 Joseph Summers, *The Muse's Method* (Cambridge, Mass.: Harvard University Press, 1962) 113.

21 Ibid., p. 112.

22 William Riggs, *The Christian Poet in Paradise Lost* (Berkeley: University of California Press, 1972) 15–45, shows that Milton anticipated Romantic theory by including several elaborate parallels between Satan and the poem's narrator within the poem.

– good emerging from evil, light from darkness. We hesitate, as he appears to have, which of the two structures to stress. What can we make of this?

The major changes in his perception and organization of the poem all occur in the second half and make more nearly accurate what the narrator says at the beginning of Book VII: "Half yet remains unsung." Three new pairs of books replace the two pairs that made up Acts Four and Five of *Ed. I*. The first of these pairs is the new Books VII and VIII, one long book in *Ed. I*. The new arrangement reveals a previously buried or subordinate aspect of the poem, one which now begins to assert itself – the increasing focus on Adam and his progressive understanding. In *Ed. II* one book is now devoted entirely to the magnificence of the creation, and then a further book to Adam's anxious questions about it, the astronomical speculations, and to his allied reflections upon his feelings for Eve (she it was who first posed the questions about the stars which Raphael answers).[23] No longer only a preparation for the Fall, the dialogue with Raphael turns the otherwise mysterious and transcendent process of creation into something which has direct and decisive relevance, though problematic, to Adam's and mankind's situation. Indeed Adam has himself something to offer to this dialogue, his own account of the birth or rather the creation of Eve. From this point of view, the dialogue that is Book VIII leads towards Adam's assumption of the narrative duties and skills of Raphael, at least on a smaller scale, and so illustrates Raphael's hint that things on earth and in heaven may be "Each to other like" (V 576).

The next new pair of books has a similar structure; the old climax of the Fall becomes now the first movement of a process which is compensated by the gradual repentance of Eve and Adam in the Book X of *Ed. II*. In that process Adam begins to realize the significance of the sentence passed on mankind by Christ, with its initially mysterious references to Eve's heel and serpent's head. The repentance scene may now be seen more clearly to include within it the contrast with the unrepentant Satan's triumphant return to Hell. That return is no longer what it chiefly had been in *Ed. I*, the beginning of Satan's power over earth, his successful colonization. The final pair, also made out of one book in the original, may now be seen to turn about a similar pivot as the previous pair, and indeed as the whole poem now does: the break be-

[23] Compare IV 657, 675, V 44 with VIII 15–25, 100–106, where the idea is reiterated that the stars must shine in vain unless someone watches them. The idea forms a part of Satan's temptation of Eve.

tween Books XI and XII, newly established for *Ed. II,* comes between the Flood and the Rainbow, or, as one of the new lines puts it, "Betwixt the world destroyed and world restored" (XII 3). Here too, as we shall see, Adam gradually moves toward a deeper understanding of his role in the larger scheme, and of the meaning of that scheme. So each of the new books created out of the second part of a long book in *Ed. I* is devoted to Adam's education by an angel.

Barker briefly proposed that other buried structures became more visible in the second edition. The new possibility of 3 groups of 4 books, for example, would allow for a triad of disobedience, woe, and restoration – but for this idea he has recently been castigated persuasively by Shawcross, who does not find that triad where Barker points.[24] Yet such possibilities will continue to provoke new readers to find, or construct, fresh structural patterns. I would propose, for example, that two of the new books, VIII and XII, now invite alignment with Book IV. All three contain important birth scenes: Eve's in IV, Adam's and Eve's in VIII, and Christ's in XII. This arrangement suggests the progress of love, a preoccupation of these three books, from bliss in IV, through troubled discussion of the subject in VIII, to the renewal of divine and human unity in XII – so at least Adam seems to understand the birth of Christ from his own loins and God, saying "So God with man unites" (XII 382).

However we define the new possibilities opened by the book divisions of *Ed. II,* it seems as if the critics who discuss the question need to find a way in which, as I also am arguing, the new organization serves to reassert or restore the divine plot by which Satan's plot is contained and converted. The second edition more nearly imitates this divine plot than the first. From the point of view emphasized by the first edition, the sequence of episodes shows his God doing what Milton appears to have done himself in the second edition, reacting to the power accorded to Satan. Book III, of course, like the poem's earliest event, God's speech in Book V, purports to resolve this difficulty by showing that God anticipated all of the events and allowed them their place in his scheme. Yet is there really so much difference, granted an omniscient God, between reacting to an anticipated deed and picking up the pieces after it has happened, even if the new structure one makes from the pieces is better, in some sense, than the old? However we may react to or conceive of Milton's God, whether with Empson and the Romantic tradition, or with what Empson called the "illiberal approach" which dominates the

[24] Shawcross, p. 64.

Milton industry and which has recently been asserted in a book called *Milton's Good God*,[25] it is clear that most of the problems the poem poses resolve themselves ultimately, as Milton saw, into the problem of God. It is the ways of God that call for justification, and Milton's chief means of doing so, since this is a poem rather than a treatise, is to imitate and so reveal in narrative structure the divine form. But what is remarkable about *Paradise Lost*, as the various discussions of its structure have revealed, is how closely it weaves together Satan's plot and God's, and how much they come to look like each other, as the rebel and victorious angels do. As a famous passage in *Areopagitica* asserts, the doom that Adam fell into was to know good and evil, and the context of this remark, it should be remembered, is the argument that men be allowed to enjoy this doom without the interference of censors: the bishops, like God, should permit us to read bad books and make our own discriminations.

> Good and evill we know in the field of this World grow up together almost inseparably; and the knowledge of good is so involv'd and interwoven with the knowledge of evill, and in so many cunning resemblances hardly to be discern'd, that those confused seeds which were imposed on *Psyche* as an incessant labour to cull out, and sort asunder, were not more intermixt.[26]

Milton applied the same doctrine to the reader of *Paradise Lost* as he applied to all potential readers in *Areopagitica*. The changes between the two editions show him engaging in the process of discernment himself.

The new break that introduces Book XII coincides with another shift in the poem's manner, the moment when Michael ceases to be a Prospero-like producer of a magic-lantern show and becomes simply a narrator. "Henceforth what is to come I will relate,/ Thou therefore give due audience and attend" (XII 11–12), he explains, and so echoes the Miltonic narrator, who also hoped that he would "fit audience find, though few" (VII 31). Michael's reason for the change, he says, is that "I perceive/ Thy mortal sight to fail" (XII 9), and he thus picks up a central aspect of the blind narrator's language, he who spoke of "things invisible to mortal sight" (III 55). Michael's words thus link Adam with Milton as well as with the poem's reader.[27] And the second edition increased the structural responsibilities that this tiring Adam must bear.

[25] Dennis Danielson, *Milton's Good God* (Cambridge: Cambridge University Press, 1982).

[26] *Areopagitica*, cited from *The Prose of John Milton*, ed. J. Max Patrick (New York: Doubleday Anchor, 1967) 287.

[27] A good discussion of the relations between angelic and Miltonic narrators is Riggs, (note 22), ch. 3.

Adam proves a good reader (or listener), if a little overenthusiastic. He still gets things wrong and has to be chastened by Michael. When he hears about the birth of Christ, for example, he reacts by seeing the structural implications, looking both backwards and forwards at once: "O prophet of glad tidings, finisher/ Of utmost hope!" (XII 375–6). He goes on to say that he now understands the meaning of the obscure promise of Book X that the seed of woman shall bruise the serpent's head. So far so good, but immediately Adam goes wrong again: "Say where and when/ Their fight, what stroke shall bruise the victor's heel" (385–6). He reacts like the father of a boxer whose son has just been offered his big chance, and he wants tickets for the fight. In a sense, that is exactly his position – he has just said that Christ will proceed from his loins – but Michael is obliged to explain the inward nature of the battle: "Dream not of their fight/ As of a duel" (386–7). In this and similar passages, Adam becomes a figure for the reader's efforts to construct an accurate version of the poem's – and God's – plan.

Learning from this chastening, Adam greets the final paradox of the poem's history with an ambivalent response. His final discovery in the poem is a crucial event, in every sense, for the interpretation of its structure. Since Lovejoy's essay, this moment has been called, rather incautiously, the discovery of the Felix Culpa or Fortunate Fall – the Redemption or Atonement story, which makes the Fall fortunate. This apparent key to the poem's meaning Adam greets at first with wonder:

> O goodness infinite, goodness immense!
> That all this good of evil shall produce,
> And evil turn to good; more wonderful
> Than that which by creation first brought forth
> Light out of darkness! (XII 469–73)

Lovejoy pointed out that it was a major innovation of Milton's to have Adam perceive the doctrine himself, but he did not point out that Adam's first reaction is essentially a structural one: Adam is piecing together the poem's meanings, and he here links the Redemption to the process that Milton had made the centre of the second edition: the emergence of light from darkness, the creation which follows the war in heaven. Lovejoy went on to show that Adam's next reaction, doubt, was also a Miltonic innovation, but again I suggest Milton's originality goes further. The word "doubt" retains, I think, its Latin meaning of hesitation alongside its psychological and religious meanings. What Adam hesitates between are two reactions to the poem's informing structures. As we first hear his lines, they suggest the dominant plot of the poem, or at least the active and obvious one, the Satanic plot that Milton tried to contain in *Ed. II:*

> Full of doubt I stand
> Whether I should repent me now of sin
> By me done and occasioned, or rejoice

The line end at "rejoice" makes us think, until we follow the enjambement on to hear the relatively innocuous sequel, that the Satanic plot of the poem is the one that succeeds in more than the sense in which Eve and Adam were induced to eat the apple. All the intervening lines, the Son's judgment, the bitter recriminations, Michael's teaching, have all led towards the same rejoicing as Satan's on his return to Hell. Adam, as we hear him first, doubts not only whether he should repent, sufficiently disturbing alone if one follows the logic of the thought, but whether he should not rejoice at what he has done. Just as Satan does. Just as all the romantic or humanist readers have done.

The rest of the speech, however, soon absorbs or converts that threat, just as the larger plot does. Adam is hesitating whether to repent or to rejoice

> Much more, that much more good thereof shall spring,
> To God more glory, more good will to men
> From God, and over wrath grace shall abound.

What Adam might be inclined to rejoice at, it turns out, is not what he did, but what God will do. But even there the syntax is not quite so explicit. Adam does not incline to rejoice at God's active achievement but rather at his passive or indirect presence: "To God more glory" and "more goodwill to men/ From God" – parallel prepositional phrases at the beginning of succeeding lines which both put God in oblique cases. Grace, it is true, shall abound over wrath, but also "good *thereof* shall spring" – where the antecedent of "thereof" is Adam's sin. What Adam perceives here, then, in the complexity of his syntax and the perplexity of his mind, is not so much the active deity as the results of his plotting – or to put it another way, the compensatory, redemptive and converting plot of the poem as Milton, in God's wake, had constructed it, and as, with his final godlike act, he had reinterpreted it, allowing the main epic plot to emerge from, and compensate for, the "dark materials" (II 916) of the dominant tragic plot he had first invented.

Several critics have in fact argued that we do not find the doctrine of the Fortunate Fall in *Paradise Lost,* even in the hesitant and ambivalent way I have suggested.[28] Clearly the doctrine was dangerous ground. The

[28] Lovejoy's argument (note 11 above) has been challenged by Virginia R. Mollenkott, "Milton's Rejection of the Fortunate Fall," *Milton Quarterly* 6 (1972)

risk is that, if the logic of the paradox were spelled out, then the Fall is Fortunate because necessary to the Redemption. Thus the Satanic plot is not merely converted but ignored, and so the whole delicate doctrinal and architectural structure of Milton's poem would collapse, leaving only a bland, if cosmic, smile, a Buddha face, in place of the awful sense of sin, the dread proximity of damnation, that Milton evokes in the figure of his lost archangel. So dangerous was the doctrine that many Christians, and Milton's contemporaries among them, denied the idea altogether, as Danielson has recently insisted in arguing for an entirely Unfortunate Fall. It is indeed true that *Paradise Lost* provides for Adam and Eve to graduate from Paradise by a better route than the sorrowful way in which they do leave it. God says as much, for example in a speech from the heavenly throne in Bock VII (155–60). It is also probable that Milton included such passages, as Dennis Burden argued, because he was

> worried about the idea of the Fortunate Fall. It is one thing to say that Adam is, as a result of the Atonement, better off than he was in Paradise, but something altogether different to suggest that he is better off than he would have been if he had stayed obedient. God's mercy cannot be allowed to make nonsense of his justice.[29]

That is well said, but, equally, it is one thing to argue, with Burden, that Milton was worried about the Fortunate Fall, and something quite different to argue, with Danielson, that he therefore scrupulously avoided it. Milton was not in the habit simply of avoiding dangerous issues, and this one goes to the heart of his project to justify the ways of God to men.

That Milton did not so oversimplify the problem is evident, I think, not only in the lines which Lovejoy used to demonstrate his point, and which I have been further analysing, but also in the following quotation from earlier in the poem:

> From this descent
> Celestial virtues rising, will appear
> More glorious and more dread than from no fall.

1–5, by John C. Ulreich, Jr., "A Paradise Within: The Fortunate Fall in *Paradise Lost*," *Journal of the History of Ideas* 32 (1971) 351–66, and most recently by Danielson, (note 25), pp. 202–33.

[29] Burden, (note 17 above), p. 37. The dangers of the doctrine are amply illustrated by the citations in Lovejoy's essay, as well as by the new material gathered by Danielson's fine research. In spite of the various objections, however, the assumption continues in Milton criticism that the paradox explains the poem: see, for example, Steadman (note 5 above), p. 30.

This is as clear a version as one could wish, much clearer than Adam's hesitant response, of the doctrine of the Fortunate Fall. The words, however, are Satan's, part of the speech in which he encourages the troops at the opening of the great consult (II 14–16). The sentence does not end with the last line of my quotation, but continues: "And trust themselves to fear no second fate." We are thus required to reassess the meaning of "virtues" in line 15: it is not the abstract term, but the title of a rank of angels, and this literal meaning is all that Satan has in mind. One of the many ironies of the poem is that this apparently straightforward version of the doctrine that informs it should be given to Satan, only for us to discover he doesn't understand it.

So the doctrine of the Fortunate Fall is present in the poem, but ever threatening to become a Satanic parody of itself. Any interpretation of the poem's structure and meaning is always likely to turn into its opposite: even the informing structural principle exemplified by the Fortunate Fall, that good emerges from evil, is heralded and balanced by Satan's defiant anticipation of it

> If then his providence
> Out of our evil seek to bring forth good,
> Our labour must be to pervert that end,
> And out of good still to find means of evil.[30]

And the principle is set at risk by his later heroic cry, "Evil be thou my good" (IV 110).

Both points of view, then, the Satanic and the divine, are required by and woven together in the overall plot of the poem. As the state of man

[30] I 162–65, J.R. Watson, "Divine Providence and the Structure of *Paradise Lost,*" *Essays in Criticism* 14 (1964) 148–55, cites this among other examples of the symmetry which the poem now shows about its central point between Books VI and VII, and also suggests that it was Milton's perception of this symmetryx that caused him to renumber the later books. Watson's approach is reminiscent of Cedric Whitman's to the *Iliad,* in *Homer and the Heroic Tradition* (Cambridge, Mass.: Harvard University Press, 1958), who discovers "geometric design" and what he calls "pedimental structure" as informing devices. William H. Marshall, however, "*Paradise Lost: Felix Culpa* and the Problem of Structure," *Modern Language Notes* 76 (1961) 15–20, finds that the didactic and dramatic elements of the poem clash, so that the conclusion "involves repudiation rather than subordination, of what we have felt during the first nine and a half books." But if Marshall had seen that there is no "explicit assertion in the final books of the Paradox of the Fortunate Fall," as he puts it, but only the hesitant Adam's perplexity about it, he might have seen how the delicate balance is maintained by these symmetries, and reinforced in the second edition.

now is, it is necessary they be intermixed since it is the Miltonic reader's task to distinguish them. Adapting Milton's words in *Areopagitica,* we might say that Satan's plot is necessary in order that, however dimly, we may see God's.

Just how much Milton made them look like each other, how difficult they are, even for Milton, to sort, may be seen if we return, finally, to our first and apparently trivial illustration of the change between the two editions. Even as he shifted the major centre of his poem to Christ's activity across Books VI and VII, Milton dethroned the ascendant Christ from the numerological centre and replaced him with a line that suits better the landscape of Hell: "Of smoke and bickering flame and sparkles dire". The odd word "bickering" is glossed by Fowler as "darting, flashing," but this is the earliest use of the word in that sense: all other such uses, defined as poetic by the OED, are allusions to that line of Milton's. The OED's basic meaning for the word is frequentative, akin to, but stronger than, its modern English sense: quarrel, skirmish, battle. It was Milton who extended and altered this sense by aligning it with the word "flame" and so producing the alliterative suggestion of "flickering." In their context the words are attached to Christ's rather than Satan's warlike rage. But whether consciously or by inadvertence Milton has made the poem's central words feel Satanic even as they are observed into the larger activity of Christ which now commands the poem's middle books. The balance is different, but only slightly, and these minor shifts, to and fro between Satanic and divine foci and between first and second editions show how close and necessary to each other are the poem's two informing structures. Adam and Milton, the first two readers of *Paradise Lost,* both hesitate between the two plots in the process of reconstructing the structure of this text. To stand, but full of doubt, seems to be the necessary, even salutary, position of the Miltonic reader.

Swift: The Satirical Use of Framing Fictions

Jean-Paul Forster

Swift's satires are often rather loosely described as blending different genres with one another: allegory, parody, mock encomium in *A Tale of a Tub*, and travel book, imaginary voyage, utopia and autobiography in *Gulliver's Travels*. At the same time, it is obvious that Swift did not so much follow classical models as borrow the least literary forms of his time, immortalising its ephemeral writings, while mocking its achievements. That the champion of the "Ancients" in the quarrel between "Ancients" and "Moderns" should so resolutely have chosen to play the "Modern" and express his views in the least traditional and most fugitively fashionable genres of Queen Anne's reign is just one of a number of contradictions for which Swift's work is famous. This utilization of contemporary genres and the combination of disparate elements warrant investigation as one of the crucial, though little studied, strategies used by the author to produce the corrosive effect of satire.

The gesture towards, and implicit reliance on, a contemporary context now largely fallen into oblivion, except in the case of historians, makes Swift difficult to approach by way of modern formalistic theories, notions of literary inter-textuality and conceptions of non-referentiality in literary criticism, as Edward Said has noted.[1] To such theories satire has, in any case, usually been something of a problem, because satire refers to a situation outside the text and insists that the reference be considered as part and parcel of the economy of the text. This reference often takes the form of a mimetic and "isomorphic" representation of reality, which does not totally preclude formalistic approaches. With Swift the problem of referentiality is more fundamental since the act of satirising the contemporary world does not take place only at the level of

[1] Edward W. Said, *The World, the Text and the Critic* (London: Faber, 1984), pp. 55–56.

its representation, but begins with the choice of a form of publication or genre as part of a complex structure. The purpose of the following analysis is to describe the structural rôle and function of this choice of contemporary genres in the satirical fictions.

In his satires Swift parodies the forms and genres that he follows. However, the purpose behind the parody is different from that of his contemporary and friend Alexander Pope. The latter, in his mock-epics, aims, through the use of a deliberately debased form, to suggest the remoteness of modern life from the classical ideals celebrated by the great epic poets. The attitude manifested by the handling of form is conservative and nostalgic. Swift's parodies evidence no such indirectness. They are straightforward imitations of the *discourses* of contemporary journalism, science – or philosophy, as it was then called –, and literary criticism. Whatever may be said of Swift's political and religious ideas, there is no trace of conservatism and nostalgia here.

Strangely enough, it is Swift's use of masks or *personae* that has attracted most attention, and not his caricature of contemporary genres. Of course, his impersonations of various types of scribblers is a striking feature of his fiction-making, but it is not present in all his satires, and, where it is found, it is subordinated to, and a mere emanation of, the playful imitation of a discourse. Discourse has priority over persona. Discourse is an apt concept to describe Swift's satires and, in particular, their framework, which is the object of this study, for two reasons. On the one hand the framework, however discreet it may be, is always argumentative, in contradistinction to narrative or dramatic structures. On the other hand the term refers to a new conception of language that emerged at the end of the seventeenth century and aimed at representing the world and experience in such a way as to give a faithful verbal picture of them, and with a view, likewise, to their verbal analysis.[2] Swift's mimicking of typical genres and forms of publication has the same purpose. It presents them as discourses, in other words as the ways in which certain groups of people – one is tempted to say pressure groups – think and speak of certain subjects: religion, politics, science or madness. The importance taken by the mimicking of contemporary genres supports Swift's own claim that his parodies do not primarily intend to ridicule people, "John, Peter, Thomas, and so forth," as he once put it in a letter.[3] It is more correct to say that they isolate samples from diverse

[2] Michel Foucault, *Les Mots et les choses* (Paris: Gallimard, 1966).

[3] *The Correspondence of Jonathan Swift,* edited by Harold Williams (Oxford: Clarendon, 1963), vol.iii, p. 103.

discourses to hold them up for inspection and criticism. To be immediately identifiable, the individual samples of fashionable discourses must present the typical characteristics of the genre in a concentrated form: hence the necessity of some degree of caricature. So the parodic quality that results from underlining typical features achieves two things: it introduces the distancing that makes a critical evaluation possible and it draws something like a circle around the sample which reveals it as a fake. The circle is the starting point of the fictionalising process. Swift makes it sufficiently visible for the fictitious to be easily distinguished from the real thing. He does so mainly by a device that criticism calls "framing." By including – framing – one type of discourse within another, he presents the phenomenon of communication as complex and the relation between text or original intention, and reader or reception, as problematic.

Swift's use of framing is of a kind that seems to have had a particular appeal for his contemporaries. The early novels sometimes purported to be the editing of private papers, memoirs or letters. If no full account was given of their provenances, the title pages at least vouchsafed their authenticity. Defoe's *Journal of the Plague Year* is subtitled: "Written by a Citizen who continued all the while in London. Never made public before." This minimal sort of framing underlined the fact that there was some direct connection between real life and fiction. In short, it claimed for the artefact the status of a truthful document. It pretended to give the public not something novel or new, as is often understood today, but news of the world. A narrative introduced by this kind of device is called framed. A similar kind of staging characterises most of Swift's satires and, here too, framing may be roughly equated with the editing of purportedly true pieces of writing.[4] There the similarities end, however. Swift does not write narrative or pretendedly documentary fictions, even when his satires take a narrative turn. It is well known that satires usually promise one thing and end up by offering another. Swift's parodies of forms of publication, genres, and more generally discourses, do precisely this. They do not fulfil their promises. They are editing tricks which promise information but frame fanciful tales or made up stories. Consequently the framing plays a different rôle from that in the novel, where it authenticates the fiction.

[4] Everett Zimmermann has recently pointed out that "Swift's major satires analyse the context in which the novel arose, engaging the hermeneutical and epistemological concerns that are implicit in the new form." (*Swift's Narrative Satires: Author and Authority*, Ithaca: Cornell University Press, 1983), p. 14.

Swift is a parodist of genius, and he pushes the art of parody further than any early novelist. There is no genre, however humble and non-literary, that he cannot turn to advantage in his satirical fictions. In general the forms he chooses for his framing devices are those that he also handles in the other important aspect of his production, the polemical writings: prefaces, forewords, advertisements to readers, digressions, letters, pamphlets, apologies, petitions, manuals, proposals, elegies, songs, lampoons and broadsides. Their diversity is considerable, and no discussion of the subject can do more than propose a few illustrations.[5] Here is a list of those that will be mentioned in the course of the analysis. Apart form *A Tale of a Tub, Gulliver's Travels* and *A Modest Proposal,* which are too familiar to need presenting, the following works come in for discussion: *The Battle of the Books,* familiar for its allegory and mock-epic battle, but which begins – the fact is usually ignored – like an eighteenth-century disquisition on the moral causes of wars; *A Meditation on a Broomstick,* which mocks a favourite genre with churchmen; *The Mechanical Operation of the Spirit,* subtitled a "discourse", but written in the leisurely style of an epistolary exchange; *A Critical Essay upon the Faculties of the Mind,* a mock psychological, or, in eighteenth-century language, physiological essay; *The Bickerstaff Papers,* a collection of texts whose nucleus is the imitation of an almanac and whose core is public polemics; *A Complete Collection of Genteel and Ingenious Conversation,* which satirises manuals of good manners; two news items or reports, *A Hue and Cry after Dismal* and *A New Journey to Paris;* two letters, *A Letter from the Pretender to a Whig Lord* and *The Story of the Injured Lady. In a Letter to her Friend, with his Answer;* two petitions, one in verse, *Mrs Harris's Petition,* and one in prose, *The Humble Petition of the Footmen of Dublin;* a public protest, *An Examination of Certain Abuses, Corruptions and Enormities in the City of Dublin;* a prose broadside, *The Last Speech and Dying Words of Ebenezor Elliston;* and finally two poems, "A Description of the Morning" and "A Description of a City Shower."

This list immediately invites two remarks. The first is that Swift's satirical fictions are never offered to the reader as literature, as the work of a highbrow man of letters like Pope, but as contributions to a vast public debate of ideas on politics, religion, superstition, education, social life and relationships, as well as literature. Their forms, down to the

[5] John G. Blair discusses some aspects of the problem facing any examination of literary variety in his essay on *Moby Dick* included in the present volume, see pp. 209–220.

use of disguises, which was a common feature of all journalistic writing, are those typical of this public debate. By Pope's standards, and on the basis of the criterion of genre, Swift's satirical fictions can only be classed as low and answering mostly practical purposes. The second clearly concerns the difference between the satirical parodies and the polemical writings themselves. Though the caricatural element in the former helps to detect the fake in most cases, they remain outwardly so closely akin that only the degree of fictionalization resulting from the use of a framing device and their different finalities mark off the fakes from the real thing. A study of framing is then doubly useful: it explains the peculiar nature of the satirical fictions and their very different appeal to readers, compared to the polemical writings.

Considering the variety of the satirical fictions, it would be illusory to try to reduce all the satires to the same pattern. First of all, though the major works and a large proportion of minor pieces use the device, other pieces do not. Most satirical verse had better be regarded as unframed narrative or descriptive satire. Furthermore – and this is important for what follows –, the nature of the framing varies considerably from one work to another. In some cases it is minimal and consists only in a signal external to the text, the material support of the framed tale or made up story. In other cases it develops into a full parody and forms the wrapping of another fiction. At this end of the spectrum the framing becomes heavy and sometimes even threatens to swallow up the framed fiction or allows it only the ghost of an existence. *An Examination of Certain Abuses* is so full of its supposed author's presence and concerns as to leave little room for the development of the fictional message it contains: a picture of universal conspiracy. In *A Tale of a Tub* the reader has to get through no less than seven pieces of introductory material, four declared digressive chapters and a fifth unannounced one, to which must be added several minor digressions within the narrative, as well as a number of footnotes, before he comes to the end of the tale of the three brothers. In *Gulliver's Travels*, on the other hand, the framing, though fully developed, is kept within bounds and tailored so as not to interfere with the travelling tale. In these cases the framing constitutes a complete fiction in itself, as well as the parody of a discourse. From this discourse there sometimes emerges the personality of a purported author. The nature of the relation between this author and the framed fiction which he prefaces and proposes to the reader reveals one or both discourses to be burlesques, so that the writing cannot be taken for serious polemics.

At the other end of the spectrum there are cases of minimal framing, which one hesitates to call fictional and which simply anchor the parody in the literary and intellectual debate of the time. Sometimes all the framing consists in a title, a subtitle, or the lay-out of the printed text as in letters. Sometimes it is only present by implication, in the margins of the text, as when the material support of the item could be said to be all the framing there is. *A Hue and Cry after Dismal, Ebenezor Elliston*, and several of the songs were distributed as half-sheets and fulfilled a function similar to that of special newspaper editions today.[6] As for the two poems, "A Description of the Morning" and "A Description of a City Shower", they may have appeared framed to their first readers, who discovered them in *The Tatler* and no doubt first saw in them true instances of reportage on city life, something like the equivalent of today's magazine photographs. Such instances come close to the pretence of serious editing found in the novel of the age. Editing some writing of a particular kind will usually imply that the editor takes its content seriously and has given it what he believes to be appropriate diffusion as news, pamphlet or declaration. If the attitude implied by the editing and the genre of the writing or its place of appearance contradict the nature of the contents, of the framed fiction, the disjunction draws attention to itself and is sufficient to trace around the satire the circle that frames it and shows it to be a fake. Whether in the case of heavy or minimal framing, it is always the nature of the framed fiction and the relationship it bears to the framing device that makes the satirical intent clear. Even where the framing device does not look much like fiction in itself, it is fiction in so far as it pretends to be what it is not, i.e. something true and authentic.

As a structuring device, framing looks both inward towards the organization of the individual works and outward towards the world outside the text. As such it is the articulation of a complex relationship, only a few of whose traits can be examined here. To begin with the internal structure of the work, it is a commonplace of criticism that this structure is in its broad outlines dictated by the conventions of genre. As a rule, the more elementary the genre, the stricter the plan of the work. There are not several ways of reporting a piece of political news. In *A Hue and Cry after Dismal* the subtitle already gives the essential element, like the boldface type at the beginning of a modern article: "Being a full and true Account, how a *Whig* Lord was taken at *Dunkirk*, in the

[6] *The Prose Writings of Jonathan Swift* (PW), edited by Herbert Davis (Oxford: Blackwell, 1969–1973), vol.vi, p. 210. All references to Swift's prose are to this edition.

Habit of a Chimney-Sweeper, and carryed before General *Hill.*"[7] Here follows a brief reminder of the general political situation that led to the event:

> We have an old Saying, *That it is better to play at small Game than to stand out:* And it seems, the Whigs practice accordingly, there being nothing so little or so base, that they will not attempt, to recover their Power.

After which, the story of the arrest is given with all the details desired: "On Wednesday Morning the 9th Instant, we are certainly informed, that Collonell Killegrew (who went to France with General Hill) walking in Dunkirk Streets met a tall Chimney-Sweeper with his Brooms and Poles" (PW, vol.vi, pp. 139–141). Needless to say, not a word of the anecdote is true. Swift enjoyed creating fully developed little fictions like this one or that of *A New Journey to Paris* as a relaxation from his serious work as a Tory pamphleteer.

In a similar way, once it is realised that *A Tale of a Tub* satirises the editing practices of a new generation of scholars,[8] whom Swift accuses of boosting their reputation by publishing the stories or writings of others instead of doing original work, its structure becomes clear. The bookseller's note corresponds to our modern dust jacket notices; a preface, an introduction and notes are in the order of what any reader has come to expect of a good scholarly edition, and today the digressions would be relegated to the end of the volume and they would be called appendices. Swift even invites the reader to follow my suggestion when he writes that "if the judicious Reader can assign a fitter [place to one of his digressions, he does] here empower him to remove it into any other Corner he please" (PW, vol.i, p. 94). The multiplying of introductory material and its peculiar nature evidence Swift's intention to caricature a new practice and show that he would have been delighted by Bernard Crick's editing of George Orwell's *1984*, had he lived today. As for the structure of *Gulliver's Travels,* it is equally straightforward and in keeping with conventions. Gulliver introduces the story of his four incursions into fairyland with a brief account of his person, quality and life. Each voyage begins and ends with a glimpse of his life in England or aboard Western ships. Even the long discursive passages that intersperse the otherwise chronological narrative are in keeping with the genre of the

[7] Udo Fries calls this part the "summary" of the article in "Summaries in Newspapers: A Textlinguistic Investigation", included in the present volume, pp. 47–63. This study suggests that there has been a remarkable stability in the genre since the seventeenth century.

[8] Miriam K. Starkman, *Swift's Satire on Learning in "A Tale of a Tub"* (Princeton: Princeton University Press, 1950).

memoir. Swift adopts conventions and follows them faithfully. There is no search for renewal or sophistication on this head, nor does one expect any, as the structure must remain to the end a reminder that a discourse is being satirised by means of parody. Generic transparency plays a capital rôle.

Similarly, by anchoring the fiction in the literary, political or religious context of the time, the framing fiction fictionalises reality. On this point its rôle is different from that in the novel of the period. In the latter the framing fiction simply claims for the framed fiction the status of an authentic document. It is not the claim which is problematic but the relationship of the framed fiction to the circumstantial reality of the time. The fantasy of Swift's framed fictions and the grotesqueness of some of their purported authors prevent the reader's taking the fictional satire for anything but a hoax. But, at first sight, things look different. It is as though the framing fiction, the genre of the piece, or at least its material support, were in part dictated by the circumstances occasioning the purported author's gesture, and as though Swift wanted his fictitious discourses to pass off for real contributions to the intellectual debate of the period, a period of virulent paper controversies as historians tell us. He shows his purported authors to be directly involved in the activities of the period, acting in a socio-political context and reacting to it, as he himself was doing as a friend and later political opponent of Addison and Steele. When it is remembered that the authority of print, what Lennard J. Davis calls its "legitimising effect,"[9] was unquestioned, the power of authentication of Swift's fictions must have been irresistible. Readers must have thought at first that they were dealing with true journalistic or polemical writings. As they began to realise that what they were reading was a counterfeit, a joke, their whole idea of the intellectual and political debate of the time became tainted by analogy. What had looked serious was shown to be what could be designated by the metaphor of a game, and this metaphor turns reality into an implicit fiction.[10] It is true that many of the fakes were written to embarrass Swift's enemies, so that the polemical bias cannot be ignored. But when he invented events, Swift was conscious of doing something different. Issues were forgotten, imagination took over, the limited objectives of polemics were abandoned and human activities were caricatured and aped as activities, as ludicrous and pointless agitation.

[9] *Factual Fiction: The Origin of the English Novel* (New York: Columbia University Press, 1983), p. 148.

[10] A metaphor used in a different sense by Peter Steel in *Jonathan Swift: Preacher and Jester* (Oxford: Clarendon, 1978), p. 143.

By far the most ambitious and complex attempt to inscribe a fiction in the circumstantial reality of the period, and to fictionalise reality through it, resulted in *The Bickerstaff Papers.* On Swift's side, the *Papers* consist of a series of five publications, a whole polemic, allegedly by several hands. It is to be noted that a plurality of pens is usually an essential feature of the literary game, which must be collective to be a game. *A Tale* is also the product of several pens, and *Gulliver's Travels* is Gulliver's account, published and prefaced by his cousin Sympson. In a letter prefixed to a later edition, Gulliver complains to his cousin about an "Interpolator." This interpolator, also referred to as "a Person since deceased, on whose Judgment the Publisher relied to make any Alterations that might be necessary," is accused of having tampered with Gulliver's text. Gulliver, in his letter, also claims to be cousin with William Dampier (1652–1715), pirate, explorer and author of *A New Voyage Round the World* (1697) and *A Voyage to New Holland* (1703). *A Modest Proposal* not only presupposes the existence of other proposals, it also refers to a friend of the author, who has given him a good idea. *The Bickerstaff Papers* (PW, vol.ii) form a practical joke at the expense of an almanac writer called Partridge. The game was to stir up a polemic over the seriousness of almanac writers and "the credulity of the vulgar," as a contemporary put it (PW, vol.ii, p. 196). Another contemporary, the poet Nicholas Rowe, described the hoax as a plan "to murder a man by Way of Prophecy" (PW, vol.ii, p. 233). It ran over a period of several months and was so successful that not only was Partridge forced to defend himself, but other writers joined in the fray unprompted, helping to blur the distinction between fact and fiction. The fiction shows a brilliant sense of timing. It develops like a comedy in three acts.

Act I. In February 1708 a certain Isaac Bickerstaff, who introduced himself as a serious student of astrology, which almanac writers, he claimed, were not, offered the public a counter-almanac. His first prediction for the following months concerned the death of a popular astrologer, John Partridge. The date given was 29th March, a little more than a month away. Some readers at once detected a *bite.* As for the fools and gulls, "he has them fast for some time," someone remarked (PW, vol.ii, p 195). In the meantime, the astrologer Partridge could not resist rising to the bait and publishing a reply. Act II. 29th March came and went. On the following day an account appeared reporting Partridge's alleged death on the day predicted. The author of this account was not Bickerstaff. He described himself as an acquaintance of the almanac writer and, in his "Letter to a Person of Honour," not only narrated the manner of the astrologer's death, but also attacked Bickerstaff for failing to determine the exact time of the death in question. There was, he argued, as much as four hours' difference. For good measure, there also appeared, presumably on the same day, an anonymous "Elegy on Mr Partridge, the Almanack-maker, who died on the 29th of this Instant March, 1708."[11] It was printed on a separate half-sheet. Unable to foretell the time of his own death, Partridge was discredited. He had been killed metaphorically. Act III. When, in the second half of the same year, the living Partridge ventured to publish his predictions for 1709, protesting that he was still alive and kicking, Bickerstaff was ready to pounce on him and deal him a second metaphorical blow. In a proud and solemn "Vindication," he accused Partridge of not playing fair, of having dealings with the devil as, quite obviously, he was dead and consequently could not publish a new almanac without recourse to the most devilish witchcraft. Such practice, he went on, impeded "the progress of his own art" for selfish reasons (PW, vol.ii, p. 161). Bickerstaff also defended himself against the accusation of failing to determine the exact moment of the astrologer's death the previous spring. To crown the whole, Swift forged a supposedly ancient prophecy, "A Famous Prediction of Merlin," which concluded the polemic. The comedy ends with the defeat of the villain and of the obstructive forces, unscrupulous astrology and superstition, and with the victory of the genial character, Bickerstaff. With this fiction of a polemical debate inscribed in real life, the fictitious character ends up having more presence and reality than the real people taking part in it. After such a promising beginning, Bickerstaff was guaranteed a brilliant literary career, as everyone knows. Several years later Swift was to repeat the same tactic for strictly polemical purposes. In *The Drapier's Letters,* however, the mask of the drapier is only a thin disguise for the Dean of St. Patrick's and the polemic is no longer a game but deadly serious.

The framing fictions have been seen to express two opposed, even contradictory, aims. On the one hand they fictionalise reality and on the other hand they claim for themselves the status of facts and real events. Either way the structuring of the satire blurs the distinction between real life and fiction and lends them an ambivalent character. To what end? In so far as the fictionalising of reality turns contemporary polemics, reports and the public taking of stand by private individuals into a mere game – this is, by the way, an interesting instance of what criticism today calls "troping" of reality – it casts doubt on the seriousness and honesty of the intellectual, scholarly and journalistic activities of many writers: it

[11] *Swift: Poetical Works* (London: Oxford University Press, 1967), pp. 67–70.

belittles their efforts and ridicules the low level of the debate itself. The use of framing fictions thus contributes a crucial element to the scope and meaning of the satire. The parody of a genre is prolonged beyond the text so as to become a parody of the intellectual activities of the time. If, in a novel of Aphra Behn or Defoe, the framing fiction mediates between fact and fiction and guarantees a factual fiction, in Swift's satires the framing fictions do not become factual. On the contrary, they may more properly be described as fictional facts, fictional gestures and events, in that, in them a fictitious writer, writing about his fictitious experience, publishes a materially real, credible and printed contribution to the contemporary debate of ideas. When the fictitious authors imitate their contemporaries and compose news reports, pamphlets, petitions, prefaces, digressions, notes, proposals or travel books, they give no guarantee but of their fictionality, and it is fiction that steps into reality. The fictionalising force is such, as has been seen with *The Bickerstaff Papers,* that historical figures whose example is directly called upon are metamorphosed into fictional types. This fate is incurred not only by Partridge, but by a well-known scholar of the age, William Wotton, in *A Tale of a Tub,* and by other figures as well. The fictionalization of reality that occurs when the framing fiction suggests the image of the literary and journalistic game and an active participation in it may be said to supply the fictional plots that have eluded critics.[12] Only here the plot has to be looked for outside the text, in its imaginative extension. Swift's satirical strategy does not only consist of a way of deflating partisan and various other biased views of life. The framing device contextualises the fiction at the same time as it fictionalises the context so as to make possible a fictional participation in the drama of real life.

At the point where living people are digested into the fiction, a watershed is reached. The movement is reversed and the fictionalization of reality yields to a process that is best described, to oppose it to the other tendency, as the factualization of fiction. It is not just that each framing fiction ends up being an event and a gesture inscribed into circumstantial reality. The fiction shifts and assimilates, not only contemporary figures as mentioned above, but also a large number of factual details about everyday life, so that the substance of the framing fiction appears as though contaminated by the contemporary background. The fictitious authors make repeated references to their supposed life, their profession,

[12] A notable example is John R. Clark's *Form and Frenzy in Swift's "Tale of a Tub"* (Ithaca: Cornell University Press, 1970), which looks for the *Tale*'s fictional plot in various abstract patterns.

and the life of the age. These references are usually brief and form many Hogarthian vignettes in the text. They are not intended to give the reader a sense of the individuality of the purported author. They do not build up a coherent vision of life as in a novel. Their rôle is rather to create the impression that the voice of the fictitious author is that of a real person acting in real circumstances. These Hogarthian vignettes sometimes appear purely incidental, like the following one from the bookseller's dedication "To the Right Honourable, John Lord Sommers" at the beginning of *A Tale of a Tub:*

> But, it unluckily fell out, that none of the Authors I employ, understood *Latin* (tho' I have them often in pay, to translate out of that Language) I was therefore compelled to have recourse to the Curate of our Parish, who Englished it thus, *Let it be given to the Worthiest*; And his Comment was, that the Author meant, his Work should be dedicated to the sublimest Genius of the Age, for Wit, Learning, Judgment, Eloquence and Wisdom. I call'd at a Poet's Chamber (who works for my Shop) in an Alley hard by, shewed him the Translation, and desired his Opinion, who it was that the Author could mean; He told me, after some Consideration, that Vanity was a Thing he abhorr'd; but by the Description, he thought Himself to be the Person aimed at; And, at the same time, he very kindly offer'd his own Assistance *gratis,* towards penning a Dedication to Himself. I desired him, however, to give a second Guess; Why then, said he, It must be I, or my Lord *Sommers.* From thence I went to several other Wits of my Acquaintance, with no small Hazard and Weariness to my Person, from a prodigious Number of dark, winding Stairs; But found them all in the same Story, both of your Lordship and themselves. Now, your Lordship is to understand, that this Proceeding was not of my own Invention; For, I have somewhere heard, it is a Maxim, that those, to whom every Body allows the second Place, have an undoubted Title to the First. (PW, vol.i, p. 14)

The next illustration offers a glimpse of eighteenth century life. In the text it functions as a simile. Allowance being made for Swift's animus against the Scots, the picture need not apply to Edinburgh in particular. It is as accurate a picture of city life as "A Description of a City Shower." To do their work, the purported author of *A Tale* says, critics must proceed

> in their common perusal of Books, singling out the Errors and Defects, the Nauseous, the Fulsome, the Dull, and the Impertinent, with the Caution of a Man that walks thro' *Edenborough* Streets in a Morning, who is indeed as careful as he can, to watch diligently, and spy out the Filth in his Way, not that he is curious to observe the Colour and Complexion of the Ordure, or take its Dimensions, much less to be padling in, or tasting it: but only with a Design to come out as cleanly as he may. (Ibid., p. 56)

To this method of anchoring the satire and the fictitious author's gesture more firmly in the contemporary reality the reader owes the short account that Gulliver gives of his parentage and education at the beginning of *Gulliver's Travels,* as well as a number of allusions to his family life between his voyages. The Wagstaff of *Polite Conversation* and the conversations he collects come more fully alive when he describes himself going about the fashionable world with his "Table-Book" in his pocket (PW, vol.iv, p. 100), like a modern would-be social scientist with tape-recorder and camera.

The Hogarthian vignettes considerably reinforce the reader's impression that the satire is relevant to the world outside the text. They are vivid little tableaux and have the ring of authenticity about them. They make the fabrication of the document and the fictitious author look true. They have a visual quality which enables Swift to heighten his staging effect and to make the fictitious author's gesture look dramatic like that of a character in a play.

Both when they fictionalise reality and when they pass themselves off as genuine contributions to the contemporary debate of ideas, Swift's framing fictions fulfil a more ambitious and different function than is the case in the novel of the age. Swift is not content to exploit the news / novel ambiguity like Defoe and to offer the public an allegedly truthful document. He uses his framing fictions like weapons. Whereas Addison and Steele attempted with their essays to raise the periodical newspaper above polemics and to turn their undertaking into literature in the modern sense of the word, Swift seemed, by comparison and for all his scorn of modern practices, ever ready to plunge into polemics. It is on precisely this point that his satirical strategy, with its recourse to the framing device, parts company with that of other satirists. These will generally hold up their distorting mirrors to nature at a distance. The framing fictions give Swift's satires the thrust of polemical writings. The reader has the impression of dealing directly with a message which makes a claim on his sympathy and approval. Satirists normally avoid this. The reader is called upon to take sides. Swift manipulates his response so as to provoke a new awareness about the implications of the problem or attitude presented in the fiction. When he completes the framing fiction in *Gulliver's Travels* and adds to the Faulkner edition (1735) an "Advertisement" and a letter from Gulliver to his cousin Sympson, who was the alleged author of the preface to the original edition (1726), Swift's intention is neither to make the travel account look more genuine nor to conceal his identity, as has been argued. He does so explicitly to provoke a reaction. The starting point is always that the writing should excite curiosity. Then several ways are open. Either the appeal to the reader's sympathy and approval is meant to be answered positively as in *The Bickerstaff Papers* and *A Hue and Cry* and the complicity between alleged author and reader leads to their sharing the joke at someone else's expense contained in the framed fiction; or the reader grants his sympathy, but not his approval, as in the petitions, so that the satire is directed both at the alleged author, who becomes the target of Swift's sense of humour, and at the framed fiction as tale or made-up story; or the claim on the reader's sympathy and approval becomes so embarrassing that the reader is led to reject all collusion with the polemical stance expressed in the framing discourse as in *A Modest Proposal*, but sometimes not before he has been tempted first to embrace it as in *Gulliver's Travels*. Sometimes the reader is manoeuvered into giving an impossible assent and feels taken to task. *Gulliver's Travels*, originally entitled *Travels into Several Remote Nations of the World*, takes him to task for, among other things, not discriminating between true reports and marvellous tales, *A Hue and Cry* for his thirst after sensational news, and *A Modest Proposal* for a well-meaning but callous response to the problem of poverty and exploitation of Ireland. In fact it is a great mistake to ignore the polemical side of the satires, as is often done, especially with the narrative ones like the *Travels*. The framing fictions work like shock tactics to prevent a distant and, consequently, indifferent response. Light or ferocious, the lightness or ferociousness of the satire is directed at the reader, a member of the public, even where there seems to be a particular addressee as in the case of the astrologer Partridge. Their function is to avoid at all cost the satirical fictions remaining looking-glasses in which people would recognise everyone's face but their own.[13] With Swift the satirist is no "littérateur," but a polemicist still, or, more exactly, a preacher still; also a man of action, an activist wielding power. Satire is action, even when it proposes fictions to the public. Satire cannot change the world overnight. Nor can sermons for that matter. With Swift, ferociousness becomes very direct.

To stress the fact that Swift gives his satirical fictions the thrust of polemical writings might at first sight seem to lend support to the view, rejected above, that satire is just another form of polemics, and to undermine the validity of the proposed distinction between his satirical and polemical writings. If both points were granted, and the distinction made in the preceding discussion thus reduced to the status of a simple analytical move, the procedure could still, of course, claim to have

[13] *The Battle of the Books* (PW, vol.i, p. 140).

served a useful purpose in bringing out one of the singular qualities of Swift's satires: the way they take the reader personally to task. This could be said to substantiate Edward Said's case for considering Swift "as a kind of local activist" and his writings as "reactive" gestures and "events."[14] If there is in this view a timely reminder that Swift's satirical fictions are deeply rooted in the circumstantial reality of their time, the description is, however, also unduly reductive and consequently unsatisfactory. In the first place, it does not account for the lasting fascination of *Gulliver's Travels* and *A Modest Proposal*, a fascination universally recognised. To take notice of the rôle played by the framing device in the creation of the fakes and fictions helps to understand why the distinction between satirical and polemical writings is not merely one of convenience or of degree in the sharpness of the attack. It shows it to be structural and to correspond to a different intention. Swift's strategy is to give his satirical fictions the thrust of polemical writings, but not their character. *They* give the impression of being the work of local activists. He disclaims any share in their composition and foists them on imaginary authors, thereby exhibiting an unquestionable measure of humorous aloofness. The polemical stance must be considered as part of the larger fiction of the literary and journalistic game. The polemical intent is subordinated to the satirical, and the satirical to the fictional. Reducing the satirical fictions to polemics also amounts to dismissing the imaginative element, the Hogarthian vignettes and the dramatic character, as purely decorative, which it is not. Swift's satirical art is an art of parody and mimesis as much as a visionary art. It creates prefaces, pamphlets, books or broadsides; it invents fictitious authors and situations. Swift does not only ridicule the issues in the controversies of his age. When he mimics the style of all sorts of writings that were competing in his time to satisfy, and sometimes to pander to, a new thirst for information, discussion and education, he does, for the flood of popular writings of his time, much the same as Cervantes had done for the vogue of the mediaeval romance a century earlier.

As has often been noted, criticism today is fond of spatial metaphors. Framing is one. It suggests an enclosed surface, and frames are themselves surfaces of a sort, more often than just lines: they enclose a surface between two lines. The metaphoric meaning, the vehicle of the metaphor, twice points to the notion of enclosure. In Swift's satires the enclosed spaces tend to become the spaces of an exclusion. The framing becomes the drama of a blacklisting, or proscription, of all that does not

[14] Edward Said, op. cit., pp. 77, 78, 59.

come up to the decent standards that a classical age, or just decency and commonsense, ought to promote. The space of exclusion is sometimes that of the framed fiction – which cannot be discussed here –, sometimes that of the framing and framed fictions, whenever the purported author or the discourse become unacceptable as a whole, as in *A Tale of a Tub* or *Polite Conversation.* The notion of enclosure recalls Foucault's notion of confinement of people exhibiting irregular behaviour.[15] In this context, it is interesting to note how conscious Swift is of the social dynamics of confinement and exclusion in his work. In the framing fiction of *A Tale,* his most systematic attempt to deal with various aberrant behaviours and enclose them in a fiction, he has his fictitious author propose that certain inmates of Bedlam be paradoxically brought out of their confinement and used by the state in different official capacities. Such a proposal is in keeping with the intent to fictionalise reality: it visualises the invasion of reality by fiction which the hack's framing fiction dramatises. But it also shows that the choice of genre and the typical character of the discourse can become ways of placing a class of writing, of topics or of people on a blacklist. The ridicule of the parody becomes in itself a condemnation in the virulent cases and a means of depreciation in the milder ones.

Finally, to return to my starting point, it is obvious that the question of whether Swift is a traditionalist or a Tory is irrelevant from a creative perspective. Even if the initial germ of his satires may be his attachment to inherited values, the fact that the satirical intent is effected by, and finds expression in, parodies of fashionable genres that show the prevalent discourse to be problematic makes the fictions more radical than conservative. Imitation becomes invention, the satirical fiction opens the way for a new generation of writings: for novels more aware of their fictitious character, and often more humorous or satirical as a result; for the "conte philosophique," which *Gulliver's Travels* and *A Tale of a Tub* prefigure.

[15] *Histoire de la folie à l'âge classique* (Paris: Gallimard, 1972).

The Structure of *Tom Jones.* Regularity and Extravagance

Ernest Giddey

To say that *Tom Jones* is remarkable for its structure is a trite saying. Studies on Fielding frequently allude to, or quote, Coleridge's famous statement that *Tom Jones* offers one of "the three most perfect plots ever planned."[1] And every first year student, after reading Fielding's masterpiece, knows that its eighteen books are equally divided into three groups of six books each: the first relates events taking place in the country; the second deals with incidents happening on the London road, whereas the third carries the action to London. An analysis of the novel, even if it is superficial, also shows how skilfully the author handles time and provokes a decelerating process (Books I and II cover fourteen years; Book IV, one year; Book VI, three weeks; Book VII, three days and Book IX, twelve hours) with a corresponding tightening of the dramatic tension. Themes and motifs are inserted and crop up again according to a pattern which betrays a constant attention to order and regularity. Before winning Sophia's hand, Tom has three love-affairs, one in the first part of the novel, one in the middle and one in the London section. There are also symmetrical stories within the story, and a number of parallel or contrasting occurrences placed at equal distance of the pivotal central scene, the Upton episode (Books IX and X). If the plot is examined from that pivotal centre, the organic perfection of the structure is obvious, actions performed before the Upton chapters being mirrored by circumstances happening after.

So evident is Fielding's devotion to regularity that critics seem to make a point of finding original formulas praising what they consider his greatest achievement: tightly-knit structure, consummate artistry, architectonic quality, masterly overall planning, expression of the classical

[1] "Table-Talk", 5 July 1834, *Coleridge's Miscellaneous Criticism,* ed. Thomas Middleton Rayson (Cambridge: Harvard University Press, 1936), p. 437.

spirit of the age, systematic organization of contrasts, regularity of Palladian architecture, perfection of a Mozart symphony, etc, etc. An article written in French some twenty years ago and published in the *Nouvelle Revue française* (the author is Michel Cazenave) even declares that *Tom Jones* is so beautifully designed that it becomes the novel of total clearness ("un roman de la clarté totale"); there is nothing mysterious, nothing hidden in it, "aucune trace de ce que Péguy, de si belle manière, nommait un extra-texte."[2]

*

The fact that a novel is regarded as one of the greatest books ever written does not justify uncritical admiration. It would be ridiculous, however, not to admit that *Tom Jones* is cleverly planned. Its theatrical devices remind us of some of the stage contrivances of the best comedies of the French classical theatre. Fielding himself gives abundant evidence of his interest in the theoretical principles advocated by Boileau and Rapin and supported in England by Thomas Rymer; he was conscious of the importance of rules. And the predominance of the figure three in *Tom Jones* led some critics to the conclusion that it is not preposterous to establish structural links between Fielding's world and Dante's universe, an interpretation that is not contradicted by some of the proper names chosen by the author: Tom's benefactor, Mr Allworthy, has something of the Almighty in him, which perhaps accounts for his Somerset residence being called Paradise Hall.

But it would be a mistake to insist too heavily on regularity and symmetry. The reader should not focus his thoughts on one aspect only of the working hypothesis that gave birth to *Tom Jones.* Though he greatly admires the classical writers and proclaims that they deserve reverence and obedience, Fielding often rebels against literary theorists. Doctrines are unnecessarily rigid. They should reveal the beauty of a work of art, but in fact underline the "dictatorial power" of critics. For Fielding does not trust critics. Most of them are "men of shallow capacities". They make use of rules as despots wield weapons to legitimate

[2] "A propos de *Tom Jones*", *La Nouvelle Revue française* 12 (Nov. 1964), reprinted in *Henry Fielding und der Englische Roman des 18. Jahrhunderts*, ed. Wolfgang Iser (Darmstadt: Wissenschaftliche Buchgesellschaft, 1972), p. 267. On the question under discussion: J. P. Hunter, *Occasional Form: Henry Fielding and the Chain of Circumstances* (Baltimore and London: The Johns Hopkins University Press, 1975), and particularly ch. 8 ("Occasion Large and Small: Symmetry and the Limits of Symmetry in *Tom Jones*").

tyranny. Rules are acceptable only if they are founded on truth and nature; the yoke of rules should be thrown off when they do not vindicate beauty but "serve for no other purpose than to curb and restrain genius."[3]

Fielding, like Sterne a few years later, asserts that he has a right to be digressive and extravagant, both adjectives having here their strong etymological Latin meaning. Digression and extravagance soon appear as conscious limitations of the structural economy so frequently praised in *Tom Jones.* Various expedients are adopted by Fielding to unsettle the apparent harmony of the general pattern.

To begin with, let us mention the author's ironic and disrespectful playfulness. It sometimes manifests itself in the heading of chapters. Normally a title is a way of telling the reader where he stands and helping him see the plan followed by the writer. Fielding intentionally misleads the reader by suggesting that some of the chapters are useless: "Containing little or nothing", "Containing five pages of paper", "Too short to need a Preface". Such titles are examples of what I might call Fielding's humorous escapism: how to reject the strictures of order without impairing the general structure of the novel.

Critics are wont to say that the different sections of *Tom Jones* are held together by repeated references to the same object or by the intervention of recurring themes: Sophia's muff, Tom's bank note, curtains in bedrooms; the punishment, pursuit and rescue motifs. In fact, even though they are pattern-making elements, such clues are deceptive. They are supposed to emphasize structure; they also bring about the doubts that create dramatic imbroglios. An example will help me establish what I mean: the role of the correspondence exchanged by the different characters, particularly in the London chapters. Letters are usually sent to convey information; they are written for the sake if not of truth, at least of clarity. In *Tom Jones,* letters (epistolary dispositions are perceptible in Sophia, Lady Bellastron, Honour, Mrs Hunt, Mr Allworthy, Tom, and several others) seldom contribute to the immediate triumph of truth; in many cases, they are a source of misunderstanding and confusion; their emotional colouring is not perceived with the same intensity by the persons who send and those who receive them; they sometimes reach their destination too soon or too late; and above all, they may be used with unscrupulous cunning: the letter in which Tom proposes marriage to Lady Bellaston provokes unforeseen reactions. Letters apparently have the same role as phone-calls today: their increasing number does not improve the quality of human understanding.

[3] *Tom Jones,* Book V, ch. 1 (Penguin Ed., p. 200).

Oral communication is also the origin of several errors. Characters are deceived by words. A good deal of what they hear or say is pure gossip. They are dazzled by the face-value of utterances. Any reader who tries to sum up the plot of *Tom Jones* is compelled to make use of the vocabulary of pretence or deception. He cannot avoid phrases such as "he assumed", "he was led to believe", "his apparent kindness", "an air of piety", "the wrong impression that ...", "The false report that ...". All things considered, he realizes that the plot is pushed forward by inaccurate interpretations. All the characters, at one time or another, show their lack of critical wisdom. Tom, in book V, believes that Molly Seagrim is genuinely in love with him and that he is responsible for her pregnancy. Sophia often suspects that other characters know more than they do. Now and again Mr Allworthy's natural sagacity is compromised by fits of incredible gullibility. Mr Western is easily fooled by his sister, his friends or members of his household; his pursuing a fox at the beginning of book XII, instead of following his daughter on her way to London, does not simply prove that he is the typical landowner with a passion for hunting; the incident has a symbolic significance: it shows the importance of "wandering" or "erring" as one of the key motifs of the whole novel. Extravagance (here again taken with its etymological connotations) is the word to be used.

In *Tom Jones,* we are in a world of make-believe. Mystification frequently outweighs truth. Some critics will probably attribute Fielding's propensity to distort the image of reality to his years of intense activity as a playwright and repeat that many episodes in *Tom Jones* are visibly theatrical with the unlikelihood and the use of contrasts, repetitions and reversals which are the essence of comedies or farcical interludes. I am not sure that Fielding's adaptations of Molière and his own plays are the real genesis of Fielding's masterly disorder in *Tom Jones.* I would rather say that a better explanation is provided by the spirit of the age as it is illustrated by some aspects of 18th century architecture.

*

I am not referring here to the interpretation defended by Frederick W. Hilles in his *Art and Artifice in Tom Jones,*[4] where he postulates that the three main parts of Fielding's novel partly reproduce three sides of Prior

[4] Frederick W. Hilles, "Art and Artifice in *Tom Jones*", *Imagined Worlds: Essays on Some English Novels and Novelists in Honour of John Butt,* Eds. Maynard Mack and Ian Gregor (London: Methuen, 1968), pp. 91–110.

Park, the stately house of Fielding's patron, Ralph Allen, as it had been designed by John Wood, the famous architect known as "Wood of Bath". To my mind, Hilles's argument does not carry conviction. Moreover it would only tend to emphasize the classical symmetry of *Tom Jones,* a fact so obvious that no one will venture to deny its veracity. My contention is that Fielding was influenced by contradictory tendencies: by Palladian sobriety, but also by baroque exuberance; the twisted columns of some new churches and the massive pillars of neo-classical architecture; broken pediments and the triangular fronts of pseudo-temples; wide windows opening on luminous landscapes and concealed casements indirectly revealed by the oblique sunbeams they give admittance to; imposing portals and painted entrances which prove to be sham doors. And also billowing clouds and realistically drawn alcoves, suggestive of depth where reality offers only a simple, plain surface; reflecting mirrors creating an illusion of endlessness ... Reality may contradict the first preception of the eye. Dreams may be more valid than blank facts; running water more expressive than stable stone.

Houses and mansions built for the aristocracy under the first Georges, though often traditionally classical in their general planning, sometimes reflect a vague desire for a new form of wealth. The peace and smoothness that create taste are troubled by unexpected undercurrents, like the surface of a lake ruffled by a sudden breeze. Harmony and symmetry are no longer sufficient to define beauty. "There is nothing in Nature that is great and beautiful, without Rule and Order", John Dennis had written a few decades before, "and the more Rule and Order, and Harmony, we find in the Objects that strike our Senses, the more Worthy and Noble we esteem them."[5] And Pope, though he did not like Dennis, whom he attacked in *The Dunciad,* had also praised the quality of well-proportioned architecture:

> No monstrous height, or breadth, or length, appear;
> The Whole at once is bold, and regular.[6]

By the middle of the century, the vision is no longer the same. Taste does not necessarily reject eccentricity. There may be nobleness in Gothic singularity. Nature can be improved by those *chinoiseries* which

[5] Quoted by A. R. Humphreys, *The Augustan World: Life and Letters in Eighteenth-Century England* (London: Methuen, 1954), p. 223. On literature and visual arts in the 18th century: John Stegmann, *The Rule of Taste: From George I to George IV* (London: Macmillan, 1936); J. W. H. Atkins, *English Literary Criticism: 17th and 18th Centuries* (London: Methuen, 1966).

[6] *Essay on Criticism,* lines 251–252.

in France had been revealed by the genius of Watteau. Elegance is not marred by the presence of a ruined tower in a park. What is apparently incongruous may give a castle or an abbey its intrinsic life. Robert Adam, the great architect, and his brother James had insisted on the role of movement, which is "the rise and fall, the advance and the recess, with other diversity of form, in the different parts of a building, so as to add greatly to the picturesque of the composition."[7] A new conception of architectural refinement was being developed, with the irruption of a form of dynamic extravagance animating the traditional stability of masses. In 1747, two years before the publication of *Tom Jones,* Horace Walpole bought Strawberry Hill, near Twickenham, and made it into an imitation of a Gothic building. At the same time, an alhambra, a pagoda and a mosque were erected in the gardens of Kew. In order to define these alterations of the classical taste, various by-roads must be explored; and in such an investigation, we stumble upon concepts and words which, without being synonyms, concurred to produce a new artistic code: baroque and rococo, gothic and oriental, grotesque and burlesque, picturesque and sublime.

Was Fielding really conscious of the importance of such changes? Though he keeps repeating that his masters are the great writers of Athens and Rome, he was probably seduced by the new aspirations of his own time. His ideal house does not offer the Palladian regularity John Wood recommended when he designed Ralph Allen's stately house. It had, like Fielding's major novel, unconventional outgrowths. Fielding rarely speaks of external nature in *Tom Jones.* But he carefully describes Paradise Hall, Mr Allworthy's residence:

> The Gothick stile of building could produce nothing nobler than Mr Allworthy's house. There was an air of grandeur in it, that struck you with awe, and rival'd the beauties of the best Grecian architecture; and it was as commodious within, as venerable without.
>
> It stood on the south-east side of a hill, but nearer the bottom than the top of it, so as to be sheltered from the north-east by a grove of old oaks, which rose above it in a gradual ascent of near half a mile, and yet high enough to enjoy a most charming prospect of the valley beneath.
>
> In the midst of the grove was a fine lawn, sloping down towards the house, near the summit of which rose a plentiful spring, gushing out of a rock covered with firs, and forming a constant cascade of about thirty foot, not carried down a regular flight of steps, but tumbling in a natural fall over the broken and mossy stones, till it came to the bottom of the rock; then running off in a pebly channel, that with many lesser falls winded along, till it fell into a lake at the foot of the hill, about a quarter of a mile below the house on the

[7] Humphreys, *op. cit.*, p. 233.

> south side, and which was seen from every room in the front. Out of this lake, which filled the center of a beautiful plain, embellished with groupes of beeches and elms, and fed with sheep, issued a river, that, for several miles, was seen to meander through an amazing variety of meadows and woods, till it emptied itself into the sea; with a large arm of which, and an island beyond it, the prospect was closed.
>
> On the right of this valley opened another of less extent, adorned with several villages, and terminated by one of the towers of an old ruined abbey, grown over with ivy, and part of the front, which remained still entire.
>
> The left hand scene presented the view of a very fine park, composed of very unequal ground, and agreeably varied with all the diversity that hills, lawns, wood, and water, laid out with admirable taste, but owing less to art than to nature, could give. Beyond this the country gradually rose into a ridge of wild mountains, the tops of which were above the clouds.[8]

Fielding's dream of the perfect dwelling-place – his earthly Paradise – does not obey the rules of symmetry and harmony defended by the classical theorists. It has no architectural unity, being Gothic outside and Grecian inside, uniting the opulence of stately mansions and the charm of ruined abbeys. The park has little in common with the *jardins à la française* so lavishly admired on the Continent; it has its own informal singularity, which results from the freedom granted to nature and the apparent absence of restraint in the treatment of ground and water as architectural material.

Placed at the beginning of *Tom Jones,* the description of Mr Allworthy's country house seems to indicate how the pages and chapters that follow should be interpreted. It warns the reader against the dangers of a one-sided analysis. Paradise Hall proclaims the "admirable taste" of its master, but discards any form of intolerance, just as Tom, who embodies benevolence, sometimes succumbs to "a tendency to vice"[9] without losing the reader's sympathy. A balanced perception of values, either artistic or moral, is gained only through experience and not by listening to the pedantic lessons of narrow-minded philosophers and critics.

"Every book", Fielding says in *Tom Jones,* "ought to be read with the same spirit, and in the same manner, as it is writ."[10] The spirit that inspired his novel more than two centuries ago and still animates its plot is an original amalgamation of the reverence for the neo-classical principles of the Augustan age and a vital craving for new forms of intellectual and sentimental intoxication. This blending is the root and essence of Fielding's realism.

[8] *Tom Jones,* Book I, ch. 4 (Penguin Ed., pp. 58–59).

[9] *Ibid.*, Book XVIII, Chapter the Last (Penguin Ed., p. 873).

[10] *Ibid.*, Book IV, ch. 1 (Penguin Ed., p. 151).

Addison as Semiotician: The Threefold Structure of *Spectator* 28

Werner Brönnimann

In Swiss political life the letter to the editor published in Addison's *Spectator* 28 would seem to be a plea for *mehr Staat*, i. e. more state intervention. The letter begins:

> Sir, Observing that you have Thoughts of creating certain Officers under you, for the Inspection of several petty Enormities which you your self cannot attend to; and finding daily Absurdities hung out upon the Sign-Posts of this City, to the great Scandal of Foreigners, as well as those of our own Country, who are curious Spectators of the same: I do humbly propose, that you would be pleased to make me Superintendant of all such Figures and Devices as are or shall be made use of on this Occasion; with full Powers to rectifie or expunge whatever I shall find irregular or defective.[1]

This proposal – to create a governmental post for the supervision of street signs in the city of London – may seem absurd. Indeed it is meant to be absurd, but it points to a genuine phenomenon of eighteenth-century London: aids to orientation in that town were picturesque rather than efficiently unified. In the Penguin *Selections from the Tatler and the Spectator* Addison's number 28 is therefore anthologized in the section on "The Town and Daily Life", as a document preserving what to the modern reader adds a touch of quaintness to the usual image of London as a thriving and expanding commercial and cultural center.

But Addison's introductory remarks preceding the letter to the editor invite other readings:

> I shall here present my Reader with a Letter from a Projector, concerning a new Office which he thinks may very much contribute to the Embellishment of the City, and to the driving Barbarity out of our Streets. I consider it as a Satyr upon Projectors in general, and a lively Picture of the whole Art of Modern Criticism.

[1] All quotations from the *Spectator* are from Donald F. Bond's edition, 5 vols. (Oxford: Clarendon Press, 1965), vol. I, pp. 115–118.

This introdutory paragraph shifts the reader's mental set three times. The reader first expects a genuine letter to the editor; he is then told to expect a satire on political opportunists and busybodies; and he is finally advised that this number of *The Spectator* is an allegorical presentation "of the whole Art of Modern Criticism."

The first sentence of the "letter" can thus be read on three levels:

1. As opening a genuine letter by a somewhat naive schemer who thinks he has found a sinecure.
2. As opening a fictitious letter that is meant to satirize the type represented by this particular schemer. Indeed the negative connotations of the word "Projector" undermine the reliability of the purported letter writer from the beginning, and the word "Satyr" defeats the pretense that the so-called letter is genuine, because the "Projector" will hardly voluntarily indulge in self-parody.
3. As opening an allegorical text, where street signs stand for a systematic structure of signs called 'texts', and where the "Superintendant" represents the literary critic, who not only supervises the use of "Figures and Devices", i. e. rhetorical figures and tropes, but also acts as a censor, because he may "rectifie or expunge" texts that are "irregular or defective."

This discussion of *Spectator* 28 will concentrate on the third, the allegorical level, where street signs stand for literary texts and the "Projector" for the literary critic. Addison does not say that he presents a *satirical* view specifically of "Modern Criticism", he calls his allegory a "lively Picture" of criticism; "liveliness" does not necessarily imply satire, nor does it exclude it. Indeed the medley of genres that make up *Spectator* 28 – genuine letter, fictive satire, allegory – makes the picture of criticism so "lively" that we do not always know where Addison really stands, in that we are uncertain when he is being serious and when he is being satirical. Nevertheless we can posit a dual structure of the allegorical level by dividing up the "Superintendant" of "Figures and Devices", i. e. the critic, into a naive prescriptive censor-critic resembling the "Projector", and a sophisticated descriptive observer-critic or "anti-pedant."[2] Addison's point-of-view (being Mr. Spectator's point of view) ideally coincides with the descriptive observer-critic's opinion.

> For want of such an Officer, there is nothing like sound Literature and good Sense to be met with in those Objects, that are every where thrusting them-

[2] For the "critic as anti-pedant" see Lee Andrew Elioseff, *The Cultural Milieu of Addison's Literary Criticism* (Austin: Univ. of Texas Press, 1963), especially p. 38.

> selves out to the Eye, and endeavouring to become visible. Our Streets are filled with blue Boars, black Swans, and red Lions; not to mention flying Pigs, and Hogs in Armour, with many other Creatures more extraordinary than any in the desarts of *Africk*. Strange! that one who has all the Birds and Beasts in Nature to chuse out of, should live at the Sign of an *Ens Rationis!*

To the *Projector* street signs containing "blue Boars", "black Swans", "red Lions", "flying Pigs", and "Hogs in Armour" are unnatural and monstrous. To the *prescriptive* critic invented and fantastic entities should not occur in literary texts because they are only products of the imagination and not of nature. To the *descriptive* critic the presentation of imagined beings presumably is not objectionable.

> In the second Place I would forbid, that Creatures of jarring and incongruous Natures should be joined together in the same Sign; such as the Bell and the Neats-Tongue, the Dog and gridiron. The Fox and Goose may be supposed to have met, but what has the Fox and the Seven Stars to do together? and when did the Lamb and Dolphin ever meet, except upon a Sign-Post?

The prescriptive critic establishes rules for the combination of signs: unlikely collocations must be avoided, and an unlikely collocation is defined as one that only occurs in texts – not in nature: "And when did the Lamb and Dolphin ever meet, except upon a Sign-Post?" To the pedantic critic literary tradition does not diminish the strangeness of unusual collocations, whereas the observing critic knows that "art is born of art, not of nature."[3]

> I must however observe to you upon this Subject, that it is usual for a young Tradesman, at his first setting up, to add to his own Sign that of the Master whom he serv'd; as the Husband after marriage, gives a Place to his Mistress's Arms in his own Coat.

Even the censorious critic must accept combinations of signs based on intertextuality if "certain [unspecified] rules" are followed, just as the projector must accept that tradesmen exhibit the sign of their masters within their own. On the allegorical level, this probably means that integrating the *styles* of literary predecessors is permitted. On this topic the difference between the prescriptive and the descriptive critic seems to be minimal, a mere matter of tone: the notion of the author's work as his intellectual property is beginning to establish itself.

In fact, the Projector's comments on the integration of other tradesmen's signs can be interpreted differently, i. e. as not referring to the integration of *styles* of literary predecessors:

[3] E. H. Gombrich, *Art and Illusion: A Study in the Psychology of Pictorial Representation* (London: Phaidon Press, 1960), p. 20.

> I would therefore establish certain Rules, for the determining how far one Tradesman may *give* the Sign of another, and in what Cases he may be allowed to quarter it with his own.

This sentence could also refer to the problem of plagiarism and thus of copyright. If so, the descriptive critic and much-plagiarized Mr. Spectator would probably be in favor of even stricter rules than the prescriptive critic; he certainly agrees with him later in the text, where it is claimed that literary predecessors should be acknowledged:

> But though it may not be necessary for Posterity thus to set up the sign of their Fore-fathers; I think it highly proper for those who actually profess the Trade, to show some such Marks of it before their Doors.

In the first two paragraphs Addison's critic has discussed the relation of the literary text to the world of existing things, and the intertextual relation of texts to previous ones. In the third paragraph he turns to the relation between the signifier and the signified and posits the iconic sign as an aesthetic ideal:

> I would enjoin every Shop to make use of a Sign which bears some Affinity to the Wares in which it deals.

The pedantic critic simply holds, but does not justify the opinion that the relation between signifier and signified should be somehow plausible and not contradictory:

> What can be more inconsistent, than to see a Bawd at the Sign of the Angel, or a Taylor at the Lion? A Cook should not live at the Boot, nor a Shooemaker at the Roasted Pig; and yet, for want of this Regulation, I have seen a Goat set up before the Door of a Perfumer, and the *French* King's Head at a Sword-Cutler's.

The dull critic *does* perceive that unlikeness is the associational link between sin and virtue – as represented by "Bawd" and "Angel" – or between cowardice and courage – the "Taylor" and the "Lion" – but to him unlikeness is mere contiguity, no more than senseless contradiction. What the pedant does not see is the foregrounding effect of these apparent inconsistencies: when the associational nexus between signifier and signified is unlikeness, the sign – and thus the public house – draws attention to itself.[4]

[4] For the influence of Hobbes's and Locke's theories about the association of ideas on Addison see Martin Kallich, "The Association of Ideas and Critical Theory: Hobbes, Locke and Addison," *ELH: A Journal of English Literary History*, 12 (1945), 290–315. For Dryden's role in the transmission of these theories see C. H. Salter, "Dryden and Addison," *Modern Language Review*, 69 (1974), 29–39.

The difference between the prescriptive critic and the descriptive one is thus the lack of discourse awareness. The dull critic posits: "A Cook should not live at the Boot, nor a Shooemaker at the Roasted Pig", the descriptive critic superimposes a second structural pattern over the dull critic's argument, that of a chiasmus, thus simultaneously validating and denying the censorious critic's argument. The pedantic critic's argument is *validated* – indeed a cook should live at the Roasted Pig – because the chiasmus is based on contiguity and on cause and effect: the chiasmus links the "Cook" with the "roasted Pig" and the "Boot" with the "Shooemaker"; the pedant's argument is *denied*, because the straightforward statement: "A cook should live at the Roasted Pig, and a shoemaker at the Boot" would be uninteresting. The prescriptive critic holds an opinion, the descriptive critic plays with it at the other's expense; discrete textual structures reflect discrete views on criticism.

The tendencies of the descriptive critic's views on criticism become more manifest in the last paragraph of the letter, where he first ridicules criticism that praises the altogether too obvious: he praises Mrs. Salmon for "ingeniously" giving her signpost the shape of the very same fish, and then exposes the follies of a criticism that turns to the abstruse and ludicrous, to folk etymology and clichéd psychologizing. But this tendency of Addison's to situate himself between the extremes, in the present instance between dullness and what he elsewhere calls "false wit", is not the only expression of opinion on criticism in *Spectator* 28. There is a discrete strand of fascination with the possible arbitrariness of the sign that runs through this text.

The hypothetical descriptive critic does everything he can to extend the range of signs. He does not limit the referents of signs to the world of nature, he implicitly also allows referents that belong to the world of the imagination, including flying pigs. This critic also likes to expand the limitations that are imposed on the choice of signifiers by the strict laws which govern associations between the signifier and the signified; his play with ironically incongruous associations shows the comic potential inherent in the foregrounding of surprising contiguities. The "*French* King's Head at a Sword-Cutler's" is an example of such a playful incongruity of signifier and signified. From this example we can extrapolate: a non-arbitrary relation between signifier and signified in literary texts is only desirable for certain *effects,* primarily for effects of wit, just as on the level of sounds the relation between signifier and signified is arbitrary except for onomatopoetic effects. "Modern Criticism" – Addison implies – is wrong in its insistence on the iconic sign, a sign "which bears some Affinity" to its signified; the relation between the signifier and the signified is conventional or arbitrary.[5]

If – hypothetically – we accept this view as Addison's, we must examine the consequences. They are far-reaching.

The town is structured like a language: we all read its conventional signs. Literary texts have an analogous structure: critics read its conventional signs. It is individuals – be they ordinary citizens or the specialized readers of signs called critics – who impose significance on the signifying structures of our textual surroundings. All individuals become imposers of meaning, thus creators and authors – although only what I have called descriptive critics are aware of this role. Pious Addison thus lays the foundations of secular individualism and of critical hubris.

Furthermore, the relation between signifier and signified is an analogue of the free market: we as individuals decide which relations of signifier and signified count, which rules we accept. What seem to be natural rules governing street signs are boring, what seem to be natural rules governing the structure of literary texts stifle the imagination and true wit, what seem to be natural rules governing early mercantile society in an absolutist state stifle the free exchange of goods. Addison wants criticism to encourage a literature that deliberately breaks these natural rules. Hohendahl in *The Institution of Criticism* puts it more radically: "Literature served the emancipation movement of the middle class as an instrument to gain self-esteem and to articulate its human demands against the absolutist state and a hierarchical society."[6] It is the critical discourse of Joseph Addison in particular which, for all its "blandness", contains unruly elements suggesting that social hierarchical structures are arbitrary, that the signifier "birth" only by convention signifies

[5] Saussure's concept of the arbitrariness of the sign can be found in Hobbes and Locke. See Stephen K. Land, *From Signs to Propositions: The Concept of Form in Eighteenth-Century Semantic Theory* (London: Longman, 1974). Land quotes Hobbes, ed. W. Molesworth, vol. I, pp. 14–15 (p. 16): "And of signs, some are *natural* ... and others are *arbitrary*, namely, those we make choice of at our pleasure, as a bush hung up, signifies that wine is to be sold there; a stone set in the ground signifies the bound of a field; and words so and so connected, signify the cogitations and notions of our minds." And Locke, *Essay Concerning Human Understanding*, III.II.1: "Thus we may conceive how *words*, which were by nature so well adapted to that purpose, came to be made use of by men as *the signs* of their *ideas:* not by any natural connexion that there is between particular articulate sounds and certain *ideas*, for then there would be but one language amongst all men; but by a voluntary imposition whereby such a word is made arbitrarily the mark of such an idea."

[6] Quoted in Terry Eagleton, *The Function of Criticism: From* The Spectator *to Post-Structuralism* (London: Verso, 1984), p. 10.

"command", that this relation can be ironically juggled with, although it is of course only the *French* king's head which is – quite prophetically – involved in this juggling. Addison's critical discourse, in short, is not as harmless as it looks; his critique of contemporary criticism, the "lively picture of modern criticism" presented in *Spectator* 28, attacks the remnants of absolutist hierarchies in the criticism of his time: he attacks the belief in natural rules, in iconic signs. "In the early eighteenth century ... the bourgeois principle of abstract free and equal exchange is elevated from the market-place to the sphere of discourse ..."[7] Although Addison is thus a proponent of a rational discourse that permits free exchange of opinions, a discourse that reflects and enlivens the free exchange of goods, this free discourse does need fixed rules when it comes to property: forefathers and predecessors must be properly acknowledged.

Admittedly the correlation of the indexical or iconic sign with conservatism, and of the conventional or arbitrary sign with progressivism is a schematic simplification – a simplification which needs some elaboration.

In a recent controversy between Murray Krieger and E. H. Gombrich in *Critical Inquiry,* Krieger commits the error of slicing Gombrich in two: into a humanistic, progressive proponent of the arbitrary sign and a scientific, conservative proponent of the non-arbitrary sign. The main point of dissension is the issue of whether perspective in art is a mere convention, or whether perspective is a more "natural" mode of representation than others. To Krieger this is an ideological issue: to him the view that perspective is non-conventional, the view that perspective is a more "natural" mode of representation, necessarily implies that e.g. Egyptian art is inferior to the Greek tradition, and this he considers a reactionary view. Krieger accuses Gombrich of having abandoned his former progressive views; Krieger's text belongs to a new genre: the liberal complaint:

> One change (from the early to the recent Gombrich) is the denial of the antique distinction in aesthetics between natural and conventional signs, that is, between signs which look like their referents and arbitrary signs related to their referents only by convention: in short, between pictures and words. For all representation – even that apparently depending on its resemblance to external reality – comes to be similarly viewed as responding to the perceptual and cultural norms brought to it – in short to be similarly viewed as conventional signs. And these norms, through usage, establish an authority that does not depend upon fidelity to what (in a neutral, naturalistic sense) is being represented. All signs must be read, not – as with the natural-conventional sign distinction – some signs seen and some read.[8]

[7] Eagleton, p. 26.

[8] Murray Krieger, "The Ambiguities of Representation and Illusion: An E. H. Gombrich Retrospective," *Critical Inquiry,* 11 (1984), 184–185.

Krieger accuses Gombrich of reintroducing the notion of "seeing" pictures, rather than "reading" them. Presumably only arbitrary signs demand that one *learn* to "read" them.

> In spite of those daring early moments that got us all going, it does seem to be his constant conviction that this tradition [i. e. the tradition of perspective], with its perfection of perspective devices, solved the problem of representation in a way that permits the viewer to see immediately (that is, without semiotic mediation), to see without having to read. In effect, it reestablishes the distinction between natural and conventional signs and the mode of response appropriate to each.[9]

This tendency in Gombrich Krieger calls an "anticonventionalist theoretical conservatism."[10]

The Krieger-Gombrich controversy proves the importance of the arbitrariness – non arbitrariness issue in today's critical theory and the ideological implications of the issue. As to the relevance of the controversy for Addison's *Spectator* 28, Gombrich's statement in *Art and Illusion* may be pertinent: "The test of the image is not its lifelikeness but its efficacy within a context of action."[11] The test of criticism for Addison was not its absolute truth, but its efficacy in a new public sphere.

[9] Krieger, p. 188.
[10] Krieger, p. 190.
[11] Gombrich, p. 94.

Multum in parvo: Moby-Dick, the Swiss Army Knife, and the Poetics of Infinity

John G. Blair

"It is hard to be finite upon an infinite subject, and all subjects are infinite."[1]

Since my title has elicited skepticism among those who doubt that the Swiss Army Knife is mentioned in *Moby-Dick*, let me begin by acknowledging that I rely on the spirit of the text more than the letter. Literally, the epitome of knifeliness evoked therein by Melville came from Sheffield, but no reader of our time is likely to miss the aptness with which its 20th-century avatar from Switzerland is evoked in the process of characterizing the carpenter:

> He was like one of those unreasoning but still highly useful, *multum in parvo*, Sheffield contrivances, assuming the exterior – though a little swelled – of a common pocket knife; but containing, not only blades of various sizes, but also screw-drivers, cork-screws, tweezers, awls, pens, rulers, nail-filers, countersinkers (Chapter 107, 388–9).

There are those who feel that *Moby-Dick*, in its literary kind, is also "a little swelled," but the scale of the work becomes relevant here in the context of structure, the compact concatenation of tools shared by the Swiss Army Knife and *Moby-Dick* as a text.[2]

[1] "Hawthorne and His Mosses" (1850), as reprinted in *Moby-Dick* ed. Harrison Hayford & Hershel Parker (New York: Norton Critical Edition, 1967), 551. This source provides all quotations from *Moby-Dick*, identified by chapter and page number within my text.

[2] Northrop Frye rightly identifies the relevant genre of *Moby-Dick* as, like *Gargantua and Pantagruel*, *The Anatomy of Melancholy* or *Tristram Shandy*, an anatomy, a form which almost inevitably follows the structure of openended sequence: 1, 2, 3 … n. See *Anatomy of Criticism: Four Essays* (Princeton: Princeton University Press, 1957), 313. See also the extension of the concept in A. Robert Lee, "*Moby-Dick* as Anatomy," in *Herman Melvil-*

The Swiss Army Knife as a structure incorporates a certain arbitrariness of scale: the officer's model has more blades and implements than the foot soldier's model, yet obviously both share the same basic structure. The structure of *Moby-Dick* has proved more elusive, though widely probed in search of an explanation for the peculiarities of a work which has never fitted very comfortably into standard categories, no matter what literary fashions have been in style.[3] Investigating the ways in which the Swiss Army knife can be understood as a model for the fictional text will inevitably question the rationale for the length of *Moby-Dick*, which has exercised so many readers from would-be abridgers to faithful apologists.

Another issue at stake concerns the kind of glue that holds together the multiform parts of this text, hence a search for a coherent explanation of why in a work ostensibly dedicated to the search for "veritable gospel cetology" so much of what is said constitutes mere "higgeldy-piggeldy whale statement" (Extracts, 2). The Extracts and the Etymology, in this context, may prove proleptic simulacra of an interminably openended structure, in which case *Moby-Dick* will appear as unconcludable. Certain critics are indeed conscious of the "howling infinite" that Melville opens up for contemplation. For example, Morton L. Ross in a widely praised article rightly calls attention to some of Melville's favorite diction as negative and infinity-bound: "nameless," "measureless," "ungraspable", "boundless", "unfathomable," "illimitable," "resistless," and so on. To Ross "These terms hint at the outer limits of the chaos which Ishmael otherwise seeks to constitute, classify, and delimit."[4] The problem with Ross's way of putting it is that negative diction pointing toward infinity can never even suggest a credible outer

le: Reassessments, ed. A. Robert Lee (London & New York: Vision/Barnes & Noble, 1984), 68–89.

[3] So many critics have commented on the structure of this fiction that to list them would seem prohibitive. The tendency in recent years has been to distinguish sharply between Ahab's presence and Ishmael's. For example, John Seelye writes: "Ahab's quest is associated with the kinetic, linear element of the story – the onrushing narrative. The cetology chapters, with their relatively static, discursive movements, act to block and impede the forward movement of the narrative, much as the ideas which they contain qualify Ahab's absolutism." *Melville: The Ironic Diagram* (Evanston, IL: Northwestern University Press, 1970), 63. My interpretation presumes the same distinction but reverses the weighting. Instead of privileging the narrative, I see Ishmael-narrator as centrally committed to an interminable cetology, an infinite regress from which narrative in the form of the Ahab-Pequod story saves him and his book.

[4] "*Moby-Dick* as an Education," *Studies in the Novel,* 6 (1974), 70.

limit, despite Ishmael's heroic efforts. When he apotheosizes Bulkington for his dedication to landlessness, "the highest truth, shoreless, indefinite as God" (Chapter 23, 97), we have to take him at his words because nowhere in the text does he locate any thematic limit which might shelter humanity from the terrors of the unlimitable infinite. Even Ishmael's sometime conversion to "the wife, the heart, the bed, the table, the saddle, the fire-side, the country" in "A Squeeze of the Hand" (Chapter 94, 349) is belied by the evidence for his having returned to whaling yet again after his Pequod experience as we shall see shortly.

That infinity was on Melville's mind at the time of writing is clear from the epigraph to this study, which is drawn from his essay in praise of Hawthorne written in the summer of 1850 as the work on *Moby-Dick* gathered momentum. In the original context Melville is drawing the essay to a close rather playfully by implying that he can never say enough in praise of his as-yet-unmet friend-to-be. But that very same problem turns out to be crucial in the construction of the book subtitled "The Whale." How could a writer ever create a book that was appropriate to the scale of such a subject? How could he "get it all in?" Indeed Ishmael-narrator's overall aim is explicitly to make a book "up to" the whale, though this project by its very conception may prove impossible.

> From his mighty bulk the whale affords a most congenial theme whereon to enlarge, amplify, and generally expatiate. ... Since I have undertaken to manhandle this Leviathan, it behooves me to approve myself omnisciently exhaustive in the enterprise; ... How, then, with me, writing of this Leviathan? Unconsciously my chirography expands into placard capitals. Give me a condor's quill! Give me Vesuvius' crater for an inkstand! Friends, hold my arms! For in the mere act of penning my thoughts of this Leviathan, they weary me, and make me faint with their outreaching comprehensiveness of sweep, as if to include the whole circle of the sciences, and all the generations of whales, and men, and mastodons, past, present, and to come, with all the revolving panoramas of empire on earth, and throughout the whole universe, not excluding its suburbs. Such, and so magnifying, is the virtue of a large and liberal theme! We expand to its bulk (Chapter 104, 378–9).

Here our cheerfully punning writer-narrator is exercising a habitual self-mockery of his enterprise, but the operative word is ALL. Any book written to whale scale would be unprintable, unbindable, unreadable, and, of course, unsaleable. A whale-book spelled out in the placard capitals school teachers used in the early 19th century to parade their pupils through spelling bees would stretch from New England to the other side of the world and perhaps beyond.[5] Taken literally, the ALL-

[5] A set of placard capitals that illustrates the proper chirography for a whale of a

project is palpably impossible, a subject not to be spoken of without a jocularity appropriate to assuring that both writer and reader acknowledge how preposterous the idea is.[6] Taken literarily, however, the ALL-project may not seem simply foolish since literature has means to transcend the literal by way of the figurative. The project itself, in short, generates the need for figuration, itself compactly figured in the Swiss Army knife.

Multum in parvo, a phrase apparently invented in the 18th century as the motto of *The Gentleman's Magazine*[7] and used in 19th-century advertisements for Sheffield knives, aptly echoes the paradoxical sleight of hand by which literature figuratively escapes its apparent limitations. In the present case the most obvious limit is the impossibility of pursuing and testing all knowledge about either Moby Dick or the whale in general. A second-level approach would appear more manageable. That project would involve trying out the explanatory power of the variety of tools wherewith human beings have sought to carve out useful knowledge, whether about whales or anything else. Tools for knowledge are clearly less numerous than facts and presumably more manageable within a textual structure. Blade after implement, then, the Swiss army knife epitomizes this intellectual-literary endeavor as focused through Ishmael-narrator.

If Ishmael mocks the ALL-project even in the act of stating it, he nonetheless goes to great lengths to test against the whale the viability of diverse philosophies, codes of knowledge, and approaches to making sense of phenomena. In every case the figurative tool, whatever its origins, is shown to be inadequate to describing, interpreting, or otherwise capturing the whale. Conceptually speaking, then, as of some point adding to the number of screw-drivers, tweezers or rulers available offers no further promise of success, given the large number of possibilities tested and found wanting.

The structure of such a project constitutes an openended sequence obedient to the formula 1, 2, 3 ... n. Not only is there no inherent limit

book is preserved in the schoolhouse of Hancock Shaker Village, a few miles west of Pittsfield, Massachusetts, from the period when both Melville and Hawthorne visited the Shakers. Each capital letter takes a card roughly 20 cm by 30 cm.

[6] This "godly gamesomeness" of Ishmael's acquires fresh resonance in Warwick Wadlington, *The Confidence Game in American Literature* (Princeton: Princeton University Press, 1975), esp. Chapter 3.

[7] I am grateful to Peter de Bolla of the University of Geneva for this information, which improves on the OED.

in the amount of whalelore that might be considered, but there turns out to be no inherent limit to the number of cognitive strategies for knowledge about whalelore that might be tested. The ostensibly more limited project proves no easier to close: a smaller infinity remains nonetheless interminable. As we shall see in time, the length of the actual series will be determined by factors extrinsic to itself. For the moment it is essential to acknowledge now my own problems of exposition as a critic who would speak of such matters which is homologous to the difficulties facing Ishmael, who would try all the interpretive tools he can think of. In Ishmael's words: "It would be a hopeless, endless task to catalogue all these things. Let a handful suffice" (Chapter 24, 99). But how many instances suffice to make the point – either for Ishmael or myself?

My first instance is Chapter 99, "The Doubloon," since it offers a structural microcosm of the basic problem. A total of nine crewmembers respond to the doubloon and see themselves in it as surely as ever Narcissus confronted the forward projection of himself. Starting with the second interpreter, Ahab, the order or presentation follows roughly the hierarchy of authority on board with Pip coming last, but Ishmael-sailor comes first, defining the relevance both of his young-sailor self and his narrator's perspective.[8] At first Ishmael speaks largely in the past tense, signaling that we are to take his discourse as describing the physical doubloon he saw as a young sailor; it is presumably an accurate portrayal of what would have been visible to any observer on board the Pequod. In his second paragraph, however, Ishmael without warning shifts to the present tense, signaling the synchronic unconfined time frame dominant in his narration: "And some certain significance lurks in all things, else all things are little worth" (Chapter 99, 358). Granted the pun on "certain," Ishmael is here reaffirming his basic motivation for going a-whaling in the first place and its continued relevance to his present attempt to write his way into some way of understanding whales and such. All this chapter, and indeed the whole exercise, can offer is, in the words of Stubb, "another rendering now; but still one text. All sorts of men in one kind of world, you see" (362). The parade of doubloon interpreters yields some insight into their personalities and outlooks, but none into the doubloon itself. In Pip's summation it boils down to a grammatical paradigm: "I look, you look, he looks; we look, ye look, they look" (362). In short neither narrator nor reader has made any progress in

[8] John Seelye is simply wrong when he excludes Ishmael from the list of major characters who interpret the doubloon; Ishmael's description is intimately expressive of his habitual interpretive stance in relation to phenomena. See *Melville: The Ironic Diagram*, 67.

understanding the world, though the structural pattern of an openended sequence of alternatives has been exemplified in compact form: *multum in parvo*.

In terms of the figure of the Swiss Army Knife, a series of blades has been tried and found wanting. They just can't cut the mustard. Both narrator and reader are invited to feel that it would be pointless to extend the number of characters who join the parade. Simply adding another instance or two would offer no promise of progress in the desired direction. This same realization applies to a whole array of attempts to come to terms with the world which in an openended series structure the vast middle of *Moby-Dick*.

Ishmael-narrator tries and finds wanting all sorts of codes, philosophies, myths, epistemic strategies that human beings have developed for interpreting the significance "that lurks in all things." These are necessarily figurative in that they inevitably go beyond the literal. The most literal-minded and materialist interpreter of all, Flask, even makes a mistake in figuring out how many cigars the doubloon could buy (361), reminding us that such orders of reality as well are subject to interpretation, or in this case, miscalculation. Naturally Ishmael cannot test all possible interpretive schemes, but he must try out enough so that he himself and the reader can feel confident that there would be no point in continuing.

Ahab, of course, embodies the single most compelling worldview that surfaces in Ishmael's story so that Ahab's paranoid-heroic quest to locate the higher powers in or behind the white whale quite understandably dominated readings of *Moby-Dick* for a long time.[9] But even his domineering personality encounters the catastrophic limit of what he can master. From the point of view of Ishmael-narrator his experience as a young sailor dragged along in Ahab's wake has not sufficed to drown his fascination with the "problem of the universe" (Chapter 35, 139). As Paul Brodtkorb, Jr., suggested two decades ago, he apparently returned to whaling again even before the renewal of his experience represented by the act of writing.[10] In addition to these further experiences at sea, he has had time to accumulate a great deal of reading about whales in particular and the universe in general so that as narrator-author he is

[9] More recently, say for twenty years or so, interpreters have emphasized the role of Ishmael-narrator as the locus of formal coherence. See, for example, Edgar Dryden, *Melville's Thematics of Form: The Great Art of Telling the Truth* (Baltimore: Johns Hopkins University Press, 1968), esp. Chapter III.

[10] See *Ishmael's White World: A Phenomenological Reading of* Moby-Dick (New Haven & London: Yale University Press, 1965), esp. 102–3.

prepared to try out a much wider range of interpretive tools than his younger sailor self could possibly have conceived or tested himself. These are richly constitutive of the so-called cetological chapters of *Moby-Dick;* in them the blades and augers and measuring sticks of the mind are tried and, each in turn, found inadequate to the task.

Though an exhaustive list may remain beyond reach, I can at least exemplify the limitations Ishmael-narrator finds in the tools he tests. With an Ishmaelian sense of the arbitrary ordering of any such endeavor,[11] one might as well begin with a visual representation, whose inescapable limitation is stated explicitly after several chapters evaluating existing portraits of whales:

> Any way you look at it, you must needs conclude that the great Leviathan is that one creature in the world which must remain unpainted to the last. True, one portrait may hit the mark much nearer than another, but none can hit it with any very considerable degree of exactness. So there is no earthly way of finding out precisely what the whale really looks like (Chapter 55, 228).

Alternative approaches to the whale remain open, of course, including direct experiential engagement as in Ahab's hunt, but such persistent attempts to stick it to the whale come to ends which are profoundly unsatisfactory.

A second avenue to knowledge that Ishmael tests was prestigious in his day as well as ours: science. In particular the chapter entitled "Cetology," sometimes maligned as supererogatory, plays a key role in evaluating the biological taxonomies which occupied so much scientific attention in the 18th and 19th centuries. Ishmael's critique in effect asserts the fruitlessness of the whole endeavor:

> It is some systematized exhibition of the whale in his broad genera, that I would now fain put before you. Yet it is no easy task. The classification of the constituents of a chaos, nothing less is here essayed. ... Nevertheless, though of real knowledge there be little, yet of books there is a plenty. ... It is by endless subdivisions based on the most inconclusive difference that some departments of natural history become so repellingly intricate (Chapter 32, 117, 118, 121).

Unexpectedly, these once musty issues are still alive today. The 1980s have seen revisionist biologists (the "cladists") complain that the established taxonomic categories are unconvincing because they fail to define precisely and identify consistently the characteristics which are theoreti-

[11] Ishmael's sense of arbitrary order in his presentation surface in asides such as "this seems as good a place as any" (Chapter 33, 128).

cally the basis of the classifications.[12] These are precisely the grounds on which Ishmael refuses confidence in science and decides that he might as well rely on the homely wisdom of his fellow Nantucket whalemen, who observe that the whale is a spouting fish with a horizontal tail. Ishmael's ultimate judgment on science, "Physiognomy, like every other human science, is but a passing fable" (Chapter 79, 292), is as *au courant* as contemporary scepticism about the scientific objectivity.[13]

After Ishmael's strenuous testing shows up the limitations in these two tools for human understanding, a third trial directly engages word-mongering, which is endemic to literature: the attempt to make sense of the stuff of the world by a careful use of words and the distinctions they generate. Ishmael's attempt to define the character of the whale's spout serves as a crux:

> But why pester one with all this reasoning on the subject? Speak Out! You have seen him spout; then declare what the spout is; can you not tell water from air? My dear sir, in this world it is not so easy to settle these plain things (Chapter 85, 312).

In short the grounding of words in relation to things is itself so problematic that any conclusion based on such distinctions is necessarily suspect. Small wonder that our punster-narrator leaves the issue in mistiness: "Still, we can hypothesize, even if we cannot prove and establish. My hypothesis is this: that the spout is nothing but mist." (313).

Another source of understanding dear to literature gets its comeuppance in Chapter 42, "The Whiteness of the Whale," when symbolism turns out to offer only ambiguity and unresolved questions:

> Is it by its indefiniteness it [whiteness] shadows forth the heartless voids and immensities of the universe, and thus stabs us from behind with the thought of annihilation, when beholding the white depths of the milky way? Or is it, that as in essence whiteness is not so much a color as the visible absence of color, and at the same time the concrete of all colors; is it for these reasons that there is such a dumb blankness, full of meaning, in a wide landscape of snows – a colorless, all-color of atheism from which we shrink? ... And of all these things the Albino whale was the symbol. Wonder ye then at the fiery hunt? (Chapter 42, 169–170)

The openended series of rhetorical questions itself echoes the inconclusiveness of symbolism as cognition.

[12] See, for example, Tom Bethell, "Agnostic Evolutionists: The Taxonomic Case Against Darwin," *Harper's*, Vol 270, No 1617 (February, 1985), 49–61.

[13] The seminal text here is Thomas Kuhn's *The Structure of Scientific Revolutions*, 2nd edition (Chicago: University of Chicago Press, 1970).

The formula which controls the structure of my discourse as well as the vast center of *Moby-Dick* (and my Swiss Army Knife) is 1, 2, 3 . . . n. A large and undeterminable number of further instances might be examined under "n." The "cetological center," whose testing procedures dominate the text from Chapter 23 through Chapter 106, is spacious and rich in examples. Like Melville I feel uncertain of just how many instances will suffice to communicate my point. Also like him I worry that my reader might feel that I have cut short the presentation for lack of examples. Nonetheless space and the editor's patience are short so I proceed more summarily.

Law as an instrument of truth and justice is tested in terms of a whaler's distinction between free-floating whale carcasses which are marked for ownership and those which are not:

> These two laws touching Fast-Fish and Loose-Fish, I say, will, on reflection, be found the fundamentals of all human jurisprudence; for notwithstanding its complicated tracery of sculpture, the Temple of the Law, like the Temple of the Philistines, has but two props to stand on (Chapter 89, 33–34).

After the ominous allusion to the Temple of the Philistines which Samson brought down, Ishmael proceeds to list historical examples which demonstrate again and again that law boils down to power games of possession or non-possession.

Exegesis of texts is a venerable intellectual strategy useful over the centuries to sustain favored interpretations of honored texts so Ishmael understandably weighs its worth:

> Another reason which Sag Harbor (he went by that name) urged for his want of faith in this matter of the prophet [Jonah], was something obscurely in reference to his incarcerated body and the whale's gastric juices. But this objection likewise falls to the ground, because a German exegeticist supposes that Jonah must have taken refuge in the floating body of a *dead* whale (Chapter 83, 307, Melville's emphasis)

In short if a single argument from a single "authority" can produce a nonsensical reading which would be incompatible with other aspects of the larger Jonah story, then it is far from constituting a reliable source of knowledge. Ishmael implies that all too many interpretive endeavors proceed self-cancellingly by means of "the best of contradictory authorities" (Chapter 82, 306).

Should my listing of instances go on? I could cite the futility of scholastic reasoning in Chapter 83, "Jonah Historically Regarded," or the mocking of traditional orthodoxies in Chapter 69, "The Funeral," or the absurdity of quantification, which yields numbers so meaningless that they ultimately boil down to "simple child's play" in Chapter 103, "Measurement of the Whale's Skeleton." Once again, "it would be a hopeless, endless task to catalogue all these things" so a handful must suffice.

Ishmael similarly tests and finds wanting madness, statistics, allegory, metaphor, religious enthusiasm, history, prophecy and so on. Sooner or later both he and we must acknowledge that even the most persistent attempts to find trustworthy access to the reality of the whale must be abandoned as hopeless. At that point his examples must seem to have excluded no promising possibility and to have ranged so widely that no further instance holds out promise of more favorable results. Like my own listing of examples, his goes on till he anticipates that all parties are convinced that going further would add nothing significant.

The order in which Ishmael presents these instances is less important than the range he covers. Ishmael orders us to "look at this matter in other lights; weigh it in *all* sorts of scales" (Chapter 24, 99, my italics). He lets us learn through his example how our readings cannot expect verification no matter how far the openended sequence of possible epistemic strategies is extended. When that realization finally seems inescapable, there is no way out except to return to "what there may be of a narrative in this book" (Chapter 45, 175). That is, once there is no point in pursuing any more tools for knowledge, the Ahab story itself serves as a means for Ishmael-narrator to escape from infinite regress. That story line does go somewhere: to its catastrophic end. Then the book can end because narrative has provided a refuge from interminability.

Even so, Ishmael's quest and its implications continue without inherent limit beyond the confines of the text. He ends the Epilogue with the final reiterated metaphor of circular movement which, if it keeps him alive, gets him nowhere. It issues into yet another all-embracing perspective: all human hearts, at one time or another, will feel the pull of this chase for the phantom significance (Chapter 52, 204). There is no predicting from *Moby-Dick* when Melville would become convinced that there was nothing to gain by turning more stones, by testing yet another approach to the world, searching for a more effective Swiss Army Knife.[14]

The impact of this reading of *Moby-Dick* is to reformulate the terms in which we conceive structure as a Melvillean strategy. The length of

[14] In fact that point was reached six years later at the point of a nervous breakdown with the last fiction Melville was to complete during his lifetime. See John G. Blair, *The Confidence Man in Modern Fiction* (London: Vision Press, 1979).

the work reflects the extraordinary lengths to which Ishmael-narrator is willing to go to test a dazzling variety of possible approaches to the whale and to knowledge in general. As far as I know, no one has yet, in print or in person, suggested that the text is too short. Until someone comes forward to defend seriously such a proposition, I must conclude that Melville succeeded remarkably well since no one seems to disagree with the implicit judgment that nothing would be gained from a prolongation.[15] This mastertext, then, ultimately depends on the paradoxical magic of figuration: though *multum* may be written *in parvo*, as *Moby-Dick* demonstrates again and again, yet no matter how extensive the work, it seems paltry in facing up to the realities it tries to figure out.

[15] I have devised a short test whereby any reader can evaluate this proposition. Imagine that you are Herman Melville who has just finished *Moby-Dick* when the mail brings in a magazine which announces new facts: in the Himalayas fossil whales have been discovered which show that 50 000 000 years ago whales were leaving land life to become sea creatures (actually reported in *Science* in early 1983). Should you hold up the manuscript already overdue at the publisher's? Adding one more whale fact would change nothing unless it led you to modify the categories of your understanding of whales. In Piaget's cognitive terms "assimilation" of the new fact to established categories would not modify understanding and at some point no further "accommodation" of categories to facts would seem necessary. For a discussion in depth of these terms as applied to literature, see Marie Christine de Montauzon, "William Faulkner's *Absalom, Absalom!* and Interpretability: The Inexplicable Unseen" (doctoral diss. University of Geneva, publ. Bern: Peter Lang, 1986).

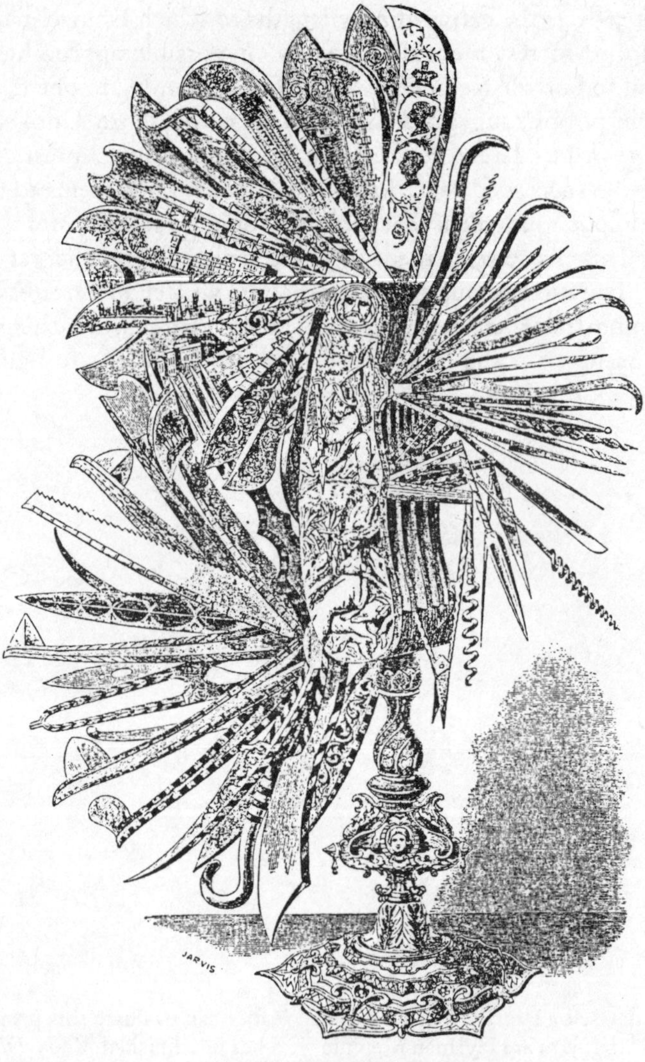

SPORTSMAN'S KNIFE

containing eighty blades and other instruments ... with gold inlaying, etching and engraving, representing various subjects, including views of the Exhibition Building, Windsor Castle, Osborne House, the Britannia Bridge, etc. The handle is 12 inches long, of mother-of-pearl, carved with subjects emblematic of the chase, from designs by Wehnert.
(Rodgers & Sons, Sheffield.)

The Carpenter: "He was like one of those unreasoning but still highly useful, *multum in parvo,* Sheffield contrivances, assuming the exterior – though a little swelled – of a common pocket knife; but containing, not only blades of various sizes, but also screw-drivers, cork-screws, tweezers, awls, pens, rulers, nail-filers, countersinkers." – Chapter 107, "The Carpenter," *Moby-Dick* (1851)

Anthropological Narrative and the Structure of North American Indian (Auto-)Biography

Hartwig Isernhagen

1. Native American Literature and Anthropology: The Life History as (Auto-)Biography

I would like to suggest in this brief essay that the development of North American Indian narrative is currently towards a greater degree of *dialogicity* and that this development is coupled with an increase in the importance of the genre of the life history, as developed by American anthropologists between the two World Wars.[1] As part of the same trend, the life history is acquiring the status of *a literary genre,* rather than a subliterary or purely documentary one; it becomes relevant outside the boundaries of the discipline of anthropology. At the same time, though, it has to undergo changes in its actual form that are correlates of changes in function. The decline in status of the traditional fictional forms of narration, one would presume, leaves a sort of gap that is filled by the life history, which is itself transformed in the process.

Other forms of narrative and other anthropological approaches *are,* of course, made use of in Native American literature,[2] but it is undeni-

[1] "The life history method in anthropology emerged out of research on American Indians." L. L. Langness and Gelya Frank, *Lives: An Anthropological Approach to Biography* (Novato, Cal.: Chandler & Sharp, 1981), 17.

[2] Cf. works like the following: Jane Willis, *Geniesh: An Indian Girlhood* (Toronto: New Press, 1973), and Emerson Blackhorse Mitchell and T. D. Allen, *Miracle Hill: The Story of a Navaho Boy* (Norman: Univ. of. Oklahoma P., 1967), two largely autobiographical novels; or Anthony Apakark Thrasher, *Thrasher ... Skid Row Eskimo.* In collaboration with Gerard Deagle and Alan Mettrick. (Toronto: Griffin House, 1976), a case story; or Joseph E[ngasongwok] Senungetuk, *Give or Take a Century: An Eskimo Chronicle* (San Francisco: Indian Historian Press, 1971), an essayistic medley of different kinds of texts, including a great deal of anthropological information.

able that *biography* of different sorts is one of the dominant genres. It has always played a prominent role in the process of minority self-reflection, self-identification, and self-demonstration – and for quite obvious reasons. The more general term covers "true" biography, autobiography, and a 'mixed' (auto-)biography of the "The Life of X as Told to Y" type, which is also the predominant type of *life history* in twentieth century anthropology. In it, the reader is placed inside the dialogue between two voices or perspectives, between the subject (informant) and the interviewer (anthropologist); this is, in the simplest terms, what we refer to as the extra degree of dialogicity that distinguishes the *life history (auto-)biography* from the other two – the "purer" – forms of "biography."[3]

Dialogicity in Native American and Canadian life histories is, then, *initially, though not ultimately,* due to the presence of the two *auctores* in interview situations and in the general making of the text. It results in a doubleness (or even duplicity) that manifests a general concern with the problematical character of *meaning* in that intercultural space where radically different world views attempt to communicate with one another. The *structure of the text* is determined by the two "voices" in such a way that it embodies the epistemological problems of the intercultural communication situation. Dialogicity has something to do, therefore, with questions of mediation, truth, and (above all) legitimacy, which will concern us in the remainder of this section of the essay.

Part of the *dialogic* nature and function of the genre is to mediate between individual and group, as well as between the native and the white "sides". The practical work of anthropology, writes Kennelm Burridge,

> entails a movement of the mind between the Aborigines themselves and their cultures, and the investigators and their cultures: a quadratic relationship whose intricacies the mind has to hold and map.[4]

That this relationship does not only exist on the level of content, but also on that of form is evidenced by the status of the individual (the "charac-

[3] One might add that it only makes explicit the implicit dialogicity of the other modes; cf. Langness and Frank on the collaboration of anthropologist and subject in biography (96 ff.), and on the resulting text as a "double autobiography" (99).

[4] *Encountering Aborigines: A Case Study: Anthropology and the Australian Aboriginal* (Elmsford: Pergamon, 1973). Quoted by Marjorie Myers Halpin, "William Beynon, Ethnographer: Tsimshian, 1888–1958," in: Margot Liberty, ed., *American Indian Intellectuals* (St. Paul: West Publishing Co., 1978), pp. 141–156, quotation p. 152.

ter" of conventional narrative) in the text. Margaret B. Blackman suggests:

> "Culture" as lived by the individual represents the ultimate inside view ... The life history ... complements the ethnographic account by adding to the descriptive an affective or experiential dimension. ... In many cultures the lives of natives span periods of critical and rapid cultural change; the life history affords a personalized, longitudinal view of these changes. Kluckhohn ... adds that life histories can be avenues to understanding status and role, individual variation within cultural patterns of behavior, personality structure, deviance, and idiosyncratic variation.[5]

This, the anthropologist's, view stresses the function of *particularization,* both within the native world and within the framework of the "white" scientific interest in the individual; to the literary scholar, who regards life histories as forms of autobiography, directly complementary statements that stress the function of *universalization* suggest themselves, once again in both realms. He would argue that such texts add to the inside view a perspective from outside, that they attempt to objectify in a greater degree than the normal biography, and that they show the patterns of the native culture and of *culture* as such underneath the individual fact, as well as the norm next to the variation. Obviously, the genre occupies a position in which it is possible to bring the particular and the universal together in a view of the individual.[6]

Charles C. Hughes makes an interesting point about the status of such views, which seems to reflect the basic concerns of the Frankfurt *Geistes-/Sozialwissenschaften* debate of the Sixties:

> The uniqueness of any event – or, indeed, of any life – can ... be turned to double account: on the one hand, toward a focus on what separates it from all other occurrences, the idiographic approach, in a manner resembling the artistic and humanistic strategy; and, on the other, toward those features which, when made explicit, render it a member of a class or classes of phenomena, in the ethos of a scientific, or "nomothetic," approach to understanding.[7]

The status of whatever meaning the text may offer is, then, uncertain on theoretical and methodological grounds. It is also uncertain for a very

[5] Margaret B. Blackman, *During My Time: Florence Edenshaw Davidson, a Haida Woman* (Seattle: University of Washington P.; Vancouver: Douglas & McIntyre, 1982), 4.

[6] And the question of the typical individual is one of the more fundamental questions of anthropological sources in general.

[7] Charles C. Hughes, *Eskimo Boyhood: An Autobiography in Psychosocial Perspective* ([Lexington]: The University Press of Kentucky, 1974), 6.

practical reason that leads on to further problems. As Blackman points out

> it goes without saying that the relationship between anthropologist and life-history subject is critical to the telling of the story in the first place and ultimately to the understanding of the final record.[8]

That this relationship is a playing-off of differences against one another, becomes apparent, for example, where the interests of the interviewer come up against a barrier characteristic of the genre: where the ordinary and everyday is not remembered as clearly as the extraordinary. Thus, Florence Davidson sometimes

> was unable to remember something in the detail that I would have liked, reminding me quite appropriately, 'It wasn't important to me then; how was I supposed to know that white people might be interested in it years later?'[9]

At the same time, Blackman's questions do bring to light remembrances that would otherwise not have been actualized. Further influence is exerted in the overall shaping of the text –

> the division of the narrative into chapters is an artifact of my own thinking ... and the chronology closely parallels the traditional life stages distinguished among the Haida[10]

– and in the addition of material later elicited from the subject because Blackman

> had neglected some basic life-cycle topics: how long mothers typically nursed their children, the significance of menopause for Haida women, the learning of sexual behavior, and others.[11]

At all these points the genre of the life history encounters the problem of its own legitimacy. The question comes up even before the founding interaction begins, in the consideration that (as Blackman admits) the life history model is not compatible with all (Native American) cultures[12], and it tends to accompany the entire interaction between the *auctores* and the actual writing. Thus, Nancy Oestreich Lurie comments on her *Mountain Wolf Woman*, which is actually controlled by its subject in a remarkably high degree, that

[8] Blackman, 15.
[9] Blackman, 18.
[10] Blackman, 19.
[11] Blackman, 20. Cf. 126: "In 1981 Florence corrected her earlier [dating of the making of a canoe]. ... Because the narrative has been reorganized topically within the life cycle, discussion of the canoe was left in this chapter."
[12] Blackman, 14.

> an element of coercion was involved with both Crashing Thunder [who had been paid by Radin] and Mountain Wolf Woman; Radin took advantage of his informant's poverty and I manipulated the kinship structure for my own purposes. [She was her subject's adopted niece.] However, while neither informant would have written an autobiography without the stimulus provided by an anthropologist, both informants were chosen because it was possible to interest them in the work and they were eminently qualified to perform the task.[13]

It is in accordance with this notion of the text being based on the subject's aptitude and inclination that Lurie can later stress the differences of the two autobiographies and account for them by pointing at the different personalities of their subjects.[14] Out of the same notion comes one decisive test of the adequacy of the final text to the personality – the question whether the subject will accept it as his or her own story; Mountain Wolf Woman did.[15]

The underlying axiom here seems to be that the text is only legitimate when it is based on a fundamental equality of the participants in the dialogue, or on a certain (egalitarian or full) kind of dialogicity. Wherever *it* is not given, there is a danger of manipulation, violation, and exploitation of the subject. The question of legitimacy has turned the argument back, once again, upon the very notion of dialogicity. For it is only on this notion that such legitimacy can be founded, and the more recent texts seem to demonstrate this, and to shape themselves according to the insight.

2. *Varying Shapes of Dialogicity: Standpoints and Degrees of Their Accommodation*

That all "anthropologization" of the narrative constitutes a departure from a more or less spontaneously generated personal narrative does not make the text inauthentic. The "deformation" is not easily discountable one way or another, for it is not only *ultimately* sanctioned by the subject, but often also sanctioned *in each of its individual stages;* thus,

[13] Nancy Oestreich Lurie, ed., *Mountain Wolf Woman, Sister of Crashing Thunder: The Autobiography of a Winnebago Indian.* Foreword by Ruth Underhill. (Ann Arbor: Univ. of Michigan Press, 1961), 93.

[14] Lurie, 102.

[15] Cf. Spradley (James P. Spradley, *Guests Never Leave Hungry: The Autobiography of James Sewid, a Kwakiutl Indian* [New Haven: Yale Univ. P., 1969]) reporting that "when the final draft was read back, he [Sewid] responded to it as his own story and made very few changes." (5)

Blackman is asked by Florence "to 'fix it up' and 'make it look right.'"[16] That such "fixing-up" is in accordance with the conventions of a basically white genre does not diminish the authenticity of the process in the self-presentation of a woman who *has* taken over many things from white civilization and whose right to use the anthropologist as a sort of *scribe* cannot be denied. The process can, positively, be described as the infusion of a theoretical aspect into the rendering of the text *and into the self-reflexion of the subject.* "Everything about the inquiry relationship itself," says Bourdieu,

> betrays the interrogator's 'theoretical' (i. e. 'non-practical') disposition and invites the interrogatee to adopt a quasi-theoretical attitude: the situation in which the interrogation is carried out rules out any reference to the use and conditions of use [of the native notions].[17]

If "formal methods ... cancel out the practical function of notions, creating important changes in their status"[18] and if informants present to the interrogator a certain "theoretical" set of notions "as long as they see themselves as spokesmen mandated to present the group's official account of itself"[19], *this may be an impediment to the normal forms of anthropological research, but it becomes an asset as soon as it is made the base situation of the life history.* Under conditions of culture contact, it there serves, in some manner and degree, to set up an intercultural space as a sort of *Öffentlichkeit,* i. e., as a public space in which public discourses need to be used – or, in many cases, to be established. On the other hand, the focus on the private life as the material basis of the story (and as ultimately its only legitimizing matter) prevents the public aspect from taking over completely.

The mediation, in such cases, is of course towards the white world, and this is the direction in which many of the great earlier life histories went. Clellan Ford's (auto-)biography of Charles Nowell, for example, is not characterized by any great editorial interference with the original narrative, but the anthropologist's perspective and interest have been internalized by Charles Nowell. That the informant knows what is expected of him and delivers it, becomes apparent when Nowell, having

[16] Blackman, 19.

[17] P. Bourdieu, *Outline of a theory of practice.* Cambridge Studies in Social Anthropology 16. (Cambridge: Cambridge Univ. P. 1977) Quoted by Ladislav Holy and Milan Stuchlik, *Actions, norms and representations: Foundations of anthropological inquiry.* Cambridge Studies in Social Anthropology, 45. (Cambridge: Cambridge Univ. P., 1984), 61.

[18] Holy and Stuchlik, 67.

[19] Holy and Stuchlik, 75.

talked about his life as a baby and making a bee-line for the stories his father told him, says that "he also tells me about fairies and monsters – all kinds of stories which Dr. Boas has already taken down."[20] More important than the full representation of the life of the individual is the newness of the material, in the sense of its not yet having been recorded, and *the structure of the text,* in the sense of the selection and combination of the material that goes into it, is determined by the needs of the science of anthropology.[21]

The autobiographical here is in an ancillary role. The same is true of the (auto-)biography of "Chris" by Opler, a text published only in 1969, but based on material collected in the thirties and wholly informed by the standards of the time;[22] it may actually be true of most of the earlier texts. The autobiographical is ancillary in that the lived life and its cultural context do not yield the tools to interpret it/them, but that they require a perspective (anthropological, of course) from without to become comprehensible and "real" (i. e., discursively real). Both Charley Nowell and "Chris" do, however, show at the same time that the anthropological perspective becomes a lived one – not just a discourse chosen for rare and isolated moments of interaction with a white field worker. In this sense, there does exist a real dialogue of cultures, whose *form,* however, is determined exclusively or almost exclusively by the white science of anthropology. With regard to the interaction of the cultures, this implies a high degree of acculturation in discourse, which may perhaps be possible because there is comparatively much cultural substance left on other experiential levels to balance such adaptation; with regard to the question of genre, it implies that the life history is a source for the white science, rather than a literary expression of the native culture. The more contemporary life history, by way of contrast, seems to be a form of native historical writing that makes use of anthropological patterns.

In such texts, now, the mediation implies or includes the native side on more clearly formal levels – for example, with regard to the evaluative framework for actions and events in the story. In conventional western

[20] Clellan S. Ford, *Smoke from Their Fires: The Life of a Kwakiutl Chief* (New Haven: Yale Univ. P., for The Institute of Human Relations, 1941), 41.

[21] Ford, 56.

[22] Cf. in this regard chapter titles like "Childhood Play" (2), "Growing Up" (5), "Girls" (6), "Adult Life" (9). It needs to be pointed out, however, that there are others that are exclusively historical – which some of the quoted ones are, too, in part. Obviously, the distinction between anthropological pattern and individual history is not an absolute one.

autobiography, the criteria would seem to be related to a shared view of culture, and the autobiography would appear to deal with the individual's contribution to and/or experience of it, as well as with the culture's, and his or her, changes in the process. Conflict exists, but the areas of conflict and hence the shapes that conflict can take are fairly well determined – they need not be established by the work itself.[23] Tacit assumptions about the cultural meaning of the actions and events that make up the life, as well as a sustained implied reference to the cultural field in which the life is acted out, serve to structure the telling by establishing a pattern of relations (conflicts, alliances, parallelisms, and what not) in the reader's mind, within which he automatically places and accords greater or lesser importance to individual actions and events.

Where the shared fund of assumptions, codes, etc. is greatly limited or perhaps only uncertain, such patterning needs to be established by the text itself. This is what happens, for example, in several Inuit texts,[24] where *hunting*, which is at first merely a necessarily repeated event, attains the status of a natural and cultural *norm* associated with problems of survival and finally even with a fundamental *desire* that gives impulse and experiential reality to the subject's life. *I, Nuligak*, for example, uses a modified chronicle pattern that attempts to deal with the problem of repetition by condensing some periods.[25] Such abbreviation, which is much helped by the absence of year-by-year dating, also mimetically renders the decline of Nuligak into a less active old age, in which, however, the essentials of the past experience become clearer. One such essential is the excitement of the hunt.[26]

It is not unimportant that the very end of the book returns to this theme. When Nuligak, in his old age, regrets most that he cannot any longer go hunting,[27] there is a loss of essential vitality and almost of personal identity implied that can make for a desire to die – so that one may return for another cycle of life. The anthropological *fact* is used to structure the narrative and to elicit from a mass of events the meaning of the life that the subject wishes to present.

[23] If the merchant's son decides he is going to be an artist, rather than a merchant or lawyer, the reader need not be informed about the implications or about the general *setting* of the conflict between father and son that "normally" results.

[24] Nuligak, *I, Nuligak*. Ed. & transl. [into French] Maurice Metayer, [into English] Olive Koyama & The Canada Council. (Markham, Ont.: Pocket Books, 1971, 3rd print., 1975); Hughes.

[25] E. g. pp. 160–62, which take the reader (and Nuligak) from 1941 to 1952.

[26] Nuligak, 152, cf. Hughes, 3.

[27] Nuligak, 171 f.

In such texts a unified structure is given to the life by imputing a dominant and unifying motive to it; other texts stress the disruptive force of diverging motives. Such uses of dialogicity serve to exhibit and enact conflicts. A case in point is James Sewid, whose ability to adapt successfully to a culture conflict situation is stressed several times by Spradley. The strategy used is basically simple and immediately perceptible on the surface of the text. Insecurities and ambivalences are clearly articulated, though the speaker always manages to bring some ultimately positive aspect to the front; he usually does so by affirming a norm that has sustained him in living through the conflict, e. g.:

> Going to school was new to me and I found it awfully hard, especially such things as adding and arithmetic. Somehow I just couldn't put it in my head and I used to find it awfully hard. I really enjoyed school and that was the main reason I came to Alert Bay. I wanted to go to school pretty badly, and there was no school in Village Island, and that is why I started thinking about going to live with my grandmother. I enjoyed school very much but I had a lot of enemies there as a small boy.[28]

3. *The Benefits of Dialogicity and the Implied Functions of Life Histories*

The value of such patterns of mediation and conflict as have been briefly pointed out seems to be immediately apparent: they are, patently, in the interest of communication between the cultures that engage, through their representatives (native subject, white interviewer, native reader, white reader), in what amounts to a multiple dialogue – two voices with different timbres talking to one another. The question, however, still remains what precisely the qualities of that communication are and what kinds of benefits can be derived from it. One can, of course, say that communication *per se* is beneficial, and in a sense I shall come around to just that answer; but I shall do so by way of a detour that may clarify our notion both of *communication* and of *benefit* a little.

At the beginning stands the observation that life histories seem to make concrete and to act out some of the central problems of the science of anthropology. Among these are: (1) the fact that symbols have meaning only for those who use them and as they use them, which becomes particularly obvious in situations of rapid cultural change in which the meanings are insecure in content and status; and (2) the varying validity

[28] Spradley, 47.

of explanatory systems, according to which an action may or may not make sense.[29] Life histories, then, communicate a sense of the tentative nature of cultural meanings, and this is beneficial if we value an attitude of scepticism.

Also, Holy and Stuchlik's two basic distinctions – of "society, or structure, [as] an objective reality to whose demands people respond in specific ways" and "society or structure emerg[ing] from, and [being] maintained or changed only by what people do," and of "notions" and "actions,"[30] problematical as they may be as anthropological categories, can under certain conditions be *experiential* ones that recur in life histories and characterize the historical situation.[31] Thus, for example, the subject can feel him/herself to be swept along by an over-powering social system, while attempting to make it *or a somewhat different one* come into being through his/her actions, or the subject can feel that his/her notions and actions, in a given context – a particularly crippling one, let us say – cannot be made to tally with one another. Life histories, then, offer an integral discourse for the articulation of alienation.[32]

One could continue in this vein and list several more aspects in which the genre of the life history seems to fill a very specific and fairly important niche in the continuum of currently available forms of narrative. The more general argument may be more important, because it ascribes a privileged status to the genre. It goes something like this: *In articulating (or seeming to articulate) current problems of the discipline of anthropology, the life history deals with problems that our culture has with itself and with its own history of interaction with other cultures.*

Johannes Fabian, at least, in *Time and the Other*, sees anthropology historically involved in a contradiction between "research involving personal, prolonged interaction with the Other" and "a discourse which construes the Other in terms of distance, spatial and temporal," on which "the scandal of domination and exploitation of one part of mankind by another" is based. "The Other's empirical presence turns into

[29] Holy and Stuchlik, 36 ff., 40.

[30] Holy and Stuchlik, 2 et passim.

[31] Cf. the discussion of changes of norms occurring quite rapidly under the pressure of comparatively rapid socio-economic change, 91 ff.

[32] One might even go so far as to suggest that the incongruence of notions and actions, as discussed by Holy and Stuchlik (in terms of kinds of data, pp. 5 ff., and of the problematic status of norms vis-à-vis actions, p. 83) is one of the constitutive themes of autobiography – for if there were no such incongruence, one of the defining aspects of individuality (which lies somewhere in the mediation between notions or norms and actions, or in the transformation of the one into the other) would be missing.

his theoretical absence."[33] "Evolutionist anthropologists ... *spatialized* Time," to that "ever since ... anthropology's efforts to construct relations with its Other by means of temporal devices implied affirmation of difference as *distance*."[34] On the basis of this insight, Fabian posits as the project of an emancipated and emancipatory anthropology "the radical contemporaneity of mankind,"[35] which would realize itself in "a problematic simultaneity"[36] of cultures.

Contemporary life histories may very well be a genre that at least facilitates, and perhaps even necessitates, such contemporaneity; for the subject, at least, can they internalize the difference between the two cultures and (in living and telling them in the one life and the one act) effect their concrete, and concretely presented, interaction. Traditionally, "what makes the savage significant to the evolutionist's Time is that he lives in another Time"[37]; the existence of the subject of a life history denies the distinction, or – if it is imposed from without, by the general culture – it can contain both times and make them coeval. It may abolish the "temporal slope" between observer and observed of which Fabian talks,[38] since it implants the one time in the other. And it may thereby "image" in the subject, or create between subject and anthropologist, that "intersubjective time" that Fabian briefly alludes to as the most acceptable of time notions so far in use.[39] It may finally directly address what Fabian takes to be the real (or perhaps one had better say, the ultimate) referent of anthropology: the relationship or "contradiction" between "the West and the Rest."[40]

If – in the sense that "the object's present is founded in the writer's past" – "facticity itself ... is autobiography," as Fabian argues in accordance with Weizsäcker, if the temporal distance between the two times is converted into coevalness in situations of dialogicity, and if finally "somehow we must be able to share each other's [sic] past in order to be knowingly in each other's present,"[41] then the life history is a genre, once again, that does not only rely for its constitution on these aspects

33 Johannes Fabian, *Time and the Other: How Anthropology Makes Its Objects* (New York: Columbia Univ. P., 1983), X/XI.
34 Fabian, 15/16.
35 Fabian, XI.
36 Fabian, 146.
37 Fabian, 27.
38 Fabian, 30 f.
39 Fabian, 24.
40 Fabian, 28.
41 Fabian, 89/92.

and projects of anthropology, but that is about them, in so far as both the personal and the cultural pasts of the participants in the dialogue converge, in so far as the facticity of the life is a doubly autobiographical one (being grounded in the biographies of both participants), and in so far as the subject's present is founded in the past of two observers – both the subject's, as he or she observes him/herself, and the observing interviewer's.

Coevalness and dialogicity do not completely allay the specter of exploitation that Fabian describes, in the very general ways of the present discussion, as the removal of "possessions" from the native past into the Western present.[42] But the life history, as a possession, once again exemplifies and may (in various ways) reflect upon this process; and it will only rarely be the result of a simple act of exploitation – if only for the reason that it tends to emancipate the subject from the authority of the researcher by placing some of the latter's "theoretical" (see above) authority in that subject.[43]

What Fabian, at the end of his book, has to say about the danger of appropriation hidden in a bad kind of coevalness[44] is less important in the context of this essay than his concern with the ways in which the old paradigms of anthropology exemplify the separation of the object of consciousness from the mind, and of the mind from the practical life of the individual. The gap between the western self and its non-western other is regarded by him in the last analysis as one phase in the alienation of Western consciousness from itself; and he suggests that

> the only way to think of consciousness [materialistically, i. e.] without separating it from the organism or banning it to some kind of *forum internum* is to insist on its sensuous nature.[45]

In this context, the life history can most programmatically be characterized as communication-as-praxis, and as being of a beneficial kind: the production of language in a dialogic mode that embodies the differences of the participating persons' cultures in the coevalness of one

[42] Fabian, 95 f.; Fabian does not, however, concentrate on the aspect of commodification that (significantly enough) only comes to the fore as objects are being removed from their original context and use – cf. the example of "primitive" art that he does briefly allude to.

[43] This does, of course, not preclude exploitation along the same lines as of any author in western society, for example, by unfavorable arrangements or downright cheating.

[44] Fabian, 154.

[45] Fabian, 161 f.

verbal act which attempts to overcome the alienation of the participants from one another and from themselves. The structure of the text is determined, then, by the implied socio-cultural and epistemological project of the narrative.

Determining the Postmodernist Text

Gregory T. Polletta

What if we were to start by saying that postmodernism is a critical fiction, a critic's fiction, rather than a determinate artistic program or movement? What if we say that postmodernism is the creation and production of the art institution or polity rather than a live and real force in the making of art – specifically, in the making of novels, poems, or other literary texts? "Postmodernism," Malcolm Bradbury observes, "has in some ways become a critic's term without ever quite being an artistic movement."[1] The argument then would go that postmodernism is less an exigency for artistic experimentation, less the latest program or position for "making it new" by writers, and thereby a term for describing and defining what is happening now in the arts, and started happening somewhere about the late 50s, in the wake of modernism, than a term for taking critical or theoretical positions in the institution of literary studies.

All the more reason, should that be the case, for engaging the question, and indeed my own discussion here will focus on the uses to which postmodernism is being put in the making of literary history and critical discourse within or in opposition to the institution of literary studies. However "fashionable" may be the "theme of postmodernism,"[2] whatever the modishness that may attach to the name of the game, the subject bulks too large and figures too seriously in the activity of criticism right now to write it off indifferently; it has generated too voluminous a discursive practice or "discursivity" – to cite the notion of Roland Barthes that has been so influential in "theorizing postmodernism."[3] And it

[1] "Modernisms/Postmodernisms," in *Innovation/Renovation*, ed. Ihab Hassan and Sally Hassan (Madison: University of Wisconsin Press, 1983), p. 326.

[2] Fredric Jameson, "Foreword" to Jean-François Lyotard, *The Postmodern Condition*, tr. Geoff Bennington and Brian Massumi (Minneapolis: University of Minnesota Press, 1984), p. vii.

[3] Quoted by Hal Foster, "Re: Post," in *Art After Modernism: Rethinking*

should become clear as we go along that this is not some trivial or faddish pursuit for proper nomenclature but an attempt at a critique of discourse formation.[4] What may be at stake, besides propriety, is property, authority, ownership, and all those other words, root or branch, which signify, by tradition, possession. *Placing* the postmodernist text may be less a question of disinterested classification than of determining where, if not to whom, it belongs. Determining postmodernism turns on, to borrow the locutions of Gerard Manley Hopkins, the *keepings* as well as the *markings* of a literary text.

One approach – arguably the most productive or powerful approach – in determining the postmodernist text is by way of "deconstruction," that is, by applying the body of deconstruction critical theory associated with the work of Jacques Derrida, or that larger and looser congeries of critical theory and practice we have taken to naming "poststructuralism."[5] Indeed, we are told by a growing number of critics that the exemplary postmodernist text is Derrida's *Glas,* which Geoffrey Hartman has called "a new nonnarrative art form."[6] Whatever the merit of

Representation, ed. Brian Wallis (New York: The New Museum of Contemporary Art, and Boston: David R. Godine, 1984), p. 200. Foster's piece is included in the section of this anthology entitled "Theorizing Postmodernism."

[4] Cf. Abigail Solomon-Godeau, "Photography After Art Photography," in *Art After Modernism,* ed. Wallis, pp. 81–82: "What is at stake in art photography or postmodernism concerns their respective agendas and how as art practices they are positioned – or how they position themselves – in relation to their institutional spaces. I refer not only to the space of exhibition, but to all the discursive formations – canons, art and photography histories, criticism, the marketplace – that together constitute the social and material space of art."

[5] Derrida is quizzical about the overwhelming attention that has been given to "deconstruction" and the neglect of the other terms of his philosophical investigations. See *The Ear of the Other: Texts and Discussions with Jacques Derrida,* ed. Christie V. McDonald, tr. Peggy Kamuf (New York: Schocken Books, 1985), pp. 85–86, where he explains "why the word 'deconstruction' has always bothered me" – "this word which I had written only once or twice" and "all of a sudden jumped out of the text and was seized by others who have since determined its fate." Derrida, it should also be noted, holds no particular brief for "modernity," let alone postmodernism: "As for me, I'm no fan of modernity. I have no single belief in the irreducible specificity of 'modernity'," ibid, p. 84. Nevertheless, as so many of the essays in *Art After Modernism* display, deconstruction has become a staple of postmodernist discourse, along with what are putatively the terminologies and methods of poststructuralism.

[6] *Saving the Text: Literature/Derrida/Philosophy* (Baltimore: The Johns Hopkins University Press, 1981), p. xix.

this claim, there is no denying that Derrida's book exhibits one of the markings so frequently advanced as distinctive to the postmodernist text, and that is the way the postmodernist writer crosses freely between the borders of narrative and non-narrative, fiction and non-fiction, fictive invention and critical commentary, literary and non-literary verbal compositions – the way postmodernist writing effaces the so-called traditional boundaries, demarcations, and separations of genre, stylistic decorum, register, mode, and so on through virtually the whole anatomy of received literary structures.

Glas aside, poststructuralism has been exceedingly influential in determining what a text is or should be. In fact, to speak now, as I am doing, about the postmodernist text rather than the postmodernist poem or novel is to be drawn into the poststructuralist universe of discourse, and in speaking of a text on the occasion of this conference on "The Structure of Texts," we can hardly fail to take notice of that immensely complex and consequential turning in the recent history of critical theory whereby a concern with the "structurations" *(signifiance)*, "structurings," and "signifying practices" of a text has supplanted investigations of determinate structures and sign-systems based on the Saussurian model of linguistics (with its binary relation of signifier to signified): in short the swerve from *structuralism* to *poststructuralism*. Barthes, having so forcefully promoted structuralism early in his career, remains as one of the most authoritative and influential spokesmen for the present poststructuralist disposition towards the "theory of the text," and in his 1973 essay with that title he speaks of "the crisis of the sign" which precipitated the turn, the "overturning of former categories."[7] But it was Derri-

[7] Roland Barthes, "Theory of the Text," tr. Ian McLeod, in *Untying the Text: A Post-Structuralist Reader*, ed. Robert Young (London: Routledge & Kegan Paul, 1981), pp. 33–35. On Derrida's critique of the Saussurian foundations of structuralism, see Young's "Introduction," pp. 15–19. For Barthes' own account of the change in his persuasion, see the passage from a 1971 interview quoted by Young, p. 8. The "overturning of former categories" refers to Barthes' famous and immensely influential 1971 essay, "From Work to Text" (tr. Stephen Heath, repr. in *Art After Modernism*, p. 170), which itself inscribes the passage in his career from one, a preoccupation with the structures of the work, to the other, a preoccupation with the structurations of the text. Edward W. Said remarked some time ago that "the structuralist activity" Barthes was promoting early on "cannot show us why structure structures; structure is always revealed in the condition of having structures, but never, as Jean Starobinski has observed, structuring, or in the condition of *being structured*, or failing to structure," "*Abecedarium Culturae:* Structuralism, Absence, Writing," in *Modern French Criticism: From Proust and Valéry to Structuralism*, ed. John K. Simon (Chicago: University of Chicago Press,

da who provoked "the crisis of the sign"; it was Derrida who exposed the contradictions in the conceptions of sign and structure – the "logocentrism" or suppositions of metaphysical presence – upon which structuralism was founded. And while both Barthes and Derrida conceive of a text as *writing*, rather than as any determinate structure or composition of significations, while both poststructuralism and deconstruction foster an aesthetics of textual indeterminacy, they differ profoundly in their philosophical assumptions, methods, and purposes. How they differ is too complicated a question to entertain here,[8] but, returning to our subject, what seems to have happened is that the two are customarily spoken of together, without much discrimination, so that not only is the postmodernist text a text which may be described and determined by poststructuralism and/or deconstruction – but the terms have become all but interchangeable, in the sense that what the theory holds a text to be is what the postmodernist text is in every particular: that one is virtually a simulacrum of the other. Hence the claim would be that poststructuralism and deconstruction theory underwrites, authorizes, or even engenders the postmodernist text – rather than the other way around.

Moreover, as Fredric Jameson asserts, in an article I shall discuss at length presently, "theoretical discourse" itself "is also to be numbered among the manifestations of postmodernism."[9]

Elizabeth W. Bruss goes further by declaring that "literary theory" itself has become "our representative literary genre." She is doubtless right in claiming that theory has become engrossingly "literary" in its writing, but she adds a final, an insupportable, turn of the screw by arguing that the writing *of* theory by her exemplary authors of "beautiful theories" – William H. Gass, Susan Sontag, Harold Bloom, and Barthes – is more innovative and experimental and imaginative than so-called "creative" postmodernist writing.[10] This turnabout in the relationship of theoretical discourse to literary texts *per se*, as we used to say, is one of

1972), pp. 378–79. For an example of what Barthes produced when he took up the "structurings" of a text, see his 1973 "Textual Analysis of Poe's 'Valdemar'," in *Untying the Text*, pp. 135–60.

[8] See Young, "Introduction," *Untying the Text*, p. 19 for a sketch of these differences.

[9] "Postmodernism and Consumer Society," in *Postmodern Culture*, ed. Hal Foster (London: Pluto Press, 1985), p. 112. This anthology was first published as *The Anti-Aesthetic* (Port Townsend, Washington: Bay Press, 1983).

[10] *Beautiful Theories: The Spectacle of Discourse in Contemporary Criticism* (Baltimore: The Johns Hopkins University Press, 1982). pp. 79; 481 et passim.

the most perplexing and mystifying novelties in recent criticism. Although the motives may have been justifiable initially – to devalorize, deconstruct, or demystify the attachments to "literature" of such notions as originality, authenticity, and authorship; or, as Barthes urged, to establish the permeability of textual practice[11] – the outcome has been an indefensible valorization of the writing of theory. It is one thing for Barthes to proclaim, "Let the commentary be itself a text," or for Hartman to call into question the traditional divisions, in the institutional practice of literary studies, between primary and secondary texts, between creative and critical texts, and quite another to be asked to accept the primacy and superiority of what was formerly held to be a secondary activity or form of writing.[12] Besides, if we are going to speak of deconstructing "literature," we should be clear that Derrida has repeatedly stressed that there are no logocentric literary texts, only logocentric interpretations or appropriations of the writing.[13] More importantly, for our purposes, it should be recognized that literature came before theory in posing these problems: it is the writers of literary texts who have been grappling all along with the question of what is or is not literary in literature.

In the event, we may remark how changed the present situation is from the task Ihab Hassan set himself in championing postmodernism. Hassan was a pioneer in the territory, but what is worth noting is that he urged the need to reform and revise the then contemporary critical theory because it could not account for what was happening in the arts. The reigning "modernism" in the institution of literary studies had to be dethroned by what was happening in the postmodernist practice of the arts.[14]

One of the obvious consequences of a position such as Hassan's is whether we shouldn't treat postmodernism as a historical episode, and proceed according to tried and true methods of identifying and placing the postmodernist text in a historical period. Christine Brooke-Rose, for

[11] "Theory of the Text," in *Untying the Text,* p. 41: "We cannot by right restrict the concept of 'text' to what is written [to literature] ... All signifying practices can engender text: the practice of painting pictures, musical practice, filmic practice, etc."

[12] Barthes, "Theory of the Text," p. 44. Geoffrey H. Hartman, "Understanding Criticism," *Criticism in the Wilderness: The Study of Literature* (New Haven: Yale University Press, 1980).

[13] See Young, "Introduction," *Untying the Text,* p. 19.

[14] *Paracriticisms: Seven Speculations of the Times* (Urbana: University of Illinois Press, 1975), pp. 24–25.

instance, brusquely dismisses both terms, modernism and postmodernism, as "purely historical, period words." She contends that the inventory of properties proposed by Hassan as representative of postmodernism can be found over the whole map and history of past literature and "what would seem to be new is their combination" – that is, only the ensemble of properties, and their rearrangement in new configurations, is what identifies a text as postmodernist.[15]

But determining the postmodernist text is not a simple matter of repeating the old moves of periodization in making literary history, for the term may be less a periodizing enterprise than a critique of period-making and the functions that activity performs in the institution of literary studies. Nor is determining the postmodernist text a simple matter of establishing distinctive stylistic markings or identifying structural properties. For as one critic has observed: "However restricted its field of inquiry may be, every discourse of postmodernism ... aspires to the status of a general theory of contemporary culture."[16] This may sound grandiose and it may so total the field of inquiry as to obliterate meaningful differentiations, such as the differences between a theoretical text and an art-or-literary text, but the position is worth citing as testimony that postmodernism, both as discourse and as artistic production, inescapably compels us to include the terms of a cultural analysis as well as anything reductively stylistic or formalistic or "literary."

To look at this another way, the attempt to determine the postmodernist text in stylistic terms, strictly stylistic terms, is dubious in that it so easily invites or becomes a stratagem for discrediting the writer and the writing. Postmodernism, it won't take much exposure to see, is not one style but many styles, pluralism is the order of the day, and eclecticism, we are told repeatedly, is what postmodernism is all about, its single clearly identifiable feature. But before we make the next familiar move in fabricating literary history and affirm that hence we should speak of postmodernisms, as we should speak of modernisms, the discriminations of these blanket terms, we ought to ponder whether the effect of the proceeding, if not its purpose, isn't to defuse and disperse that collaboration of energies by which writers take fire from one another and begin tearing periods apart. A common way of disarming the new is by identifying a certain repertory of formal properties in order to assert: And what's so new or modern about that? It has been

[15] Christine Brooke-Rose, *A Rhetoric of the Unreal* (Cambridge: Cambridge University Press, 1981), pp. 344; 350.

[16] Craig Owens, "The Discourse of Others: Feminists and Postmodernism," in *Postmodern Culture*, ed. Foster, p. 61.

done before, everything been done before, though not in the same combination. The rejoinder, of course, is to say that the norm is what counts, the stylistic norm of a historical period, rather than the singular appearances. Both the attack and the defense, however, are likely to miss or mask the point the painter Barnett Newman made when he tartly remarked:

> This shrewd popularization of the big lie, that modern art isn't modern, succeeded in establishing the respectability modern art now enjoys with museum directors and professional art lovers, but wrought havoc with the creative forces struggling for a footing wherever this false thesis took hold.[17]

Which I take to mean that denying the *modernity* of what gets called modernism and postmodernism is a way of housing their productions, their texts, safely – a means by which control is exercised over the holdings, the keepings. The very profession of the art institution is to devise categories and classifications and cataloguings by which the holdings are placed and kept out of harm's way, guarded for free access, to be sure, but made secure – and in the more suspect senses of these words, so that, for instance, the devising of period concepts by which a field of activity is organized for systematic study may also be an agency by which the objects of study are neutralized and subjugated, a means by which the text is, so to speak, de-textualized. Whereas the writing, or the painting, of the modern text, by resisting any containment in a book or a museum or any canonical ordering, undoes or disowns whatever we say determines and fixes its identity or use or power. The writing that makes the text, the text that is the writing, unsettles any terminal or determinate status we try to impose upon it. The authority of the writing disturbs whatever authoritative use we want to make of the text – dispossesses our efforts to hold it fast and house it in some final resting place.

What is curious about so many discourses of postmodernism, however, is precisely the way in which they try to find a place for themselves by ascribing a terminal or determinate status to modernism. It is obvious right from the name itself that "postmodernism" turns about and returns us to the term it envelops or encloses: the "modernism" which lies behind and came beforehand. Like so many post-prefixing terms in literary or art history, post-modernism returns us to a precedent and compels us to determine what the modernism is with which the relationship is posed and/or opposed. And, of course, there is an equivocation. The word poses a discontinuity which implicates a continuity, or a

[17] Quoted in Harold Rosenberg, *Barnett Newman* (New York: Abrams, 1977), p. 27.

disaffiliation which avows an affiliation it professes to disavow, a rupture or a break that is not clean and definite – even though a number of critics, Hassan most exuberantly, will play on dis-un-de forms of undoing or unmaking, as when he asserts that "postmodernism is an aesthetics of playful discontinuity." Setting aside the rhetoric of these formulations, the problem is whether in all such discourses the postmodernist text isn't being determined, by its partisans and adversaries alike, by imposing a determinate and terminal status, a fixed state, on its precedent in order to be allowed an indeterminate freedom of expression. The question is whether the term "postmodernism" finds its place in critical discourse only by stabilizing "modernism" and making it marmoreal – in particular, as has become the fashion among certain promoters of postmodernism by conjuring up a ghostly entity called "the modernist paradigm."[18] And to move to the other side, the question is whether postmodernism is to be demeaned or discredited by making touchstones and monuments of the great achievement of modernism.

As an illustration of how the activity of determining the postmodernist text proceeds by opposing periods or paradigms, I should like to examine three discourses of postmodernism, the foremost of which is an essay of 1982 by Jean-François Lyotard entitled "Answering the Question: What is Postmodernism?" This was in part a rejoinder to a piece by Jürgen Habermas entitled "Modernity versus Postmodernity," originally a lecture delivered in 1980, and reprinted recently with the title, "Modernity – An Incomplete Project." The third is an essay of 1982 by Fredric Jameson entitled "Postmodernism and Consumer Society."[19]

Let me begin with a passage from Jameson's piece. He names a number of recent artists and performers, as "varieties" of postmodernism, and then he says:

[18] The following quotation from Fredric Jameson's *Fables of Aggression* (1971) by Foster, "Re: Post," p. 194, is representative: "The contemporary post-structuralist aesthetic ... signals the dissolution of the modernist paradigm – with its valorization of myth and symbol, temporality, organic form and the concrete universal, the identity of the subject and the continuity of linguistic expression – and foretells the emergence of some new, properly postmodernist or schizophrenic conception of the cultural artifact – now strategically reformulated as 'text' or '*écriture,*' and stressing discontinuity, allegory, the mechanical, the gap between signifier and signified, the lapse in meaning, the syncope in the experience of the subject."

[19] Lyotard's essay, tr. Régies Durand, is in *Innovation/Renovation*, ed. Hassan, pp. 3–29; Habermas's, tr. Seyla Ben-Habib, in *Postmodern Culture*, ed. Foster, pp. 3–15; Jameson's op.cit., pp. 111–125. The quotations from Jameson's essay that follow refer, in order, to pp. 111–112; 113; 114; 118; 125; 114.

> Most of the postmodernisms mentioned above emerge as specific reactions against the established forms of high modernism, against this or that dominant high modernism which conquered the university, the museum, the art gallery network, and the foundations. Those formerly subversive and embattled styles – Abstract Expressionism; the great modernist poetry of Pound, Eliot or Wallace Stevens; the International Style (Le Corbusier, Frank Lloyd Wright, Mies); Stravinsky; Joyce, Proust and Mann – felt to be scandalous or shocking by our grandparents are, for the generation which arrives at the gate in the 1960s, felt to be the establishment and the enemy – dead, stifling, canonical, the reified monuments one has to destroy to do anything new. This means that there will be as many different forms of postmodernism as there were high modernisms in place, since the former are at least initially specific and local reactions *against* those models. That obviously does not make the job of describing postmodernism as a coherent thing any easier, since the unity of this new impulse – if it has one – is given not in itself but in the very modernism it seeks to displace.

This is fairly typical of how critical discourse has been going about its work of determining the postmodernist text, and fairly typical, too, of how literary history is being made, by using one period to place the other. Jameson is ambivalent about some of the forms that have succeeded and displaced modernism, for, in his view, postmodernism in the arts is an expression of a consumer society. Postmodernism, he declares, is "a periodizing concept whose function is to correlate the emergence of new formal features in culture with the emergence of a new type of social life and a new economic order – what is often euphemistically called modernization, postindustrial or consumer society, the society of the media or the spectacle, or multinational capitalism." And all of this is evidenced in his discussion of the formal features of the postmodernist text he identifies as *pastiche* and *schizophrenia*. There is not much I have to say about these formulations other than that *pastiche* is clearly a formal term (which Jameson gives some clever turns by distinguishing from *parody*) whereas *schizophrenia,* which looks quite misplaced, is made to serve as a formal term by signifying a collapsed sense of temporality, "the fragmentation of time into a series of perpetual presents," and thereby, according to Jameson, a postmodernist rather than a modernist form of temporal structuring.

But it might be worth pausing to examine the argument about a "new component" he adduces to explain why "classical modernism is a thing of the past and why postmodernism should have taken its place." "This new component," Jameson asserts, "is what is generally called the 'death of the subject' or, to say it in more conventional terms, the end of individualism as such." Now, there is no topic that is more imposing in contemporary critical theory than the "death of the subject," no subject that is of more consuming or productive interest, none that has more mazes of ramification, none that has liberated more energies of discourse, and, as Jameson acknowledges, the question of the subject is a preoccupation, a favored quarry, of poststructuralism. It is perfectly in keeping that a recent piece by Hélène Cixous on Joyce's story "The Sisters" should begin with a section entitled "Discrediting the Subject," and appear in a collection of essays called *Post-Structuralist Joyce.*[20] If a story which was first published in 1904 can be said to discredit the subject (in the sense of dislodging the privilege and value that have been invested in a central real consciousness or presence), that obviously calls into question the terms by which Jameson classifies a writer like Joyce as a modernist rather than a postmodernist. Again, it should be emphasized that for a poststructuralist of Derrida's persuasion a text is not constitutively modernist or postmodernist; the text does not need to be deconstructed; only the interpretations which have been imposed on the text need deconstructing: the determinations of what it is taken or meant to signify, not its signifying powers. But if we must speak historically, then the dwindling fortunes of the subject have been a preoccupation of much of the fiction and poetry of nineteenth and twentieth-century literature; it has been a major theme of long standing rather than of recent origin. If we think in terms such as the "disintegration of the subject," and take that to mean less a traumatic breaking apart of the speaking or narrating or authoring subject, a decentering of the self, than a recentering of these dramas in language, in writing, in speaking and telling and making fictions, we can discern this as traversing the whole span and terrain of whatever it is we call "modern literature." The various devices that have been proposed for determining modern fiction – devices and terms such as parody, reflexivity, digression, fragment, miscellany, *écriture,* textuality, palimpsest, aleatory or allotropic compositions and decompositions and recompositions – all of these and more may be construed as constructions for displacing and replacing *unity,* both structural and phenomenological, as the central organizing principle for making literary texts. Historically speaking, the "crisis" of the integrating subject and the move towards a dis-integration of the subject is patent in the combined efforts of Henry James, Joseph Conrad, and Ford Madox Ford at making fiction new and writing "the new novel" – but theirs is

20 "Joyce: the (r)use of writing," tr. Judith Still, in *Post-Structuralist Joyce,* ed. Derek Attridge and Daniel Ferrer (Cambridge: Cambridge University Press, 1984), pp. 15 ff.

only one example of many that might be cited in any historical account of the fortunes of the subject.

The point would be that there are more than differences in degree in the way we word the case. There is all the difference in the world between the death of the subject and the discrediting or decentering or disintegration of the subject. But however we put the question, it should be made clear that postmodernism is distinctly not a doing away with all forms of structure. The norms of structure may be called into question, or wrought to a crisis, but neither postmodernist or modernist writing tries to do without any semblance or trace of structure – however much the structuration may aspire to the condition of silence, absence, the unsaid, the unsayable, or any of the other "negations" that are often proposed as consequent upon the disappearance of the subject. Decompositions and de-structurings, it should go without much saying, are hardly non-compositions or non-structurings, except as purely grammatical expedients or inventions. And such terms are less an aporia, a doubtful assertion, a shady proposition, of postmodernist writing than an aporia of those who would speak for the text in the name of postmodernism. Postmodernist writing is a discrediting of the subject, and of the modes of structuring a text that depend on a belief in the centrality and unifying powers of a subject, doubtless wrought to extremes compared with what might be located in modernist or any earlier writing, but this is not, in any simple sense, the death of the subject.

It is, however, the *historical* crisis of these developments that so dismays and disturbs Habermas. In his essay on "Modernity versus Postmodernity" he calls into question, into very sharp questioning, the historical consequences of postmodernism – the implications of the properties and purposes of the postmodernist "text", its improprieties, its offenses, travesties, and transgressions, its de-structurings, its *destructive* consequences. He starts his argument with what he acknowledges to be a great over-simplification: that in the history of modern art we can detect a trend, a steady march, towards ever greater autonomy in the definition and practice of art, and he then cites a succession of experiments that he says have been nonsense or nugatory or dead ends. The artists have not produced an emancipatory effect but "a desublimated meaning or a destructured form."[21] Modernity is "an incomplete project" because the failure of artistic experiments in time has exposed the parlous consequences of a shattering of a vital relationship among the three structures, the three discourses or discursive practices, he calls

[21] Habermas, p. 11; the next quotation refers to p. 13.

cognitive-instrumental, moral-practical and aesthetic-expressive rationality, i. e., discourses of science, theories of morality and jurisprudence, and discourses and practices of art. The project of modernity has failed, Habermas claims, it has not been fulfilled, it has taken a series of wrong turnings, postmodernism has become an anti-modernity, and thereby a manifestation of lost causes, so to speak. Habermas makes a plea, a noble plea, to reunite that which has been split apart or torn asunder – by returning to the energies of art, culture, and society inaugurated by modernity, by resuming and reinvigorating the project of modernity: "The project aims at a differentiated relinking of modern culture with an everyday praxis that still depends on vital heritages, but would be impoverished through mere traditionalism."

Which is the point where Lyotard intervenes with his query, "My question is to determine what sort of unity Habermas has in mind,"[22] and without going into the full particulars of his response, or counter-critique, what I should like to consider is the defence Lyotard mounts in behalf of postmodernism, the postmodern condition, the postmodernist painting or writing, and the implications of his dispute with, his polemic against Habermas for anything we might say in determining the postmodernist text and how we come to terms with such a text.

Lyotard follows, like Jameson and Habermas, the common practice of opposing modernism and postmodernism. He, too, seems to make hard and fast distinctions between the two by asserting that postmodernism rejoices and revels in change, turbulence, and experiment with no regrets for a past project or agenda, whereas the modern is marked by melancholy, nostalgia, and a yearning for unified structures or structurations.[23] Lyotard, however, gives modernity its due by reminding us of what it means to be modern: "Modernity," he says, "in whatever age it appears, cannot exist without a shattering of belief and without discovery of the 'lack of reality' of reality, together with the invention of other realities."[24] I say *remind* because this is the view of modernity – not of "modernism" – that Paul de Man so compellingly put forward in his

[22] "Answering the Question: What is Postmodernism?" p. 331.

[23] See Philippe Lacoue-Labarthe, "Talks," tr. Christopher Fynsk, *Diacritics*, 14:3 (Fall 1984), "Special Issue on the Work of Jean-François Lyotard," pp. 24–25. For an exposition of Lyotard's notions of the "libidinal economy" of postmodernism, along with a useful "partial bibliography" of Lyotard's writings, see Maureen Turim, "Desire in Art and Politics: The Theories of Jean-François Lyotard," *Camera Obscura*, 12 (Summer 1984), pp. 91–109.

[24] "Answering the Question: What is Postmodernism?" p. 336.

essays into the subject,[25] and de Man's views in turn were a reminder, less of the history of the term, and least of all of the diversity of programs that have paraded under its auspices, but of the historical affirmations and re-affirmations of the concept of modernity, which is a dividing moment, idea, intention, or act: that moment when the writer or painter forgets or disowns the past. Modernity is a letting go of the past, leaving the past behind, and what that signifies in the making of art: tradition, the great tradition of that which comes beforehand, the old, the past masters, the masterpieces, the whole institution or polity of masteries and masterpieces. Modernity, in whatever age it appears, is, so to speak, "starting from scratch." This is the idiom Barnett Newman liked to use in avowing his own constant determined struggle to make his paintings modern, and it is a good, an apt, idiom because it comprehends, by the figure and the resonances of the figure, how a painter or writer inscribes himself in the history of art: that is to say, re-inscribes, rewrites, himself, from the beginning, with every beginning. For it is that – a beginning, and not merely, in Barthes' famous conceit, a *déjà-lu*. Newman made his own disavowal of tradition, which, if you like, only repeats what has been said many times over. "We do not need the obsolete props of an outmoded and antiquated legend," he asserted grandly, "We are freeing ourselves of the impediment of memory, association, nostalgia, myth that have been the devices of Western European painting."[26] However "traditional" this may sound in the so-called "tradition of the new," starting from scratch is not starting from nothing or even starting from zero but starting anew. It is an inaugural moment rather than a determinate historical episode or determination. "Modernity," in de Man's presentation of the term, is conceptual and categorical rather than descriptive and programmatic. The various programs of "modernism" may be at odds with and even the counterfeits of modernity. Modernity, then, is very much an unfinished project, in every sense of the word, an indeterminate series of beginnings.

Modernity, modern writing or painting, the modern – all of these can be made without much finessing of Lyotard's terms to be a worthy project, and salvaged from both its detractors and admirers. But postmodernity is what Lyotard wants to advance towards, postmodernity is what he is determined to deliver and inscribe in discourse rather than

[25] Particularly "Literary History and Literary Modernity" and "Lyric and Modernity," in *Blindness and Insight: Essays in the Rhetoric of Contemporary Criticism* (New York: Oxford University Press, 1971), pp. 142–165 and 166–186.

[26] Quoted in Rosenberg, *Barnett Newman*, p. 26.

merely describe and publicize. His arguments on its behalf turn on a criterion and concept of "unpresentability": in the words of the title of one of his essays, postmodernity is "presenting the unpresentable."[27] These arguments are too complex for any summary exposition and analysis, but the distinctiveness of his position, and the possibilities it opens for determining the postmodernist text, for the discourse of postmodernism, may be gathered in a passage which follows his treatment of Proust as exemplary of the modern and Joyce as exemplary of the postmodern:

> The postmodern would be that which, in the modern, puts forward the unpresentable in presentation itself; that which denies itself the solace of good forms, the consensus of a taste which would make it possible to share collectively the nostalgia for the unattainable; that which searches for new presentations, not in order to enjoy them but in order to impart a stronger sense of the unpresentable. A postmodernist artist or writer ... the text he writes, the work he produces are not in principle governed by pre-established rules, and they cannot be judged according to a determining judgement, by applying familiar categories to the text or to the work. Those rules or categories are what the work of art itself is looking for. The artist and writer, then, are working without rules in order to formulate the rules of what *will have been done.*[28]

Just how searching and novel this position is for theorizing postmodernism may be gauged by contrasting what David Lodge says in speaking of the attempts by postmodernist writers to abolish the "familiar" modes of ordering and structuring fiction:

> If postmodernism really succeeded in expelling the idea of order ... from modern writing, then it would truly abolish itself, by destroying the norms against which we perceive its deviations. A foreground without a background inevitably becomes the background of something else. Postmodernism cannot rely upon the historical memory of modernist and antimodernist writing for its background, because it is essentially a rule-breaking kind of art and unless people are still trying to keep the rules, there is no interest in breaking them and no interest in seeing them broken.[29]

[27] "Presenting the Unpresentable: The Sublime," tr. Lisa Liebmann, *Artforum,* 20:8 (April 1982), pp. 64–69. For a succinct commentary on the sources of Lyotard's notions of the sublime, see John Rajchman, "Foucault, or the Ends of Modernism," *October* 24 (1983), pp. 44 ff. Barnett Newman was preoccupied with the sublime, and he too was one of Lyotard's "sources." Although it is customary to place Newman as an Abstract Expressionist painter, a modernist, Lyotard has treated him, on several occasions, as an exemplary postmodernist artist.

[28] "Answering the Question: What is Postmodernism?" pp. 340–41.

[29] *The Modes of Modern Writing: Metaphor, Metonymy, and the Typology of Modern Literature* (London: E. Arnold, 1977), p. 245.

Lodge, with all his sympathies for the "enormous risks" taken by postmodernist writing, ends by expressing a familiar complaint about the posturings and pretense of the parodistic or parasitic strain in much of what is happening now in the arts. He voices a common worry about the excesses and abuses of postmodernist experimentation.

Lyotard, however, pulls us up sharply by warning of what has become all too common a feature of discourses about postmodernism. "From every direction," he declares, "we are being urged to put an end to experimentation, in the arts and elsewhere."[30] From every direction, left right and center, we are being urged to terminate experimentation. To shape up, to come to order, to stop playing around and be serious, to restore humane values, to retrieve vital heritages or a unity of communal experience, to recover what we have lost, to reconstruct what has been deconstructed, to be constructive, to abide by the rules. "In the diverse invitations to suspend artistic experimentation," Lyotard says, "there is an identical call for order, a desire for unity ... for security, or popularity [i.e., reaching, speaking intelligibly to, communicating with the public] ... Artists and writers must be brought back into the bosom of the community, or at least, if the latter is considered to be ill, they must be assigned the task of healing it." Not that Lyotard is urging the recuperation of the old, the discredited notions of the freedom, autonomy, social indifference, or privileged status of the artist. Precisely the contrary. "If they too do not wish to become supporters of ... what exists," he declares, "the painter and artist must refuse to lend themselves to such therapeutic uses. They must question the rules of painting or of narrative as they have learned and received them from their predecessors. Soon the rules must appear to them as a means to deceive, to seduce, and to reassure, which makes it impossible for them to be 'true'," which is to say that they must leave the old rules behind. The experimentation of postmodernism for Lyotard is an activity of new determinations of what writing and painting can or should be in what *will have been done.*

This may sound like a reprise of the rhetoric of all the old manifestoes of the avant-garde – a replay of the same old exhortations to experiment and make it new, the same unremitting pursuit of experimentation and innovation as if they were empty ends in themselves – at a time when the aporias of the avant-garde, the very concept and status of the avant-garde, are undergoing severe critical scrutiny and delegitimation.[31] Re-

[30] "Answering the Question: What is Postmodernism?" p. 329; the next two quotations refer to pp. 331, 333.

[31] See Rosalind Krauss, "The Originality of the Avant-Garde: A Postmodernist Repetition," in *Art After Modernism,* ed. Wallis, pp. 13–29. Cf. Peter Bürger,

valorizing these imperatives, moreover, may play into the hands of those who have been arguing that exhaustion is built into the premises of modern art; that there is a necessary depletion in its capacity to shock or scandalize by breaking the rules unceasingly and transgressing, forever transgressing, received decorums and limits; that postmodernism is, in the words of one highly-publicized formulation, "the literature of exhaustion" which leaves only parody or pastiche as new forms of creative experimentation.

But there are crucial differences in Lyotard's position. He is advancing a new argument. And one way of catching how and why it is so might be to pose against Ezra Pound's imperative, "Make It New," a statement by William Carlos Williams, who was, of course, no less intent on experimentation and innovation than his friend Pound. "Art" Williams declared, "can be made of anything."[32] A poem, a novel or whatever other structuration of writing, a text can be made of anything. The novelty, the art, will be discovered in what will have been done, in making something from anything, rather than in the act of will and defiance and reaction against what is traditional, conventional, or whatever it is that has been done before. Making it new is discovering what is new in the making of anything, no holds barred, no rules binding, no rules standing in the way. Not that "anything goes", as so many objections to experimentation now are phrased, but rather that "anything can be made into a text." And by Lyotard's terms it is this that would be the enabling conviction or condition for the postmodernist text.

To question the rules, then, the correct rules, the good rules, is for Lyotard what moves and determines the writing of the postmodernist text. To question the correct rules, including the innovating rules of a "modernist" text, is to commit an impropriety that calls into question what is good and proper and even new or experimental. It is, indeed, to question property, as I suggested earlier: the keepings and holdings of writing and painting. The postmodernist text is a dispossessing and dislodging of properties. A dispossession, for one thing, of the *placings* of the art institution or polity, as well as of the formal or structural properties, the rules by which a text is judged worthy of being called artistic and included in the holdings. The dispossession, for another, of the individual authority of the author, either to certify originality or to reserve all rights of interpretation and use. The dispossession, in Lyotard's

Theory of the Avant-Garde, tr. Michael Shaw (Minneapolis: University of Minnesota Press, 1984).

[32] From a letter of 1932 to Kay Boyle, *The Selected Letters of William Carlos Williams,* ed. John C. Thirlwall (New York: New Directions, 1984), p. 130.

words, the "constant dispossession of the craft of painting" and writing "or even of being an artist." The dispossession of these and so many more of the properties we attribute to the production of art in order that we may treasure the texts and hold them for our pleasure, curiosity, solace, utility, or whatever. Potmodernism is breaking the rules, consensus-breaking rather than consensus-making, calling into crisis canons of artistic judgment, received orderings or placings of masterpieces, but – and here is the new turn Lyotard gives to these already familiar propositions – the motives are less to shock, scandalize, or shatter than to remake the rules by finding new rules of artistic structuration in what will have been done. Lyotard's position, in fact, implicitly challenges the whole dramaturgy of breaking rules, rupturing continuities, transgressing limits that are the scenarios of so much contemporary critical discourse – and which curiously perpetuates the figure of art, if not the artist, as lawless, revolutionary, criminal: a heroically satanic activity.[33] For Lyotard, pushing the rules to the limit and breaking them is not what matters: it is leaving the rules behind. The postmodernist text is discovering, making, inventing the rules by which it is to be determined. In that sense, then, the postmodernist text is an *undetermining,* which designates (however awkward the locution), not its indeterminate construction or meaning, not even its indeterminable status, but its determination, its resolve, to invent new or unimaginable or inconceivable rules of structuration in writing, in the writing, or in what will have been written.

But since many of the same things might be said of the *modernist* text, as distinct from the programmatic texts of "modernism," and since, indeed, they might equally be said of the unmodified *text,* according to the poststructuralists in general and Derrida in particular, we should take a closer look at the historical reasons why we need the term, the *postmodernist text:* a closer look at how history figures or should figure in determining the postmodernist text. For if we say that the conviction "art can be made of anything" is an inaugural moment in postmodern-

[33] Harold Bloom may be the most spectacular "dramatist," as Bruss exhibits in *Beautiful Theories,* pp. 306–7, 312–18, passim, but other dramatizations are acted out all over the stage of recent criticism, e. g. when Barthes presents the text as "that which goes to the limits of the rules of enunciation (rationality, readability, etc.)," as an "experience of limits," "From Work to Text," in *Art After Modernism,* p. 171; or when Foucault presents modern art as "an art of transgression," *Untying the Text,* p. 11, and Rajchman, "Foucault, or the Ends of Modernism," p. 43. Indeed, such dramatizations may be said to constitute the "scene" of contemporary critical discourse.

ism, there is plainly no denying that it appears at a *historical* moment, in a historical *situation*, and that this enabling condition, as I called it, produces structurations of writing that are sensibly different, historically speaking, from those that obtained beforehand. "Art can be made of anything" alters the disposition, a historic disposition, towards rule-breaking and rule-making, but its only real value is in the *event* of what will have been done, as in the writing of *Paterson*.[34] And while this does not mean that the event is historically determined, in any simple sense, or that any adequate measure of what is produced can be taken by falling back of the procedures for marking and placing that have been traditional in literary studies, some measure must be taken of the historical situation in which both the production and reception of what will have been done *take place*.

One way of doing this is to propose that we need the term the "postmodernist text" in order to mark the latest turn or the most advanced degree of the historical development by which we ask, not "what is beautiful?" but, "what can be said to be art (and literature)?"[35] and that postmodernism is the juncture at which "art can be made of anything." This line of argument might be open to the objections that have been registered about periodizing literary history. A stronger objection might be that it is too *literary* a history: that it fails to take due account of the actual historical situation of such formations, by being too formalistic or stylistic in its priorities, and that it neglects the material realities of the historical conditions in which such turns take place.

Such in fact is the position of one body of postmodernist criticism – arguably the most forceful or pertinent body of postmodernist discourse – which addresses the social, political, cultural, or ideological purposes that are served by what is being done now in the arts. For critics of this persuasion, what matters are the ends of beginning with the conviction that "art can be made of anything." And the objects of their investigations of what will have been done are not the makings of beautiful, intricate, audacious, or whatever structurations of writing and painting, but a *critique* of the historical situation within which these structurations take place – a critique of discourse formation. The purposes served by such a critique are held to be oppositional: to represent the deconstructive or demythologizing strategies and devices by which the production

[34] For a treatment of *Paterson* as a postmodernist poem, see Joseph N. Riddel, *The Inverted Bell: Modernism and the Counter-Poetics of William Carlos Williams* (Baton Rouge: Louisiana State University Press, 1974).

[35] Lyotard, quoting Thierry de Duve, in "Answering the Question: What is Postmodernism?" pp. 333–34.

of art, the art that is being produced now, postmodernist art, *indicts* the institution or polity or art – indicts in a direct, active, and consequential fashion rather than in any sense merely figuratively. Barthes presented the text as a weave or a network – a tissue very like a textile[36] – but the "oppositional" postmodernist critics concern themselves with the materially *social* network in which the postmodernist text is produced, disseminated, and received. To return to my earlier discussion of "discrediting the subject" for an illustration of what is distinctive about this body of recent criticism, it is concerned with the differences in the purposes to which the historical development of discrediting the subject are being put both in postmodernist art and postmodernist critical discourse – of *what is being made of* the issue : the various and energetic ways by which discrediting the subject are being employed as a cultural critique; in particular, by putting into question the attendant beliefs in individual creations or creativity, original art and artists, masters and masterpieces, to the point where, in Michel Foucault's provocative formulation, "we are at present witnessing the disappearance of the figure of the 'great writer'."[37]

Powerful as this approach to determining the postmodernist text may be, however appealing the seriousness of its cultural concerns, it is shadowed by a formidable array of problems, and even outright contradictions, one of which is that the terms of Barthes' or Derrida's conceptions of the text cannot be used to legitimate what may be quite contrary purposes. The oppositional and ideological ends proposed by this critic-

[36] "From Work to Text," in *Art After Modernism,* p. 171, and "Theory of the Text," in *Untying the Text,* p. 39. Cf. Derrida's reweaving of the figure in "Semiology and Grammatology," *Positions,* tr. Alan Bass (Chicago: University of Chicago Press, 1981), p. 27.

[37] "Truth and Power," tr. Colin Gordon, in *Power/Knowledge* (New York: Pantheon Books, 1980), p. 127. The context of the statement is Foucault's critique of "the whole relentless theorizing of writing which we saw in the 1960s," that includes, not only, e. g., Barthes and Derrida, but Foucault himself, as Rajchman shows in his essay on "Foucault, or the Ends of Modernism." For an example of "oppositional" postmodernist critical discourse, note the following statement by Abigail Solomon-Godeau, "Photography After Art Photography," in *Art After Modernism,* p. 80: "Seriality and repetition, appropriation, intertextuality, simulation or pastiche: these are the primary devices employed by postmodernist artists ... The appearance of such practices in the 1970s seemed to portend the possibility of a socially grounded, critical, and potentially radical art practice that focussed on issues of representation as such. Collectively, use of such devices to prompt dialectical and critical modes of perception and analysis may be termed deconstructive."

ism, however desirable in themselves, are not easily accommodated to the *theories* of deconstruction and/or poststructuralism. They can hardly be used to determine the postmodernist text. The tactics of deconstruction, the vocabulary of its concepts or principles, cannot be employed, as they are so lavishly and freely in this body of postmodernist criticism, without facing up to Derrida's obdurate insistence that "the text overruns all the limits assigned to it so far" – "all the limits, everything that was to be set up in opposition to writing (speech, life, the world, the real, history, and what not, every field of reference – to body or mind, conscious or unconscious, politics, economics, and so forth)."[38] The text, the postmodernist text, simply cannot be invested with a social or historical presence, or appropriated to an ideological field of reference, on or by Derrida's terms. Something more is needed than the putative "deconstruction" of the critiques of the historical place of the postmodernist text.

Lyotard's position may not be a way out of such an impasse, but it assumes a different vantage and a less skeptical outlook. For if we say that "rethinking representation" is the urgent imperative in "theorizing postmodernism," and if we say that Derrida has produced the most imposing philosophical critique of representation, we might then say that it is Lyotard, precisely because of his concern with "presenting the unpresentable," whose work is instructive in understanding how what is being written or painted now takes place. This is not to suggest that Lyotard is better at unraveling the knot of problems about representation than is Derrida, or more cogent as a theorist, but rather to say that he gives a more material sense of the production of a text, he is closer to the actuality of the writing or the painting of a text, he is more attentive to how writing and painting are being performed at the moment, he is more directly and actively and concretely concerned with how the postmodernist text comes to be produced: how it takes place. Lyotard has an acute awareness of the historical situation of the postmodernist text, but while he is like Derrida in resisting any determinations or delimitations of the text, his position is that none of the powers assigned to the text so far – social, political, cultural, historical, or whatever – are commensurate with, measure up to, the force, energy, and value of what will have been done in the performance of writing or painting.

Let us say, then, following Lyotard's lead, that we need the name the *postmodernist text* if for no other reason than as a certain figure of the text, of writing, a certain historical figure. The figure of a text which

[38] Quoted from Derrida's contribution to *Deconstruction and Criticism*, Harold Bloom et al. (1979), in Young, *Untying the Text*, p. 19.

leaves behind anything we determine to be the markings of even the most "modernist" of texts. A text which leaves behind the indeterminacy or radical uncertainty which contemporary critical theory has made so capital in reading, interpretation, textual analysis. The figure of a text which undoes and remakes the rules of representation, however modern or modernist we have concluded these rules to be, which undoes and remakes the modes of experimentation about which we have reached a consensus. A text wherein tradition, the past, the great tradition no longer play the role of that which the writer rebels against, and labors under in an anxiety of influence, or that which we, as readers, contend against or nostalgically yearn to restore. Let us say that the postmodernist text is the figure of a text which invites us to forget the past, to leave the past behind, not to be unmindful or unruled, but to engage new rules of making and writing and reading.

And if this looks like a phantom, a figure without a text, something which can be imagined but not named, or the figure of desire rather than the real thing, consider the case of Joyce, whose career may be taken as exemplary. *Ulysses* is a modern novel, a modern text, by any definition of the term, even by the parody or pale fire of "the modern" which has passed into the literary histories of the assorted programs of "modernism." *Finnegans Wake* is, by any definition of the term except "strictly" historical or chronological, a postmodernist text. But what is it that we want to assert by such denominations? That *Finnegans Wake* makes it new in ways that are more audacious than anything *Ulysses* attempts? Perhaps that is so, but it would be funny to invoke a "rupture" or that armory of rhetoric by which a modernist "paradigm" is supplanted by another paradigm. The two texts are written by the same hand, under the same "signature" (to use the locution by which Derrida and other contemporary critics efface the writer's presence) – by the same hand, too, that wrote "The Sisters." Do we want to divide Joyce's work by saying that *Finnegans Wake* is a postmodernist text because it is a critique or representation, a radical calling into question of received ways of writing fiction? *Ulysses* had already done this, not only in the pastiches of "The Oxen of the Sun," but across the whole body of the novel. *Ulysses* puts into question just about all the old rules by which we used to establish what makes writing a novel. And it wouldn't take much to show that Joyce wasn't really original in so doing, and therefore we shouldn't stand in awe of the figure of the "great writer" – even though the text itself of *Ulysses,* by the indeterminacy of Joyce's voices, deconstructs any such misapprehensions. All of which, to be sure, Joyce carries to extremes, as we might say, in *Finnegans Wake*.

But it isn't the search for novelty, or breaking received rules for making it new, and the stylistic markings that attach to these endeavors that count nearly so much as the leap of the writing into unimagined possibilities. *Finnegans Wake* leaves novelty behind, including the novelties of *Ulysses,* leaves, indeed, novel-making behind in order to discover new imaginations of possibility, new *rules* for constructing fiction. To engage this text is to partake of all that has been advanced in the present theory of the text – indeterminate *signifiance,* hybrid structurings, polyphony, polycentricity, transpersonal polycentricity, textual production in readership, overdetermined structurations and signifying practices – and more. More, because to read this text for its writing, as it is written, is to discover what we never imagined fiction could be or do until Joyce did it – to revel in an infinity of unseen or unheard-of structurations and signifying practices. The unseen and the unheard-of are exactly what Joyce presents: a presenting the unpresentable. It is not the novelties of the structurations of *Finnegans Wake,* or the breaks with precedent structures, that so engage and captivate us as the re-constructing and re-conceiving of what language can do in what will have been done, what rules might be discovered in writing for the language of literature. And Joyce, it should be said against those who would argue for the non-literary tendencies of postmodernist texts, Joyce is nothing but literary, however we must stretch our suppositions of what it means to be "literary." We are not drawn to Joyce's texts only, or even primarily, for their transgression of the limits of fiction. We are not drawn to Joyce's texts only, or even primarily, for all the reasons and motives and markings that have been advanced for modernism, though they are there, or for all the markings and motives of postmodernism, though they are there in every particular. We are drawn by their liberating sense of what writing can be and do in and by the writing. And to value Joyce's writing in *Finnegans Wake* in no way obliges us to reject *Ulysses:* one text does not usurp or supplant the other. It is simply to read with an enlarged and exhilarating sense of how Joyce continuously sought and constructed new determinations of what writing is or might be. Of how "art can be made of anything." And of the many things that are left behind in the access of wonder or pleasure or understanding at reading Joyce's work, one is the notion that it is his work. We do not worry about determining *his* text. The last thing we ought to worry about in reading *Ulysses* or *Finnegans Wake,* in fact, is *determining* the text.

Notes on Contributors

David J. Allerton, Professor of English Linguistics at the University of Basle, is the author of *Essentials of Grammatical Theory* (1979), *Valency and the English Verb* (1982), and a variety of other publications, mainly on syntax, morphology, text-linguistics and intonation.

John G. Blair, Professor of American Literature and Civilisation at the University of Geneva, has published *The Poetic Art of W. H. Auden* (1965) and *The Confidence Man in Modern Fiction* (1979). The manuscript of his next book, entitled 'Modular America,' received the 1985 Ralph Henry Gabriel Prize from the American Studies Association at its biennial conference in San Diego.

Werner Brönnimann is *Wissenschaftlicher Assistent* in the English Department of the St. Gall Graduate School of Economics. He is the editor of Shakespeare's *Troilus and Cressida* in the bilingual series *Englisch-deutsche Studienausgabe der Dramen Shakespeares* (Tübingen: Francke 1986).

Balz Engler is Professor of English at the University of Basle. He has published a study of R. A. Schröder as a Shakespeare translator (1974), a bilingual, critical edition of *Othello* (1976), a study of how the visual shape of texts affects the reading of poetry (1982), and articles ranging from Shakespearean textual scholarship to Vachel Lindsay's performance poetry and its effects on the teaching of literature.

Nils Enkvist, formerly Donner Professor of English Language and Literature at Åbo Akadami, is Director of the Research Institute of the Åbo Akademi Foundation and the author of more than 200 articles and reviews on stylistics, text and discourse linguistics. His books include *Linguistics and Style* (with J. Spencer and M. Gregory), *Linguistic Stylistic,* and *Tekstlingvistiikan peruskäsitteitä.*

Jean-Paul Forster, who teaches English literature at the University of Lausanne, has written *Robert Graves et la dualité du réel* (1974) and various articles on modern fiction and poetry. His current research deals with the concepts of modes of discourse, genres and forms.

Neil Forsyth has taught at Bryn Mawr College as well as at the Universities of California at Berkeley, North Carolina and Geneva. He is now Professor of English at the University of Lausanne. His book, *The Old Enemy,* will be published later this year.

Udo Fries is Professor of English Linguistics at the University of Zurich. He has published studies on Old and Middle English syntax, including an introduction to the language of Chaucer, and is the author of *Studien zur Textlinguistik,* a book on the relationship of questions and answers in English. He is currently working on an historical syntax of English and on a textbook on discourse analysis.

Ernest Giddey, Professor of English at the University of Lausanne, is the author of various books and articles on Addison, Laurence Sterne, Samuel Rogers, William Beckford, Byron, Thomas Hardy etc. In 1974 he published a study on *L'Angleterre dans la vie intellectuelle de la Suisse romande au XVIIIe siècle.*

Hartwig Isernhagen, Professor of English at the University of Basle, has published studies of Lawrence Durrell (1969) and John Dos Passos (1983), as well as various articles on literary theory and contemporary American and Third World literature.

Pierre E. Monnin teaches English at the Universities of Neuchâtel and Berne. He has published an article on French phonetics and is co-author of a Rimbaud concordance, but his main field of research is Old English poetry; he is currently preparing an edition of the OE *Metres of Boethius.*

Max Nänny is Professor of English and American Literature at the University of Zurich. He is the author of a book on John Dryden and of *Ezra Pound: Poetics for an Electric Age* (1973). He has contributed numerous articles on modernist authors to *English Studies, English Literary History, Paideuma* and *Word & Image*. He guest-edited the special number of *Word & Image* on "Iconicity in Literature" (1986).

Gregory T. Polletta, Professor of Modern English Literature at the University of Geneva, is the editor of *Issues in Contemporary Literary Criticism* (1973) and the author of articles on contemporary critical theories of writers and the writing of fiction and poetry.

Werner Senn is Professor of English literature at the University of Berne. His publications include books on the Elizabethan drama (1973) and on Joseph Conrad (1980) as well as articles on narrative, literary iconicity and contemporary Australian writing.

Barbara Sträuli is an assistant at the English Department of Zurich University, where she teaches introductory courses on Shakespeare. She is currently preparing an edition of "Henry V."

Paul Beekman Taylor teaches Medieval English and Old Icelandic languages and literatures at the University of Geneva. He has published several articles on Old and Middle English as well as Old Icelandic poetry and prose.

Richard J. Watts is Professor of English Linguistics at the University of Berne. He is the author of *The Pragmalinguistic Analysis of Narrative Texts: Narrative Co-operation in Charles Dicken's "Hard Times"* and a number of articles on language in use. He is currently working on interruption in verbal interaction.

Index